Theopneusty: Or, The Plenary Inspiration Of The Holy Scriptures – Primary Source Edition

Louis Gaussen

THEOPNEUSTY.

THEOPNEUSTY,

OR, THE

PLENARY INSPIRATION

OF

THE HOLY SCRIPTURES.

BY S. R. L. GAUSSEN,
PROFESSOR OF THEOLOGY IN GENEVA.

TRANSLATED BY E. N. KIRK.

NEW-YORK:
PUBLISHED BY JOHN S. TAYLOR, & CO.
NO. 145 NASSAU STREET.

BOSTON, TAPPAN AND DENNET.

1842.

S. W. BENEDICT, PRINT.

INTRODUCTION

BY THE TRANSLATOR.

———

THE Spirit of God has breathed afresh upon the Churches of the Old World ; and the principle of life is manifesting itself in a two-fold antagonism to the ancient superstition and the modern scepticism of Continental Europe. The new theologi_ cal school in Geneva, founded in 1831, is an effect and an instrument of that renovation. Its existence was indispensable to the awakened churches of Switzerland ; for, the city, church, and school of Calvin had abandoned the vital principles and facts of Calvin's religion.

Mr. S. R. L. Gaussen, our author, is Professor of Theology in this Evangelical Institution. He is an accomplished scholar, and an able writer ; and we hail the productions of his pen, (several of which are appearing at this moment, in an English dress,) and those of his esteemed colleague, Mr. Merle D'Aubigné, as the promise to France, that she shall yet recover all, and even more than she lost by the Vandalism, that burned her Protestant citizens and her Protestant literature at the same stake.

Of this work, we merely deem it necessary to say, that it possesses a degree of vivacity, simplicity, and richness, which are but imperfectly represented in the translation. Of its contents, we would make some few remarks, by which the reader may be better prepared to approach the subject, and meet the author as he desires to be met. He does not propose to convince the sceptic ; and yet there is much here, on which the doubter may profitably reflect. His great object is, to take the

Church off from her present, unsafe, indefensible and enfee-
bling position, of a mixed, varying and indeterminate inspiration.

He has assumed a bold position, which has to us many of the
essential signs of truth; simplicity, precision, consistency with
itself and with the declarations of the Bible, and power to establish the mind in firm assurance. It is simple; and in this,
is contrasted with that strange, confused, inapplicable theory,
so prevalent in the church, in which we are told, that some
parts of the Bible are formed by one *modus operandi* of the
Spirit, and others by another; and from which we are left to
infer, that some parts are more divine, and others more human—
and yet we have no sure guide, when we would fly from the
parts that are human, and rest on the pure word of God. Our
author's position is precise—for it does not vascillate in a mis-
ty indefiniteness between an inspiration of the men and of their
writings, as does the opposite theory. It comes directly to the
book as an existence, as a thing, and says of it, this is inspired,
all inspired, all equally so, all infallible. It is consistent with
itself, for it asserts that the whole Bible is infallible and perfect; and then forbids human reason to pronounce any passage
of the Bible unworthy of the Spirit of God. It is consistent
with the Bible; for it admits and asserts that *all* that is written, (all Scripture) is given by inspiration of God. It is confirming; for he who believes this doctrine, takes up his Bible,
saying, this is all true, all important, all worthy of God; not
one jot or tittle of it can fail.

Again and again, have we asked, in reading this book, what
do our learned writers on Inspiration propose to themselves,
by adopting the subtile distinctions borrowed from Jewish
Rabbins? There is, we admit, an intrinsic difficulty or mystery
in the whole subject of Inspiration. But it respects totally the
mode of the Spirit's influencing the minds of the writers. And
if this Jewish theory of Inspiration had been adopted, merely
in explanation of the psychology of the case—to inform us how
the writers were affected in the composition of different parts
of the sacred oracles, we should consider it to be as harmless
and useless as a thousand other theories. But when it invades
the text itself, and undertakes to classify the passages of the
Bible, as partaking more or less of human infirmity, ignorance

or sinfulness, then we feel ourselves constrained to differ and to remonstrate. It may be replied, no; we simply propose to guard against exaggeration, and to prevent the exposure of the doctrine of Inspiration to contempt; we find passages manifestly above the reach of human faculties, even for their comprehension, much more for their composition; we find others again, mere recitals of trivial incidents, expressions of ordinary feelings, such as may be seen in a school-boy's letter to his friends; and we cannot believe that the Spirit of God equally dictated all these passages. Still, we reply with the author, if you merely undertake to speculate upon the state of the minds of the writers, confine your speculations there—but suffer us to return, and tell the people to rely on the fact, that every word of the original text is, in its place, an inspired word—that God secured it there, to make part of an infallible revelation.

A great excellence of this work, is the clearness of its distinction between the inspiration of the men, and that of the book. We believe, indeed, and its author believes, that the writers were inspired; that "holy men of God, were moved by the Holy Ghost," when they spake. But the fact of *their* inspiration is one thing, that of the *book* is another. And the perusal of this work has increased our conviction, that a semi-infidelity on a vital point, has crept into the Church; that the sense of the imperfection of the writers has imperceptibly diminished her reverence for the Scriptures.

There is a formidable objection to the theory of Inspiration, to which our author has not replied. His reason for not doing so, is, that he writes for believers, and not for sceptics. Yet, we fear, that many a devout student of the Bible, and many a sincere preacher of its truths, might discover lurking in his heart, this subtle objection; which, like the unobserved "worm i' the bud," is sometimes hindering a vigorous growth, sometimes corroding vital organs. The objection may be thus stated:—God's works are all perfect in one sense, and all his teachings are infallible. But the instant he employs man to teach his teachings to other men, there is introduced a new element, which at once destroys perfection and infallibility. This arises from two sources, the imperfection of man, and that of his language. If the conceptions or feelings of a man are employed, they must necessarily limit and mar the divine thought com-municated to him. And if man speaks to his fellows, in human language, he must use an imperfect medium, always more or less imperfectly comprehended.

This is the most subtile and imposing of all the objections which have attacked our faith in plenary inspiration. Our ground of defence is here; that God calls his word perfect, that a particle of it shall never fail; that no future changes, no progress of science, no unfolding of the complicated drama of human life shall ever change or modify one shade of its statements. This may not satisfy the unbeliever; yet even he may find a relief from his own dark and chilling speculations, in the fact, that God's instruments are perfect for his purposes, however unadapted to ours. Nature is an infallible teacher, none can deny; or, in other words, all God's works are perfect instructers. And this remains true, although men are constantly prone to misinterpret their meaning. It remains true, although men's senses are imperfect instruments for the reception of truth, and material substances are imperfect media for conveying a knowledge of spiritual truth. " The invisible (spiritual) things of him are clearly seen, being understood by the things (material as well as immaterial,) that are made."

It is enough then for us to believe, that he who has made nature a perfect teacher, has made his word so, likewise. And all we oppose, is, the confounding one twig, one leaf, one fibre of this wonderful production of divine goodness, with any thing man has made and marred. If a doubt still remains, because we have not produced an analogy on the main point, the essential imperfection of the language; consider, that you would have no such difficulty, if God were to speak to you by audible words in your own language. The words then and thus spoken, although they had separately come down to you from your rude Saxon ancestors, and although they are now variously and imperfectly used by men, would never be forgotten by you, never confounded with even the holiest words of the holiest uninspired men. This is the precise impression which we desire to see the Bible produce in all our hearts. When our eye rests on its page, when its words fall on our ear, let us receive it as the very voice of God.

The whole scope of our book is to secure that effect. And

both the subject and the view of it here presented will compensate the devout and the inquiring reader for the time and pains of an attentive perusal. Here is the rock of the Christian's faith; an inspired communication, an infallible revelation. Here is the life and power of the Christian ministry; they have a voice of God to echo, an infallible "thus saith the Lord," to form the soul of their oratory and the power of their appeals. We could wish that the subject of inspiration might receive a more earnest attention, in the education of our youth; and especially of our candidates for the holy ministry. There is still too much dependence on mere authority, in training the mind. A consequence of which is, that subtile errorists, seeming to appeal to reason, have power to mislead our young men, who have nothing but the *ipse dixit* of teachers to oppose to argument. To this mode of creating confidence in the Bible is opposed, that of exhibiting the reasons which have convinced us that the Bible is inspired. Let us deal fairly with the youthful mind, by taking it to points of observation, whence it can see the beautiful, unquestionable signs and seals of a divine origin in the Bible. The best and strongest of these are indeed invisible to " the natural man." But there are others; and they are sufficient to establish the confidence, even of them who " discern not the things of the Spirit." Let a part of the instruction of the common-school, the Sunday-school, the Bible-class, the college and the pulpit, be —the inspiration of the " living oracles;" let it be repeated, until the evidence of it is clear and brilliant to the mental eye. We do not overrate the importance of this point. The effects of a more earnest and a more general inculcation of this great fact, must soon become apparent, in many ways; from such tilling, under the dews of the Spirit, and the breathings of his " south wind," would spring the most beautiful and fragrant flowers, the richest and most refreshing fruits. There would be many a negative, but blessed result; the nipping of many a poisonous germ of error in its first budding. Some of our most reckless and blasphemous revilers of the word and doctrines of God, were once under christian culture. How comes it that they can now give themselves to the constant contradiction of the plain statements of that word, to the bold and damnable contempt of the theology and the logic of the Bible ?

Surely their eyes have never seen in that book, even that which the "reason unbaptized" may see, of the presence and authority of those who spake from the smoking summit of Sinai, amid terrible glories. Much then may be done, to prevent this fatal scepticism, by a more full and faithful exhibition to those under our instruction, of the great and glorious fact of inspiration, and of the evidence of its reality. Much too may be done to press back the sweeping current of scepticism, by a faithful exhibition of this whole subject, including the incompetence of man to prejudge a Revelation, to dispense with a Revelation, or to provide a substitute for the Bible. There has constantly been, on the one hand, an exalting of human reason to a position where it promises to relieve us from the sense of helplessness; and on the other hand, there has been an equally dangerous tendency to exalt merely human writings to a level with the Scriptures. To meet these two extremes, of having no revelation and too much revelation, our doctrine must be clearly, earnestly presented to the public mind. On this point a great battle is yet to be fought. And then, when the battle waxes hot, and the enemy possesses our entrenchments closely, we shall not be surprised to find the whole out-works of a varied inspiration carried away. We see not how Rome is to be attacked in her fortress of traditions, and apocryphal books, if a part of our very Bible is made up of Paul's and Peter's uninspired sayings. You call them indeed, *superintended* sayings. But you mean, in the very adoption of that term, to express that the Holy Spirit did not give these passages to the apostles, any more than he gave the book of Tobit to its author; that he left them to say in their own way, what they knew before, and what it did not become the Holy Spirit to impart to them. If you do not mean this, you then come to our author's ground; for he believes fully in the free exercise of every faculty of the sacred writers, just where you do, and as far as you do. He merely goes a step farther, and says, God designed that they should say just what they did say; and he secured their saying it in their own way, but exactly as it should be, even to an iota and a tittle. This is a verbal inspiration. And the book so written, is the word of God, and binds the conscience of the world; and nothing else does so bind it, even though it were the writings of Paul or

Peter. This ground must be taken firmly with the apostate church.

And with the infidel, whether he be christian in name, or anti-christian, the sharp sword of a perfect inspiration will be found, at last, indispensable. If he can enter the armory, and take away a single weapon, he may take all; nay, if the ground is conceded to him, that there is a single passage in the Bible that is not equally divine with every other, then we are disarmed; for he will be sure to apply his privilege to the very passages which most fully oppose his pride, passion, and error. How is the conscience of a wicked race to be bound down by a chain, one link of which is weak? How are you going to press on human belief, the unwelcome doctrines of Native and Total Depravity, of the Trinity, of Expiation by the Blood of Christ, of Eternal punishment, of Demons, of Election, of gratuitous Justification, by a Bible which admits of human imperfections in its composition? How are you going to check the audacity that accuses Paul of false logic, when you accuse him of writing something which is not as perfect as it would have been, had God himself written it? You have entered the sacred temple, and commenced the work of desecration, in your reverential and devout way; but how can you censure him that enters and imitates your example, after his own fashion, and not after yours? You say, when Paul requested Timothy to bring his cloak, he was not speaking as fully under the Spirit, as when he prophesied of future events, or revealed the doctrine of justification by faith. With precisely as good authority, the other says, when Paul wrote the whole Epistle to the Hebrews, he was left to himself.

To this doctrine do we look for new influences to affect even the ministers of the gospel. We may have inferred too much, from the adoption of the popular theory of inspiration. But we must believe, that the difference is immense, between a faith that knows not precisely what parts of its Bible are given of God, without an imperfection; and that which plants its trusting footstep, every where in the Bible, upon the rock of a divine declaration, which cannot fail. We presume that there is indeed, in the case of many pious ministers of the gospel, an inconsistency between their theory and their general belief in this matter. They accept the entire Bible as a revelation from God, completely expressive of what he desires that man should be taught, with the exception, that he has not made it all equally divine. And as he has given no certain marks by which we may distinguish such passages, these men would, if consistent with themselves, feel a distrust of the whole Bible. They often, however, avoid this paralyzing doubt, by having settled in their own mind, that certain passages are fully inspired, and by venturing to determine which those passages are. But others, who adopt the theory of a fourfold inspiration, must feel a want of implicit resting on any one passage; as would all, if they were consistent with their theory. Much of the power of preaching depends on the degree of confidence felt by the ambassador of Christ in the perfect truth and the divine authority of every thing he has learned from the Bible, and of every thing he quotes from the Bible, in the sense and connection in which the word of God presents it. If a preacher depends for his theological sentiments, more upon human arguments than upon inspired declarations, it will be a leaven affecting all his ministrations. Faith comes by hearing; but whatever faith he imparts, will be a faith in argument, but not in divine testimony. And we apprehend moreover, that some of the strongest, the sweetest, the most momentous truths of the Bible are but faintly and rarely exhibited by some good men, from the want of a deep impression that every thing in the Bible is inspired. It both prevents their searching into those deep sayings, whose meaning is never found, without prayer and earnest study, and yet which most powerfully beat down the unbelief of the heart; it likewise prevents the earnest, cordial and frequent utterance of those awful, stern and overwhelming views of the justice of God, and of the evil nature and consequences of sin, which are the sword of the Spirit for the destruction of pride, self-righteousness, and contempt of the cross.

The progress of piety likewise, is intimately connected with the fulness, clearness and firmness of faith in the inspiration of the Scriptures. We believe with devout thankfulness, that the unlearned children of God have never gone so far as to determine, with their teachers, which passages God gave the apostle, and which he had without Divine aid. They believe in verbal inspiration, without knowing that there is any other kind. Such however, as carry to their Bible-readings this confused impression of four kinds of inspiration on the minds of the sacred writers, must have an unobserved and unreproved vein of unbelief affecting all their communion with the living oracles. When the Christian retires to his private oratory, he seeks the presence of God, and of God alone. He does not want even Paul there. There may be seasons, we admit, when holy men can greatly aid our private devotions; but there are others, when their presence would be an intrusion. And unless the Christian has such hours, in which he is strictly alone with God, he will not cultivate the divine life with much success. But in those holiest hours, he may, he must take the Bible; not however as the book of Moses, of Daniel, of Isaiah or of Paul, but as the book of God. In every line, in every word, he must see only his Father, hear only his Savior. And he should desire no more to think of Paul and David, any farther than their various circumstances and feelings are employed by God for illustrating truth, than of the man who printed, bound and sold the volume.

But we must ask the patient reader's forgiveness for this long detention from the author, to whom, and to whose work, it is our privilege now to introduce him.

We intrude still, merely to say that the term Theopneusty and its derivatives, are retained by us, because there is more reason for having a word of Greek, than one of Latin origin, to express a doctrine of the New Testament; and because we have supposed that the Latin word, Inspiration, conveys to every classical scholar something of the pagan notion; and we prefer to have a Scriptural term, with which the true, pure doctrine of the completely divine origin of the entire Bible may be associated.

E. N. KIRK.

New York, March 15, 1842.

1

TABLE OF CONTENTS.

PREFACE.

———

At the very first sight of this book and its title, two equally unfounded prejudices may arise in certain minds. I desire to remove them.

The Greek word *Theopneusty*, although employed by St. Paul, and for a long time used by the Germans, is yet unknown in our tongue. Many a reader may therefore say, that the subject here treated, is too scientific to be popular, and too little popular to be useful. And yet I unhesitatingly declare, that if any thing has inspired me with both the desire and the courage to undertake this work, it is the two-fold conviction of its vital importance and its simplicity.

I do not think, that after the admission of the divinity of Christianity, a question can be stated, which is more essential to the life of our faith, than this; Is the Bible from God? is it entirely from God? or is it true, (as some assert,) that it contains sentences which are purely human, inaccurate narratives, vulgar errors, illogical reasonings; in a word, that it contains books, or portions of books, in which our faith has no interest, being marred by error and the natural indiscretions of the writers? A question decisive, fundamental; yea vital! It is the first that meets you on opening the Scriptures, and with it your religion ought to commence.

2

If it be true, as you say, that some things in the Bible are unimportant, have nothing to do with your faith, and no relation to Jesus Christ; and if it be true, again, that nothing in this book is inspired, but that which you may happen to think possessed of importance, related to faith and to Jesus Christ, then your Bible is a totally different book from that of the Fathers, of the Reformers, and of the saints in every age. Your Bible is fallible: theirs was infallible. Yours has chapters, or portions of chapters, sentences or phrases, which must be totally distinguished from those that are of God; theirs was " all given by inspiration of God, and all of it profitable for doctrine, for reproof, for correction, for instruction in righteousness; that the man of God may be perfect." The very same passage may then be, in your estimation, as far from that which it was in theirs, as earth is from heaven.

You have opened, for instance, at the forty-fifth Psalm, or at the Song of Solomon. Whilst you see nothing there, but that which is the most thoroughly human, a long marriage-song, or the amorous conversations between a young maid of Sharon and her young husband; they were there accustomed to see the glories of the Church, the bonds of Jehovah's love, the depths of grace in Christ; in a word, that which is most divine in heavenly things; and if they could not read them there, they knew that they are there, and there they searched for them.

Or, we take an epistle of St. Paul. Whilst one of us attributes a sentence which he does not understand, or which shocks his carnal sense, to the Jewish prejudices of the writer, to intentions entirely vulgar, to circumstances altogether human; the other there searches with profoundest respect, the meaning of the Spirit; he believes it to be perfect, before discovering what it is; and he attributes its apparent insignificance or obscurity only to his own unskilfulness and ignorance.

Thus, while in the Bible of the one, everything has its design, its place, its beauty, its use; just as, in a tree, the branches and the leaves, the vessels and the fibres, the epidermis, and even the bark, all have their uses; the Bible of the other is a tree, having, indeed many leaves and branches and fibres which God did not create, and which, therefore, do not accomplish his designs.

But this is not all. Not only shall you and we have two different bibles, but we shall be at an utter loss to tell what yours is. It is only, to a certain degree, human and fallible, you say; but who shall define this degree? If it be true that man, by putting his hand to this work, has left upon it the impression of his own imperfection; who shall determine the extent of that imperfection, and the places which it mars? It has its human parts, you say; but what are the limits of this part; who shall fix them for me? No one. Every one must do it for himself, according to the dictates of his own judgment; that is, this fallible part of the Bible will be magnified to us, just in proportion as we are less enlightened by God's light; so that a man must be deprived of the word of God, just in proportion as he has need of it; as we see idolaters making idols impure in exact proportion to their own distance from the living and holy God! Thus, then, every one will reduce the inspired Scriptures within different limits; and making to himself of this Bible, expurgated by himself, an infallible rule, will say to it—Henceforth guide me, for thou art my rule! as that image-maker of whom Isaiah speaks, " who maketh a God, and saith, deliver me, for thou art my God."

But this is not all; consequences still more serious are here involved. According to your answer, it is not the Bible alone which is changed; it is you!

Yes, even in the presence of passages which you may have admired most, you shall have neither the attitude nor the heart of a believer! How can it be otherwise after that you have arraigned these very passages with all the rest of the Bible, at the tribunal of your judgement, that they may there be pronounced by you, divine, not divine, or partially divine? What can be the authority of a passage over you, which is infallible only so far as you please to consider it so? Has it not once stood on trial at your bar, on the same footing with passages, convicted of being merely human in whole or in part? And can your spirit then assume sincerely, the humble and submissive attitude of a learner, before the very passage which you have just examined in the character of a judge? Impossible; you may perhaps render it the obedience of acquiescence, but never that of faith; of approbation, never that of adoration! You believe in the divinity of a passage, you say; but it is not in God that you believe, it is in yourself! This passage pleases you, it does not govern you; it excites your admiration, but does not reign over you; it is before you as a lamp, it is not in you as an unction from on high, a principle of light, a fountain of life. I cannot persuade myself that any pope, however conscious of his sacerdotal authority, ever prayed with great confidence to a saint whom by his own plenary authority, he had raised to the rank of a demi-god by canonizing it. How then, can any reader of the Bible, (however conscious of his own superior wisdom,) act the part of a genuine believer toward a passage which he has just canonized? Will his spirit come down from the pontifical chair, to prostrate itself before this passage, which but for his decision, had remained human, or at least, doubtful? How can he study any longer a passage which he must already have examined thoroughly in order to have assigned it its true position; how can he fully submit to an authority which he might have denied, and which he has already made dubious? We can but imperfectly adore that which we have degraded.

Moreover, let it be remarked, that as the entire divinity of such or such a passage of the Scriptures is dependent in your estimation, not on the fact of its being found in the book of the oracles of God; but on the fact that it presents to your wisdom and your spirituality certain signs of spirituality and wisdom; the sentence which you pronounce, can never be so exempt from hesitation, as that you can totally separate from it every doubt which at first attended it. Your faith must then partake of your doubts, and must itself be imperfect, undecided, conditional! And as the decision, so will be the faith; as the faith, such the life! But that is not the faith, that is not the life of God's elect!

The consideration, however, which manifests most strongly the importance of the subject we are about to discuss, is, that if the system we oppose have its roots steeped in incredulity, it must inevitably bear the fruit of yet a new incredulity. How happens it, that so many thousands can open their Bible, day and night, without ever discovering the doctrines which it teaches with the utmost explicitness? Whence comes it that they walk in darkness so many years, with the sun shining before them? Do they not regard these books as a revelation from God? Yes;—but, prejudiced by false notions of inspiration, and believing that there still exists in the Scriptures a mixture of error; and at the same time desirous of finding those parts which are sufficiently reasonable to be esteemed divine, they study, unconsciously I admit, to give them a sense acceptable to their own wisdom; and thus they not only make it impossible to discover what God would teach, but also make the Scriptures contemptible in their own eyes. They take up, for instance, the writings of St. Paul, in order to find in them justification by the law, man's native innocence, his tendency toward the good, the moral omnipotence of his will, the merit of his works. And

2*

what is the consequence? It is alas! that after having forced such doctrines upon the sacred writer, they find the language so wretchedly adapted to its supposed end, terms so badly chosen to express the meaning they have determined to find there, reasonings so badly conducted; they at last come to lose, in spite of themselves, what little respect they had for the Scriptures, and then they plunge into rationalism. Thus it is, that having commenced in incredulity, the fruit of their labor is a more advanced incredulity; they have darkness as the consequence of darkness, and so fulfil that dreadful word of Christ; "from him that hath not, shall be taken away that which he seemeth to have."

Such then, is manifestly the fundamental importance of the great question we are about to examine. By your answer, the arm of the word of God is enervated for you, the sword of the Spirit is blunted, it has lost its temper and its penetrating power. How can it thenceforward "pierce even to the dividing asunder of the joints and the marrow, and separate the soul and the spirit?" How can it be mightier than your lusts, than your doubts, than the world, than Satan? How can it give you light, force, victory, peace? No! it might be by an operation of the mere grace of God, that in spite of this deplorable state of the soul, a divine word should come and seize it suddenly; then Zaccheus would come down from his sycamore, Matthew quit his receipt of custom, the paralytic take up his bed and walk, and the dead revive. All that is, doubtless, possible. But it still remains true, that this disposition which judges the Scriptures, and which doubts in advance, their universal inspiration, is one of the greatest obstacles we can oppose to their legitimate action. "The word preached," says St. Paul, "did not profit them, not being mixed with faith in them that heard it;" while the most abundant benedictions of the same Scriptures were ever the portion of those who received it, "not as the word of men, but, (as it is in truth,) the word of God, which effectually worketh in them that believe." (1 Thess. xi. 13.)

This question is, then, evidently vital to our faith; and we have the right to say, that between the two answers made to it, there exists the same gulf that formerly separated two Jews who might have seen Jesus Christ in the flesh, and who might equally have recognized him as a prophet; but of whom, the one, in view of his carpenter's dress, his homely fare, his hands hardened by work, and his rustic attendants, believed him fallible and peccable, like any other prophet; whilst the other recognized in him Emanuel, the Lamb of God, the Lord our Righteousness, the Holy One of Israel, the King of kings, the Lord of lords.

The reader may not yet have admitted each of these considerations; but it must certainly be conceded, that enough has been said to justify the conclusion, that the study of this question is vastly important, and that, in weighing it, you hold in your hands the dearest interests of the people of God. I ask no more in the preface. This was my first object, to show the importance of our subject; my next is, to show that it is adapted to the capacities of all.

If this doctrine ought to be studied by all, we assert, that it is likewise within the reach of all; and the author distinctly avows, that, in writing this book, it has been his cherished ambition to make it intelligible to all classes of readers.

And yet, methinks, I hear the objection urged by many voices, "you are writing for men of science, your book is not for us; we were looking for religion, and behold theology!"

Theology, certainly! But what kind of theology?

That which must be studied by all the heirs of life, and
in respect to which every child ought to be a theologian.

Religion and theology!   Let us explain ourselves; for,
in setting these terms in opposition to each other, an injurious abuse is often made of both.   Is not Theology defined, in all the dictionaries, as "the science which has
God and his revelation for its object?"   But, when I was
a schoolboy, my catechisms gave virtually the same definition of Religion.   "It is the science," they said, "which
teaches us to know God and his word, God and his counsels, God in Christ."   They do not differ, then, in their object, their means, nor their end.   Their object, truth; their
means, the word of God; their end, holiness.   "Sanctify
them, O Father! by thy truth; thy word is truth."   This
is the wish of both, as it was that of their dying Master.
What distinction is there, then, between them?   This
alone; that Theology is Religion studied with more method, and by the help of more perfect instruments.   You
can, indeed, bring together an odd compound of philosophy or human tradition with the word of God, and dig-
nify it with the title of Theology; but that is scholasti-
cism, not Theology.

It is true, indeed, that the term Religion is not always
employed in its objective sense, as signifying the science
of the truths we believe; but sometimes, also, in a subjective sense, to designate rather the sentiments which
these truths produce in the hearts of believers.   These
two significations are different, and ought to be distinguished; but to place them in opposition, and call the
one Theology and the other Religion, is an utter misapprehension of the natures of both; it is indeed an absurdity,
as it presumes that there may be religious sentiments without the truths which originate them; it pretends to be a
morality without doctrines, piety without belief, Christianity without Christ, to have an effect without its cause,

life without a soul! Fatal delusion! "Holy Father, is not this life eternal, to know thee, the only true God, and Jesus Christ, whom thou hast sent?"

But if it were rather in the objective sense, that Religion and Theology are placed in opposition to each other; that is, the religion which a Christian learns, who reads the Bible in his native tongue, to that which the profoundest scholar would learn in the same Bible, by the aid of history and the learned languages; even then, I say, distinguish them, but do not place them in opposition to each other. Should not every real Christian become a theologian, just so far as he can? Is he not commanded to become wise in the Scriptures, nourished in sound doctrine, rooted and grounded in the knowledge of Jesus Christ? And was it not to the crowd around him, in the open street, that Jesus said, "Search the Scriptures?" Religion, then, in its objective sense, is to Theology just what the globe is to astronomy. They are distinct but united; and Religion renders to Theology the same service as the astronomy of geometricians offers to navigators.

A shipmaster may doubtless dispense with La Place's Mécanique Céleste, in order to reach the Chinese sea, or return from the antipodes; but even then, it is to this science that, in traversing the ocean with his elementary notions, he owes the excellence of his formulas, the exactitude of his tables, and the precision of the method which give him his longitudes, and make his course certain. Thus the Christian traveller, in order to traverse the ocean of this world, and to reach the haven to which God is calling him, may dispense with the ancient languages and profound speculations of Theology; but, after all, the very notions of religion which are necessary to him, shall receive, to a great extent, their precision and their certitude from theological science. And whilst he steers towards eternal life, with his eyes upon this compass which God

has given him, it is still to Theology that he is indebted
for the assurance that this celestial magnet is the same
now as when the apostles used it; that the instrument of
salvation has been handed down to him uninjured, that its
indications are true, and that the needle does not vary.

There was a time when all the sciences were mysterious, teaching with closed doors; having their initiated,
their holy language, and their free-masonry. Physics,
geometry, medicine, grammar, history, all were taught in
Latin. They sailed in the clouds, far above the vulgar;
and they let fall, at the utmost, from their sublime bark,
a few detached leaves, which men were to take up with
great respect, but which they were not permitted to judge.
Now, every thing is changed. Genius glories in making
itself understood by the many; and after having soared to
the ethereal regions of science, in order there to seize the
truth in her highest retreats, it employs its power in ascertaining the way back to earth, and in approaching closely
to us, that it may show us the route it has traveled, and
the secrets it has discovered. But, if such is now the almost universal tendency of the human sciences, it was
ever the distinctive characteristic of true Theology. She
owes herself to all. The other sciences can dispense with
the people, as the people dispense with them; true Theology, on the contrary, has need of the people, as the people have of her. She guards their Religion; and their
Religion, in its turn, guards her. Wo to them when
Theology languishes, and does not speak to them! Wo
to her, when the religion of the churches neglects her, and
ceases to esteem her! We must then see to it, both on
her account and on theirs, that she speaks to them, hears
them, studies in reference to them, and keeps their schools
open, as our temples are.

Whilst theology continues to teach in the midst of the
churches; by having constantly before her the realities of

the Christian life; she is also constantly reminded of the realities of science; the miseries of man, the counsels of the Father, the cross of the Redeemer, the consolations of the Spirit, holiness, eternity. Then, also, the conscience of the Church, restraining her wanderings, intimidates her boldness, obliges her to be serious, and corrects the effects of that almost profane familiarity, with which the science of the schools lays her hand on holy things. In speaking to her, every day, of that life which the preaching of the Cross preserves in the Church, (that life, without the knowledge of which all her science would be as incomplete, as would be the natural history of man, derived only from the study of carcasses,) the religion of the people takes away from theology her too prompt admiration of the sciences which do not sanctify. Religion often proposes to theology this question, originally put by St. Paul to the false science of the Galatians; "Have you received the Spirit by the works of the law, or by the preaching of the righteousness of faith?" She takes away the enchantment of human wisdom, she inspires theology with a profound reverence for the word of God, and (in this holy word) for those doctrines of justification by faith, which are the power of God our Saviour, and which ought to penetrate the very soul of her science. It is thus that religion guides theology by teaching her to associate in her researches, the labors of the conscience and affections, with those of the understanding, and never to pursue the truth of God, but by the united illuminations of study and prayer.

And, on the other side, theology renders in her turn, to the Christian Churches, services which are to them equally indispensable. It is she who watches over the religion of a people, that the "lips of the priest may preserve knowledge, and that they may be able to seek the law at his mouth." It is she who preserves in the holy ministry of the gospel, the purity of its doctrines; and in the preaching, the exact balance of all the truths. It is she who confirms the unlearned against the hostile assertions of a science which they do not understand; it is she who gathers her answers from the very region where the objections are gathered; who puts her finger upon the sophisms of the adversaries; who keeps them respectful in her presence, and who obliges them to observe before the Church, a style more guarded and less presumptuous. It is she, in fine, who signalizes the first moment, often so decisive, when the language of Religion among a people, begins to be erroneous; and when error, like a germinating tare, first shoots above the ground. She gives the timely warning, and they haste to weed it up.

Always, when the Churches have been pious, Theology has flourished; she has become enlightened; she has made study honorable; and, in order to qualify herself for studying the Scriptures profoundly, not only has she been willing to make herself mistress of all the sciences which could throw light on the Bible, but she has quickened all the others into new life; whether directly, by the example of her own labors, or in bringing elevated spirits around her, or in diffusing through the academic institutions that generous sentiment of high morality, so favorable to the development of science.

Thus in elevating the character of study, she has often ennobled that of an entire people.

But on the other hand, when theology and the people have become indifferent to each other, and the slumbering Churches were living only for this world, then theology herself has become indolent, frivolous, ignorant, or, perhaps, a lover of novelties; seeking, at any cost, a profane popularity; teaching for the few; pretending to discoveries which are said only to the ear, which are taught only in the academies, and suppressed in the temples;

holding her gates closed in the midst of the people, and at the same time, throwing among them from the windows, doubts and impieties, to evidence the existing measure of her indifference; until, finally, she sinks into scandalous conduct, either in attacking doctrines, in denying the integrity or the inspiration of certain books, or in audaciously giving the lie to the facts they announce.

And let no one imagine that the entire people do not quickly feel so great an evil. They suffer from it, even in their temporal interests; and their very national existence is endangered by it. In degrading the religion of a people, you debase their morals, you take away their moral life. Every thing in a nation may be measured by one standard; the height of their heaven. If their heaven is low, every thing here on earth feels its debasing influences; everything at once becomes more limited and more grovelling; the future becomes more circumscribed; patriotism is materialized; generous traditions are engulfed; the moral sense becomes effeminated; the worship of self is alone exalted, and all conservative principles depart, one after another.

We then conclude, on the one hand, that there exists the most intimate union, not only between the happiness of a people and their religion, but between their religion and true theology; and, on the other hand, that if it was always highly proper that this science should teach for all and before all, never was this character more necessary to it than in treating of the doctrine which is now to engage our attention. It is the doctrine of doctrines—the doctrine which teaches us all the others, and by virtue of which alone they are doctrines; the doctrine which is to the soul of the believer what the air is to his lungs—necessary for his birth, growth, and perseverance in the Christian life.

Under the inspiration, then, of this twofold thought, this book has been written.

Every thing in it, I trust, will show my serious desire to render it useful to Christians of every class.

To this end, I have cast off all the forms of the schools. Without renouncing entirely quotations from ancient languages, I have yet used them sparingly. In exhibiting the admirable unanimity of Christian antiquity on this question, I have confined myself to general facts. In disposing the order of the chapters, I have neglected the ordinary rules of the didactic, to follow those of the popular logic; which commences by presenting the objections, and closes with the proofs. In a word, when it has been found necessary to treat the different questions which relate to the subject, and which ought to be found here, for the full presentation of the doctrine, I have referred them all to a special chapter. And there, too, I have gone against the advice of some friends, in employing a mode which seems to them out of harmony with the general tone of the book; but to me, seems to make the clear and rapid comprehension of the subject more easy.

It is then under this simple and practical form, that in presenting this book to the Church of God, I am happy in being able to recommend it to the blessing of Him who preached in the streets, and who thus characterized his own ministry,—"the gospel is preached to the poor!"

Happy, if these pages confirm, in the simplicity and blessedness of their faith, those Christians who, though unlettered, have already believed, through the Scriptures, in the full inspiration of the Scriptures! Happy, if some burdened and weary souls are led to hear more attentively that God who speaks to them in every line of the holy Book! Happy, if by our words, some travelers, (like the pilgrim Jacob, by the stone of Bethel,) after having reposed their wearied spirits with too much indifference on this book of God, should at last come to recognize this mysterious ladder which rises thence to heaven, and by which alone the messages of grace can descend upon their souls, and their prayers go up to God! May I urge them, in their turn, to pour out upon this sacred object the oil of their gratitude and joy, and learn to exclaim, "Surely the Lord is here—it is the house of God—it is the gate of heaven!"

For myself, I say it fearlessly, in prosecuting this work I have often been constrained to give thanks to God for having called me to it; for I have there seen more than once, the divine majesty fill with its splendor, the entire temple of the Scriptures; I have seen all the threads of that coarse garment, with which the Son of Man was clothed, become suddenly such as no fuller on earth could make them; I have often seen this book illuminated by the glory of God, and every word appear radiant. In fine, I have felt what we always experience in sustaining a cause which is holy and true; it is, that it grows the more in truth and majesty, the more you contemplate it.

My God, grant that I may love this word, and possess it as fully as thou hast taught me to admire it!

"All flesh is grass, and all the glory of man as the flower of grass; the grass withereth, and the flower thereof fadeth; but the word of our God endureth for ever, and it is this word which is preached unto us."

THEOPNEUSTY,

OR

FULL INSPIRATION OF THE HOLY SCRIPTURES.

Our design in this book, by the help of God and the alone authority of his word, is, to expound, defend and establish the Christian doctrine of inspiration.

CHAPTER I.

DEFINITION OF THEOPNEUSTY.

THIS term expresses the mysterious power which the Divine Spirit exercises over the authors of the writings of the Old and New Testaments, to make them compose them, just such as the Church has received them from their hands. "All Scripture," an Apostle said, "is *theopneustic*."*

This Greek expression, perhaps was new, even among the Greeks, at the time when St. Paul used it. Yet, if this term was not employed by the idolatrous Greeks, it was used by the hellenistic Jews.

Josephus,† the historian, cotemporary with St. Paul, employs a very similar term, in his first book against Appion, when, in speaking of all the prophets "who compos-

---

* 2 Tim. iii. 15. Theopneust would be more exact, but less euphonic.

† P. 1036, edit. Aurel. Allobr. 1611.

3*

ed," says he, " the twenty-two sacred books of the Old
Testament," he adds, that " they wrote *after the pneusty*
(or inspiration) which *comes from God.** And the Jewish Philosopher, Philo,† himself contemporary with Josephus, in the account of his Embassy to the Emperor
Caligula, using likewise a term very similar to St. Paul's,
calls the Scriptures *theochristic oracles ;* ‡ that is, oracles
given under the *anointing* of God." Theopneusty is not
a system, but a fact. As all the other events of the history of Redemption, this fact, attested by the Holy Scriptures, is one of the doctrines of our faith.

At the same time, it should be distinctly observed that
this miraculous operation of the Holy Spirit had not for
its object the sacred writers, who were only his instruments, and who were soon to pass away; but its object
was the sacred books themselves, which were destined to
reveal to the Church from age to age, the counsels of God,
and which shall never pass away.

The influence which was exercised upon these men,
and which they themselves were conscious of in very different degrees, has never been defined to us. Nothing
authorizes us to explain it. The Scriptures themselves
have never presented to us its mode nor its measure as an
object of study. They speak of it always incidentally ;
they never connect our piety with it. That alone which
they propose as the object of our faith is the inspiration of
their word ; is the divinity of their books ; between these
they make no difference. Their word, say they, is theopneustic ; their books are of God, whether they recount the
mysteries of a past anterior to the creation, or those of a
future posterior to the return of the Son of Man ; the eternal counsels of the most High, the secrets of the human
heart, or the deep things of God ; whether they give utterance to their own emotions or record their own recol-

---

* Κατά τὴν ἐπιπνοιαν τὴν ἀπὸ τοῦ Θεοῦ.
† P. 1022. edit. Frankf.   † Θεοχρηστα λόγια.

lections, relate cotemporaneous events, copy genealogies or make extracts from inspired documents; their writings are inspired; their statements are directed by heaven; it is always God who speaks, who relates, ordains or reveals by their mouth, and who, to accomplish it, employs their personality in different degrees. For " the Spirit of the Lord was upon them, and his word upon their tongue." And if it is always the word of man, because it is always men who utter it, it is likewise always the word of God, for it is always God that superintends, guides and employs them. They give their narrations, their doctrines, or their precepts, " not with the words which man's wisdom teacheth, but with the words which the Holy Spirit teacheth." And it is thus that God has constituted himself not only the voucher of all these facts, the author of all these orders, and the revealer of all these truths, but that also he has caused them to be given to the Church in the precise order, measure and terms which he has judged most conducive to his heavenly design.

If then we are asked how this theopneustic work was accomplished in the men of God? we should reply, that we do not know, and that we are not to know, and that it is in the same ignorance, and in a perfectly similar faith, that we receive the doctrine of the regeneration or sanctification of a soul by the Holy Spirit. We believe that the Spirit illumines this soul, purifies it, quickens it, consoles it, softens it; we recognize all these effects; we know and we adore their cause; but we consent to a perpetual ignorance of the means. Thus let it be then with Theopneusty.

And if we were still asked to say at least, what these men of God experienced in their organs, in their will, or in their understanding, whilst they were inscribing the sacred pages, we should reply, that the powers of inspiration were not felt in the same degree by each of them, and that their experiences were not uniform; but we should add that the knowledge of this is almost indifferent to the interests of our faith, for that is concerned with the book and not with the men. ⟨It is the book that is inspired, and totally so. This assurance is sufficient for us⟩

Three classes of men, in these latter days, without disavowing the divinity of Christianity, and without pretending to decline the authority of the Scriptures, have considered themselves justifiable in rejecting this doctrine.

The one class has been totally ignorant, even of the *existence* of this action of the Holy Spirit; others have denied its *universality*; others again its *plenitude*.

The first, as Schleiermacher,* Dewette,† and many other German theologians, reject all miraculous inspiration, and attribute to the sacred writers only what Cicero attributes to the poets; *afflatum spiritus divini,* "a divine action of nature, an interior power like the other vital forces of nature."

Others, like Michaelis,‡ and as formerly, Theodore of Mopsuesta, while fully admitting the existence of an inspiration, is unwilling to acknowledge it, for more than *a part* of the holy books; for the first of the fourth evangelist for example, for a part of the epistles, for a part of Moses, a part of Isaiah, a part of Daniel. These portions of the Scriptures, say they, are from God, the others from men.

The third class, as Mr. Twesten in Germany, and as many theologians in England § extend, it is true, the notion of a theopneusty to all parts of the Bible, but *not to all equally,* (nicht gleichmässig.)—Inspiration, according to them, is indeed universal, but unequal; often imperfect; accompanied by innocent errors; and extended, according

---

* Schleiermacher der christliche glaube, Band 1, S. 115.

† Dewette; Lehrbuch Anmerk. Twesten: Voslesungen über die Dogmatik, tome 1, p. 424, &c.

‡ Michaelis, Introd. to N. T.

§ Drs. Pye Smith, Dick, Wilson.

to the nature of the passages, to very different degrees, of which they constitute themselvesmore or less the judges.

Many of them, especially in England, have divided inspiration into four kinds—inspiration of *superintendence*, by which the sacred authors have been constantly preserved from grave errors, in every thing which relates to faith and spiritual life; inspiration of *elevation*, by which the Divine Spirit, in raising the thoughts of the men of God to the purest regions of truth, has indirectly impressed the same characters of holiness and grandeur on their words; inspiration of *direction*, under the more powerful action of which, the sacred authors were guided by God both as to the selection and rejection of topics and thoughts; finally, inspiration of *suggestion*. Here, they say, all the thoughts and even the words, were given by God through a still more direct and energetic operation of his Spirit.

"Theopneusty," says Mr. Twesten, "doubtless extends even to the words, but only when the choice or employment of them is connected with the interior religious life; for," he adds, "we must make distinctions in this respect, between the Old and New Testaments, between the law and the gospel, between history and prophecy, between narratives and doctrines, between the apostles and their apostolic aids."

All these distinctions, we consider fanciful; the Bible does not authorize them; the Church of the first eight centuries of the Christian era knew nothing of them; and we must regard them as erroneous and injurious.

Our object, in this book, is to prove, in opposition to these three systems, the existence, universality and fulness of inspiration.

Our first inquiry is, whether the Scriptures were divinely and miraculously inspired. We affirm it. Then we inquire, whether the parts of the Scriptures which are inspired, are so, equally and entirely; or, in other words;

whether God has provided, in a definite though mysterious manner, that the very words of the holy book should always be what they ought to be, and should be free from error. This we affirm. Finally, we inquire whether the whole Bible, or only a part, is thus inspired. We affirm this kind and degree of inspiration of all the Scriptures; the historical books as well as the prophecies, the Epistles as well as the Psalms, the gospels of Mark and Luke as well as those of John and Matthew; the history of Paul's shipwreck in the Adriatic Sea, as well as that of the shipwreck of the Ancient world; the scenes of Mamre under Abraham's tent, as those of the days of Christ in the eternal tents; the prophetic prayers where the Messiah, a thousand years before his advent, exclaimed in the Psalms; "My God, my God, why hast thou forsaken me? They pierced my hands and feet; they cast lots for my garment;" as well as the narrative of the same events by St. John, St. Mark, St. Luke, or St. Matthew.

In other words, we aim to establish by the word of God —that the Scriptures are from God—that all the Scriptures are from God—and that every part of the Scriptures is from God.

At the same time, we would be understood in making this assertion. In maintaining that all the Bible is from God, we are far from thinking that this excludes man. We shall illustrate this point more clearly hereafter, but we deem it necessary to allude to it in this connection. Every word of the Bible is as really from man, as it is from God. In a certain sense, the Epistle to the Romans is entirely a letter of Paul; and in a still higher sense, the Epistle to the Romans is entirely a letter from God. Pascal might have dictated one of his Provincial letters to a mechanic of Clermont, and another to the Abbess of Port Royal. Would the first have been any less Pascalian than the other? Surely not. The great Newton, when he desired to transmit his wonderful discoveries to the world, might have procured some child in Cambridge to write the fortieth, and some servant of his college to write the forty-first proposition of the immortal book *Principii*, whilst he dictated the other pages to Barrow and Gregory. Should we thence have possessed in any less degree, the discoveries of his genius and the mathematical reasonings which were to rank in our view, all the movements of the universe under the same law? Would the entire work have been any less Newton's? Surely not. Perhaps at the same time, some man of leisure might have felt some interest in ascertaining the emotions of these two great men, or the simple thought of that child, or the honest prejudices of that servant, while their four pens, alike docile, were tracing the Latin sentences which were dictated to them. You may have been told that the two last, even when writing, were roving in their imaginations in the gardens of the city, or in the court yards of Trinity College; whilst the two professors, entering with lively transports into all the thoughts of their friend, and soaring in his sublime flight, like the eaglets upon their mother's back, were plunging with him into the higher regions of science, borne along and aloft upon his powerful wings, and sailing enchanted in the new and boundless space which he had opened to them. Yet, you may have been told that, among the lines thus dictated, there are some which neither the child nor even the professors were able to comprehend. What do I care for these details; you would have replied. I will not spend my time upon them: it is the book, Newton's book I want to study. Its preface, its title, its first line, its last line, all its theorems, easy or difficult, understood or not understood, are from the same author; and that is sufficient for me. Whoever the writers may have been, and at whatever different elevations their thoughts have ranged; their faithful and superintended hand traced alike the thoughts of their master upon the same paper; and I can there always study with an equal confidence, in the very words of his genius, the mathematical principles of Newton's Philosophy. Such is the fact of Theopneusty.

It is thus that God, who would make known to his elect, in an eternal book, the spiritual principles of the divine philosophy; has dictated its pages, during sixteen centuries, to priests, kings, warriors, shepherds, tax-gatherers, boatmen, scribes, tent-makers. Its first line, its last line, all its instructions, understood or not understood, are from the same author, and that is sufficient for us. Whoever the writers may have been, and whatever their understanding of the book; they have all written with a faithful, superintended hand, on the same scroll, under the dictation of the same master, to whom a thousand years are as one day; such is the origin of the Bible. I will not waste my time in vain questions; I will study the book. It is the word of Moses, the word of Amos, the word of John, the word of Paul; but it is the mind of God and the word of God.

We should then deem it a very erroneous statement to say; certain passages in the Bible are from men, and certain others from God. No; every verse, without exception, is from men; and every verse, without exception, is from God; whether he speaks directly in his own name, or whether he employs all the individuality* of the sacred writer. And as St. Bernard says of the living works of the regenerated man, "that our will performs

---

* *Translator's Note.*—The word "individuality" is here employed, not in its ordinary, perhaps its only true signification; which is; separate, personal existence. The translator, for the sake of avoiding circumlocution, intends it to represent throughout this work—the expression of personal peculiarities, or individuality in the style and contents of a writing.

none of them without grace ; but that grace too performs none of them without our will ;" so must we say, that in the scriptures, God has done nothing but by man, and man has done nothing but by God.

There is, in fact, a perfect parallel between Theopneusty and efficacious grace. In the operations of the Holy Spirit in inditing the sacred books, and in those of the same Spirit converting a soul, and causing it to walk in the paths of holiness, man is in some respects entirely passive, in others entirely active. God there does everything ; man there does all ; and we may say of all these works, as St. Paul said of one of them to the Philippians ; " it is God who worketh in you both *to will and to do*." And we see that in the Scriptures, the same work is attributed alternately to God and to man ; God converts, and it is man who converts himself ; God circumcises the heart, God gives a new heart, and it is man who must circumcise his own heart and make to himself a new heart. " Not only because we must employ the means of obtaining such an effect," says the famous Pres. Edwards, in his admirable remarks against the Armenians, " but because this effect itself is our act, as well as our duty ; God producing all, and we acting all."*

Such is then the word of God. It is God speaking in man, God speaking by man, God speaking as man, God speaking for man. We have affirmed it ; and now must prove it.

Perhaps, however, it will be proper first to define this doctrine with more precision.

In theory, we might say that a religion could be divine, without the miraculous inspiration of its books. It might be possible, for example, to conceive of a Christianity without Theopneusty ; and it might perhaps, be conceived that every other miracle of our religion, except that, was a

* Edwards' Remarks, &c. p. 251.

4

fact. In this supposition, (which is totally unauthorized), the eternal Father would have given his Son to the world; the all-creating Word, made flesh, would have undergone the death of the cross for us, and have sent down upon the Apostles the spirit of wisdom and miraculous powers; but, all these mysteries of redemption once accomplished, he would have abandoned to these men of God the work of writing our Sacred books, according to their own wisdom; and their writings would have presented to us only the natural language of their supernatural illuminations, of their convictions and their charity. Such an order of things is undoubtedly a vain supposition, directly contrary to the testimony of the Scriptures as to their own nature; but, without remarking here, that it explains nothing; and that, miracle for miracle, that of illumination is not less inexplicable than Theopneusty; without further saying that the word of God possesses a divine power peculiar to itself: such an order of things, if it were realized, would have exposed us to innumerable errors, and plunged us into the most ruinous uncertainty. With no security against the imprudence of the writers, we should not have been able to give their writings even the authority which the Church now concedes to those of Augustine, Bernard, Luther, Calvin, or of a multitude of other men enlightened in the truth by the Holy Spirit. We are sufficiently aware how many imprudent words and erroneous propositions mar the most beautiful pages of these admirable writers. And yet the Apostles (on the supposition we have just made), would have been subjected still more than they, to serious errors; since they could not have had, like the doctors of the Church, a word of God, by which to correct their writings; and since they would have been compelled to invent the entire language of religious science; for a science, we know, is more than half formed, when its language is made.

What fatal errors, what grievous ignorance, what inevitable imprudence had necessarily accompanied, in them, a revelation without Theopneusty ; and in what deplorable doubts had the Church then been left !—errors in the selection of facts, errors in estimating them, errors in stating them, errors in the conception of the relations which they hold to doctrines, errors in the expression of these doctrines themselves, errors of omission, errors of language, errors of exaggeration, errors in the adoption of national, provincial or party prejudices, errors in the anticipations of the future and in the estimate of the past.

But, thanks to God, it is not so with our sacred books. They contain no errors, all their writing is inspired of God. "Holy men of God spake as they were moved by the Holy Ghost ; not in the words which man's wisdom teacheth, but which the Holy Ghost teacheth ;" so that none of these words ought to be neglected, and we are called to respect them and to study them even to their least iota and to their least tittle ; for this " scripture is purified, as silver seven times tried in the fire ; it is perfect." These assertions, themselves testimonies of the word of God, contain precisely our last definition of Theopneusty, and lead us to characterize it finally, as " that inexplicable power which the Divine Spirit formerly exercised over the authors of the Holy Scriptures, to guide them even in the employment of the words they were to use, and to preserve them from all error, as well as from every omission."

This new definition, which may appear complex, is not so in reality ; because the two points of which it is composed, are equivalents : to receive the one of which, is to receive the other.

We propose them, then, separately to the consent of our readers, and we offer them the choice between the two. The one has more precision, the other more simplicity ; inasmuch as it presents the doctrine under a form more separate from every question about the mode of inspiration and about the secret experience of the sacred writers. Accept one or the other fully, and you have rendered to the Scriptures the honor and the faith which are their due.

We propose then to establish the doctrine of Theopneusty under the one or the other of these two forms; "the Scriptures are given and guaranteed by God, even in their very language;" and, "the Scriptures contain no error, that is, they say all they ought to say, and only what they ought to say."

Now, how shall we establish this doctrine? By the Scriptures themselves, and only by the Scriptures. When their truth is once admitted, it is from them we must learn what they are; and when they have once asserted that they are inspired of God, it is still for them to say how they are inspired, and how far.

To undertake to prove, *a priori*, their inspiration, in arguing from the necessity of this miracle for the security of cur faith, would be, to reason feebly, and almost to imitate, in one respect, the presumption which, in another respect, imagines, *a priori*, four degrees of Theopneusty. Again, to undertake to establish the inspiration of the Scriptures upon the consideration of their beauty, their constant wisdom, their prophetic prudence, and all those marks of divinity which are there revealed, would be indeed, to rest our proof on reasonings doubtless just, but contestable, or at least contested. We must then stand upon the Scriptural declarations alone. We have no other authority for the doctrines of our faith, and Theopneusty is one of those doctrines.

At the same time, let us here guard against a misapprehension. It may happen that some reader not fully confirmed in his belief of Christianity, mistaking our design, and thinking that from our book he may gather arguments to establish his faith, shall be disappointed, and shall feel himself authorized to reproach our argument as having the capital defect of attempting to prove the inspiration of the Scriptures by that inspiration.

Here we must vindicate ourselves. We have not written these pages for the disciples of Porphyry, of Voltaire, or Rousseau; nor has our object been to prove that the Scriptures are worthy of faith. Others have done this; it is not our task. We address men who respect the Scriptures, and admit their truth. It is to them we assert, that the Scriptures being true, declare themselves inspired; and that being inspired, they declare themselves entirely so; whence we conclude that they must be so.

Certainly this doctrine is one of the simplest and clearest of all truths, to the mind humbly and rationally submissive to the testimony of the Scriptures. We may indeed hear modern theologians represent it as full of uncertainty and difficulties; but men who have desired to study it only by the light of God's word, have not found there these difficulties and this uncertainty. Nothing, on the contrary, is more clearly or more frequently taught in the Scriptures, than the inspiration of the Scriptures. The ancients too, never found the embarrassments and doubts on this subject, which confound the learned of our day. For them the Bible either was of God, or it was not of God. Antiquity presents on this point an admirable unanimity.* But, since the moderns, in imitation of the Jewish Talmudists and Rabbins of the middle ages,† have imagined sage distinctions between four or five degrees of

---

* See on this subject the learned dissertation of Dr. Rudelbach; in which he establishes from history, the sound doctrines of inspiration as we have endeavored to establish them from the Scriptures. (Zeitschrift für die gesammte Lutherische Theologie und Kirche, von Rudelbach und Guericke. 1840.)

† See our chap. 5, sec. 2, ques. 44.

4*

inspiration, who can be astonished to find that difficulties and uncertainty have increased in their view? They contest that which the Scriptures teach, and they inculcate what the Scriptures do not teach. Their embarrassment is easily explained, but the blame of it rests on their temerity.

The Bible renders so clear a testimony to its own full inspiration, that differences of opinion among Christians on a subject so well defined, are astonishing. And the explanation of it will only add so much testimony to the power and evil of prejudice. The mind, already pre-occupied with objections which it has originated, distorts the sacred passages, and turns them from their natural sense, and by a secret labor of thought, forces itself to reconcile them with the difficulties which embarrass it. These Christians deny, in spite of the Scriptures, the full inspiration of the Scriptures; as the Sadducees denied the resurrection, because they found the miracle inexplicable; but it must be remembered that Jesus Christ has answered: "Ye do err, not knowing the Scriptures, nor the power of God." (Mark xii. 24–27.) It is then on account of this too common disposition of the human mind, that we have thought it best not to present our Scriptural proofs, until after a full examination of the objections raised against it.

That will be the subject of the next chapter.

We desire to present also, to our reader, a more precise exposition of our doctrine, and of some of the questions connected with it; but it has appeared to us preferable to defer this also to the last pages; both because it will be more acceptable when the difficulties shall have been maturely considered, and because we would not, at the beginning, repel, by a too didactic discussion, the unlettered readers who may come to these pages, seeking the edification of their faith.

We are about then, to commence, by an attentive examination of the difficulties and the systems raised up against the doctrine of a plenary inspiration. These difficulties constitute objections ; and these systems are rather evasions. We will study them both in the two succeeding chapters.

CHAPTER II.

OBJECTIONS EXAMINED.

It is objected, that the individuality of the sacred writers, deeply imprinted on their respective writings, cannot be reconciled with plenary inspiration; it is objected, that the fallibility of the translator renders illusory the infallibility of the original text; it is objected, that the use of the totally human version of the Seventy, by the apostles, renders their theopneusty more than doubtful; the objector refers to the variations in the manuscripts, imperfections in the reasonings and in the doctrines, errors in the facts; he brings up the statements which appear absurd in the light of our more perfect acquaintance with the laws of nature; he states, finally, what he calls the admissions of St. Paul. We shall answer these objections in order, and then examine in succession, some of the theories by which the doctrine of plenary inspiration is evaded.

Section I.—The individuality, or peculiarities of the sacred writers, deeply impressed on their books.

It is first objected, that this individuality, which so pervades the sacred books, furnishes a powerful testimony against the doctrine of a full and constant inspiration. We are told that it is impossible to read the Scriptures, without being struck with the differences of language, of conception, of style, which each author presents. These differences, by impressing on these writings the indisputable features of their personality, betray, every where, the concurrence of their personal action in the composition of the Scriptures. Although the title of each book should not indicate to us that we are passing from one author to another; yet we should quickly discover by the change of their character, that a new hand has taken the pen. This difference shows itself even between one prophet and another, and between two apostles. Who could read the writings of Isaiah and Ezekiel, of Amos and Hosea, of Zephaniah and Habakkuk, of Jeremiah and Daniel; who could study successively the writings of Paul and Peter, of James and John, without remarking in each one of them, the influence which his habits, his condition, his genius, his education, his circumstances have exercised over his views of truth, over his reasoning, and his language? They describe that which they have seen, and as they have seen it. Their memory has full play, their imaginations are exercised, their affections are drawn out, all their being is employed, and their moral physiognomy is clearly portrayed in their writings. We perceive that the composition of each book has depended greatly, both for its matter and its form, upon the peculiar circumstances and turn of its author.

Could the son of Zebedee have composed the Epistle to the Romans, such as we have received it from the hands of St. Paul? Who would have dreamed of attributing the Epistle to the Hebrews to him? And although the catholic letters of Peter should be deprived of their title, who would think of attributing them to John? It is so likewise with the evangelists. It is perfectly easy to recognize each one of them, although they speak of the same Master, teach the same doctrines, and relate the same incidents. This is the fact which none can dispute; but the legitimacy of their inferences we deny. It is said,

1. If it were God alone who speaks in every part of the

Scriptures, we should see, then, a uniformity which now they do not possess.

2. We must then admit that two different forces have acted at the same time upon the sacred writers, while they were composing the Scriptures—their own natural force, and the miraculous force of inspiration.

3. From the conflict, the concurrence, or the balanced action of these two forces, there must have resulted an inspiration variable, gradual, sometimes entire, sometimes imperfect, and often even reduced to the feeble measure of a mere supervision.

4. The variable power of the Divine Spirit in this combined action, must have proportioned itself to the importance and to the difficulties of the matters treated by the sacred author. It must, in fact, have withdrawn itself, whenever the judgment and the recollection of the writer were competent to the work; for God performs no needless miracle.

"Man cannot say," says Bishop Wilson,* "where this inspiration begins, and where it ends."

"That," says Dr. Twesten, "which is exaggerated in the notions of some, concerning inspiration, is not the extension of it to all parts, but the extension of it to all parts equally. If inspiration does not exclude the personal action of the sacred writers, neither does it any more destroy all the influence of human imperfection. But we may suppose this influence always feebler in the writers, in proportion as the matter relates more intimately to Christ."†

"We should recognize," says Dr. Dick, "three degrees of inspiration. There are, in the first place, many things which the writers could know by the mere exercise of their natural faculties; no supernatural influence was ne-

* Lect. on Evid. of Christianity, p. 506.
† Vorles. über die Dogmatik, Tom. i.

cessary to relate them; it was only requisite that they should be infallibly preserved from error. In the second place, there were other things, for which their understandings and their faculties needed to be divinely strengthened. Finally, there are many others still, which contain subjects that made a direct inspiration indispensable."*

Hence it results, that if this full inspiration was sometimes necessary, yet, for matters at once simple and not vital to religion, there may be in the Scriptures some innocent errors, and some of those stains which the hand of man always lets fall on that which it touches.

Whilst the energy of the Divine Spirit, by an action always powerful, and often victorious, was enlarging the understandings of the men of God, purifying their affections, and making them seek among all their recollections, for those which could be the most usefully transmitted to the Church; the natural energies of their minds, left to themselves for all the details which were of no importance to faith or virtue, may have introduced in the Scriptures some mixture of inexactness and imperfection. "We must not then attribute to the Scriptures an unlimited infallibility, as if there were no error," says Mr. Twesten. "Doubtless, God is truth; and, in important matters, every thing which comes from him is truth; but if every thing is not equally important, then every thing does not come equally from him; and if inspiration does not exclude the personal action of the sacred authors, neither does it destroy all the influence of human imperfection."

Such is then the objection.—It assumes, in its suppositions and in its conclusions, that there are in the Scriptures, some passages of no importance, and others marred by imperfection.—We will hereafter repel with all our power, both these erroneous imputations; but we must de-

* Essay on Insp. of Holy Scriptures.

fer it for the present, as we are here considering only the living and personal form under which the Scriptures have been given to us, and its supposed incompatibility with a plenary inspiration.

To this objection we may reply:

1. We commence by declaring how far we are from denying the alleged fact, while we resist the false inferences deduced from it. So far are we from overlooking this human individuality, every where impressed on our sacred books; that, on the contrary, it is with profound gratitude, with an ever-increasing admiration, we regard this living, real, dramatic, human character infused so powerfully and so charmingly into every part of the book of God. Yes, (we delight to say it to the objectors,) here it is the phraseology, the stamp, the accent of a Moses, there of a St. John, here of an Isaiah, there of an Amos, here of a Daniel, or St. Peter, there of a Nehemiah, there of a St. Paul. We recognise them, we hear them, we see them; it is all but impossible to be mistaken in regard to it. We admit this fact, we delight to study it, we admire it profoundly, and we there see, as we shall be called to repeat, more than an additional proof of the divine wisdom which dictated the Scriptures.

2. What bearing has the absence or the presence of the writer's affections on the fact of theopneusty? Cannot God alike employ them or dispense with them? He, who could make a statue speak; can he not make even an infant speak as he pleases? He who reproved the folly of the prophet by a dumb animal; can he not put in another prophet the sentiments or the words which are best suited to the plan of his revelations? He who caused the dead hand to come out from the wall, and write these terrible words: "Mene, Mene, Tekel, Upharsin!" could he not equally direct the intelligent and pious pen of his apostle to write such words as these: "I say the

truth in Christ, I lie not; my conscience bearing me witness in the Holy Ghost, that I have great sorrow and heaviness of heart for my brethren, my kinsmen according to the flesh"?

Do you know how God acts, and how he refrains from acting? Will you teach us the mechanism of inspiration? Will you tell us what is the difference between his mode of influence, when the personal qualities of the writer show themselves, and when they do not? Will you explain to us how the concurrence of the thoughts, the recollections and the emotions of the sacred writers would impair their theopneusty; and will you tell us why this very concurrence does not make part of it? Between the fact of individuality and the inference which you draw from it, there is an abyss. And into this abyss your intelligence can no more descend to oppose the theopneusty, than ours to explain it. Was there not enough individuality in the language of Caiaphas, when that wicked man, full of the bitterest gall, abandoning himself to the counsels of his depraved heart, and thinking of anything but speaking the words of God, cried out in the Jewish council: "You do not understand nor consider that it is expedient that one man die for the people"? Surely there was in these words sufficient individuality; and yet it is written that Caiaphas did not speak them of himself, (ἀφ'ἑαυτοῦ) but that being high-priest that year, he spoke as a prophet, without knowing what he said; announcing that Jesus was about to come, to gather the children of God who are scattered abroad. (John xi. 49–52.)

Why then could not the same spirit employ the pious affections of his saints for announcing the word of God, as well as use the hypocritical and wicked thoughts of his most odious adversaries?

3. When they say, that if, in such a passage, it is the style of Moses, or of Luke, of Ezekiel, or of John, it can-

5

not be that of God, they mean to tell us what is the
style of God. They will point out to us the accent of
the Holy Ghost; they will teach us to recognize it by the
turn of his phrases, by the tone of his voice; and they
will tell us what signalizes in the Hebrew language, or in
the Greek, his supreme individuality. Since you know
it, explain it to us.

4. It should not be forgotten that the sovereign action
of God, in the different fields of its exercise, never excludes the employment of second causes. On the contrary, it is in their very enlistment, that he loves to manifest his powerful wisdom. In the field of the creation,
he gives us the plants, by the combined employment of all
the elements; of heat, moisture, electricity, atmosphere,
light, the mechanical attraction of the capillary vessels,
and of the various work of the organs. In the field of
Providence, he accomplishes the development of his
vastest plans, by the unanticipated combination of a
thousand millions of human wills alternately intelligent
and submissive, or ignorant and rebellious. " Herod,
Pilate, the Gentiles and the Jews (moved by so many
different passions) have gathered themselves together to
do what thy hand and thy counsel determined before,
should be done." In the field of prophecy, it is still in
the same manner that he leads the prophecies on to their
fulfilment. He prepares, for instance, long before hand,
a warrior-prince in the mountains of Persia, and another
in those of Media; the first he had designated by name,
two centuries before his birth; he unites them at a point
named, with ten other people, against the empire of the
Chaldeans; he leads them to surmount a thousand obstacles, and at last brings them into great Babylon, at the
very moment which terminated the seventy years so long
before assigned to the Jewish captivity. In the very
field of his miracles, he is still pleased to use second

causes. He might there have said: "let the thing be;" and it would have been. But he designed, even there, in employing inferior agents, to make us comprehend more fully, that it is he who gives power to the feeblest of them. To divide the Red Sea, he causes not only the rod of Moses to be stretched out over the abyss; but sends also an impetuous east wind, which blows all night, and drives back the waters of the sea. To restore sight to the man born blind, he moistens the clay, and with it anoints the eye-lids. In the field of redemption, in place of converting a soul by an immediate act of his will, he presents to it motives, he makes it read the gospel, he sends it preachers; and thus, although it is he "who worketh in us to will and to do of his good pleasure;" yet "he begets us according to his own will by the word of truth." Why then, is it not so in the field of Theopneusty? Why, when he sends his word; should he not put it in the understanding, in the heart and in the life of his servants, as he puts it upon their lips? Why should he not associate their personality with that which they reveal to us? Why should not their sentiments, their history, their experiences make part of their Theopneusty?

5. The error of the objection to which we reply, may be further shewed by the entire inconsistency of those who use it. In order to deny the plenary inspiration of certain passages of the Scriptures, they allege the individuality impressed on them; and yet, it is admitted that other parts of the holy book, where this feature is equally produced, must have been given directly by God, even in their minutest details. Isaiah, Daniel, Ezekiel, Jeremiah and the author of the Apocalypse have just as much, impressed, each one his own style, features, manner; in a word, his own mark, on their prophecies; as Luke, Mark, John, Paul, Peter have on their histories or their letters. The objection then is not valid; if it proves any thing, it proves too much.

6. That which still strikes us in this objection and in the system of intermittent inspiration to which it is allied, is its threefold character of complication, temerity and puerility ;— of complication, for its advocates suppose that the Divine action, dictating the Scriptures, was interrupted or enfeebled in any passage, just in proportion to the diminished difficulty or importance of the passage ; and thus they represent God as successively retiring and advancing in the spirit of the sacred writer, during the course of the same chapter or passage !—of rashness ; for, not knowing the majesty of the Scriptures, they dare to suppose that they have, in some of their parts, no more than a human importance, and that they required for their composition, no more than a human wisdom !—of puerility, we say too ; for they fear to ascribe useless miracles to God ; as if the Holy Spirit, after having, as they avow, dictated, word for word, one part of the Scriptures, would have found it a less difficult task, in other parts, merely to illuminate or to superintend the writer.

7. But we go farther. That which chiefly leads us to oppose a theory that dares to classify the Scriptures as *inspired*, *half-inspired*, and *not inspired*, (as if this sad doctrine ought to be deduced from the fact that each book is characterised by the peculiarities of its author); is its direct opposition to the Scriptures themselves. The theory is, that one part of the Bible is made by man, and another part by God. Now hear the Bible itself. It protests that "all scripture is given by inspiration of God." It does not indicate an exception. By what authority then can any one make an exception which it does not admit? We are told indeed, that a part of the Scriptures required the plenary inspiration of the writer; that a part required nothing more than eminent gifts, and that still another part might have been written by an ordinary man. All this may be ; but what bearing has it

on the question ?   When the author of a book is named
to you ; you know that every thing in the book is his,
the easy and the difficult, the important and the unimportant.

If, then, " *all* Scripture is given by inspiration of God ;"
how does it affect our question, that there are passages, in
your eyes more important, or more difficult, than others ?
The least of the companions of Jesus could have composed the fifth verse of the eleventh chapter of John :—
" Now Jesus loved Martha, and her sister, and Lazarus : "
as also the most insignificant schoolmaster could have written the first line of Athalia :—" Yes, I come into his temple, to adore the Lord." But if some one had told us,
that the great Racine had dictated all his drama to some
village-mayor, should we not still continue to attribute all
its parts to him ; its first verse, the number of its scenes,
the names of its actors, the directions for their entrance
and their exit, as well as the sublimest strophes of its
choirs ? If, then, God himself declares to us, that he has
dictated all the Scriptures, who shall dare say that this
fifth verse of the eleventh chapter of John is any less from
God, than the sublime words which begin the Gospel, and
which describe to us the eternal Word ? Inspiration may,
indeed, be more clearly distinguished in some passages
than in some others ; but it is not, therefore, less real in
the one than in the other.

In a word, if there were parts of the Bible without inspiration, it would no longer be truth to say, that all the
Bible is divinely inspired ; it would no more be entirely
the word of God : it would have deceived us.

8. It is especially important to remark here, that this
fatal system of an inspiration, gradual, imperfect, and intermittent, arises from a mistake which we have more than
once found it necessary to point out. It is, that inspiration has almost always been considered as in the man ;

5*

whereas it ought to be looked for only in the book. It is "ALL SCRIPTURE," it is *all that is written*, which is inspired of God. We are not told, and we are not asked, how God has done it. It is certified to us, only that he has done it; and all that we are to believe is simply that, whatever mode he may have adopted for accomplishing it.

The contemplation of inspiration from this false point of view has given rise to the three following illusions:—

First, In contemplating inspiration in the sacred author, it has been usual to consider it in him as an *extraordinary excitement*, of which he was conscious, which carried him out of himself; which animated him, after the manner of the ancient Pythons, by a divine afflatus, or poetic fire, easily recognized; so that where the words are simple, calm, familiar, they must no longer be attributed to inspiration.

Consequently, by regarding theopneusty as in the persons, they have been naturally led to attribute to it different degrees of perfection; because they knew that the sacred writers themselves have received very different measures of illumination and of holiness. But if you regard 'inspiration as in the book, rather than in the man, then you will perceive that it cannot admit of degrees. A word is of God, or it is not of God. If it is of God, it is not so in two different modes. Whatever may have been the spiritual condition of the writer, if all his writings are divinely inspired, all his words are of God. And it is on this principle, (mark it well,) that a Christian will hesitate no more than Christ, to place the writings of Solomon by the side of those of Moses; or those of Mark or of Matthew, by the side of those of the disciple whom Jesus loved; yea, by the side of even the words of the Son of God. They are all of God.

Finally, by a third illusion; in considering the inspiration as in the writers, instead of seeing it in the writings, it has naturally been thought absurd to suppose that God miraculously *revealed* to a man *that which this man already knew.* This has led to a denial of the inspiration of those passages in which the sacred writers have merely recounted what they have seen, or have written sentences which any man of sense could have uttered without the aid of inspiration. But the case is totally changed, when inspiration is regarded as belonging to that *which is written;* for then every thing will be recognized as written by Divine dictation; whether it be what the writer already knew, or that of which he was ignorant. Who does not perceive, for example, that the case in which I should *dictate* to a student a book of geometry, is very different from the case in which, after having more or less *instructed* him in the sciences, I should request him to compose one under my supervision. In the latter case he would, doubtless, have need of me only for difficult propositions; but then too, who would think of saying that the book was mine? In the other case, on the contrary, all the parts of the book, easy or difficult, would be mine; from the quadrature of the transcendental curves, even to the theory of the straight line or of the triangle. Now, such is the Bible. It is not, as some have said, a book which God has charged men, already enlightened, to make, under his protection. It is a book which God dictated to them; it is the word of God; the Spirit of the Lord hath spoken by its authors, and his words were upon their tongue.

9. That a child may know that the style of David, of St. Luke, or St. John, can be, at the same time, the style of God.

If some modern French author, at the beginning of the century, in order to render himself popular, had imitated the style of Chateaubriand, could it not have been said, with equal truth, although in two different senses, that the style was his? And yet it was Chateaubriand's. If God himself, in order to save the French nation from a frightful explosion, by introducing the Gospel among them, should deign to send some prophets, by whose mouth He would make himself heard, they would certainly preach in the French language. But then, what would be their style, and what would you require as characteristic of the style of God? God might choose that one of these prophets should speak like Fenelon, and the other like Bonaparte. Then it would be, in a certain sense, the pithy, barking, jerking style of the great general; it would be again, and in the same sense, the flowing style, the sustained and wire-drawn period of the priest of Cambray; but, in another sense, more elevated and more true, it would be, in the one and in the other of these two mouths, the style of God, the periods of God, the manner of God, the word of God. God could, without doubt, every time he revealed his will, have uttered, from the highest heavens, a voice as glorious as that which shook the rocky Sinai, or that which was heard on the banks of the Jordan. He could have deputed no less than the angels of light. But then, what languages would they have spoken? Those of the earth, evidently. If then, in speaking to men on the earth, he must adopt the words and the construction of the Hebrews and the Greeks, instead of the syntax of the heavens and the vocabulary of archangels; why should he not also equally have borrowed their gait, their style, and their personality?

10. He has done so, without doubt; but do not think that he has done it by accident. "His works are known to him from the beginning." See how he prepares with prospective wisdom, the leaf of a tree, wrapped first in its little case; then gradually unfolding, to drink the rays of light and breathe the vital air, while the roots send up to it

their nourishing juices. But his wisdom has looked and provided still further; it has prepared this leaf for that coming day, when it may nourish the worms which are to burst their silky covering and spin their thread upon its branches. See how he prepared, first a gourd for the place and for the time when and where Jonas was to come and sit down on the east of Nineveh; and afterwards a destructive worm for the next morning, when this gourd should wither;—just too, as when he would proceed to the most important of his works, and cause to be written this prophecy which is to outlive the heavens and the earth; the eternal God knew how to prepare, long beforehand, each one of his prophets for the moment and for the testimony to which he had destined him from eternity. He has chosen them, one after the other, for their respective offices, from among all the men born of women; and he has perfectly accomplished in respect to them, this word: "Send, oh Lord, whom thou wilt send."

As a skilful musician, who has to execute alone a long score, will avail himself by turns, of the funereal flute, the shepherd's pipe, the dancer's bagpipe or the warrior's trumpet; thus the Almighty God, to proclaim to us his eternal word, has chosen of old, the instruments into which he would successively breathe the breath of his Spirit. "He chose them before the foundation of the world; he separated them from their mother's womb."*

Have you visited the Cathedral of Freyburg, and listened to that wonderful organist, who, with such enchantment, draws the tears from the traveler's eyes; while he touches, one after another, his wonderful keys, and makes you hear by turns, the march of armies upon the beach, or the chanted prayer upon the lake during the tempest, or the voices of praise after it is calm? All your senses

---

* Gal. i. 15. Eph. i. 4.

are overwhelmed, for it has all passed before you like a vivid reality. Well, thus the Eternal God, powerful in harmony, touches by turns with the fingers of his Spirit, the keys which he had chosen for the hour of his design, and for the unity of his celestial hymn. He had before him, from eternity, all the human keys; his creating eyes embraced at a glance, this key-board of sixty centuries; and when he would make this fallen world hear the eternal counsel of its redemption and the advent of the Son of God, he laid his left hand on Enoch the seventh from Adam,* and his right hand on John, the humble and sublime prisoner of Patmos. The celestial hymn, seven hundred years before the deluge, began with these words: "Behold, the Lord cometh with ten thousand of his saints, to judge the world;" but already in the thought of God and in the eternal harmony of his work, the voice of John was responding to that of Enoch, and terminating the hymn, three thousand years after him, with these words: "Behold, he cometh, and every eye shall see him, yea, those that pierced him! even so, Lord Jesus, come quickly, amen!" And during this hymn of three thousand years, the Spirit of God did not cease to breathe upon all his ambassadors; the angels stooped, says an Apostle, to contemplate its depths; the elect of God were moved, and eternal life descended into their souls.

Between Enoch and St. John, hear Jeremiah, twenty-four centuries after the one, and seven centuries before the other: "Before I formed thee in the belly, I knew thee, and before thou comest forth out of the womb, I sanctified thee, and I ordained thee a prophet unto the nations."† It was in vain that this man in his fear exclaimed: "Oh Lord, behold I cannot speak, for I am a child;" the Lord answered him: "say not, I am a child; for, thou

---

* Jude, 14.   † Jer. i. 5, 6, 7

shalt speak all that I command thee." Then the Lord
stretched forth his hand and touched his mouth, and said :
"Behold, I put my word in thy mouth."

Between Enoch and Jeremiah, hear Moses. He de-
bates too, upon Mount Horeb, against the Lord's appeal :
" Alas, Lord, I am a man slow of speech ; send rather I
pray thee, by whom thou wilt send."* But the anger of
the Lord burns against Moses : " Who hath made man's
mouth? Now therefore go, and I will be with thy mouth,
and teach thee what thou shalt say."

Between Jeremiah and St. John, hear Saul of Tarsus :
" When it pleased God, who hath separated me from
my mother's womb and called me by his grace, to reveal
his Son in me, that I might preach him among the
heathen."†

We see then, it was sometimes the sublime and untu-
tored simplicity of John ; sometimes the excited, ellipti-
cal, startling, argumentative energy of Paul ; sometimes
the fervor and solemnity of Peter ; it was the majestic
poetry of Isaiah, or the lyrical poetry of David ; it was
the simple and majestic narrative of Moses, or the senten-
tious and royal wisdom of Solomon ;—yes, it was all that ;
it was Peter ; it was Isaiah ; it was Matthew ; it was John ;
it was Moses ; but it was God !

" Are not these men who speak to us, all, Galileans ?"
cried one on the day of Pentecost. Yes, they are ; but
the word upon their lips comes from another country, it
is from heaven. Hear it ; for the tongues of fire have
come down upon their heads, and it is God who speaks to
you by their mouth.

11. Finally ; we would show that this human personality which is pointed out to us in the Scriptures ; so far
from leaving any stain there, or from being an infirmity ;

---

*Ex. iv. 10.   †Gal. i. 15.

on the contrary, impresses a divine beauty on the sacred page, and powerfully proves to us its theopneusty.

Yes, we have said it; it is God who there speaks to us; but it is also man; it is man, but it is also God. Admirable word of my God! It has been made human in its way, like the eternal Word! Yes, God has caused it thus to stoop even to us, full of grace and truth, like our words, in every thing but error and sin. Admirable word, divine word; but full of humanity, amiable word of my God! Yes, it must, in order to be understood by us, place itself on mortal lips, recite human things; and to charm us, must put on the features of our thoughts and all the tones of our voice, because God knows well of what we are made. But we have recognized it as the word of the Lord, powerful, efficacious, sharper than any two-edged sword; and the most simple among us, have been able to say in hearing it, like Cleopas and his friend: "did not our hearts burn within us while he talked with us?"

With what a powerful charm the Scriptures, by this abundance of humanity, and by all this personality which clothes their divinity, remind us that the Lord of our souls, whose teaching voice they are, himself bears a human heart upon the throne of God, although seated in the highest places, where the angels can serve and adore him! By this too, they present to us, not only this double character of variety and unity which at once so embellishes and distinguishes all the other works of God, as creator of the heavens and the earth, but also that union of familiarity and authority, of sympathy and grandeur, of practical detail and mysterious majesty, of humanity and divinity, which we recognize in all the dispensations of the same God, as redeemer and shepherd of his Church.

It is then thus that the Father of mercies, in speaking in his prophets, has had not only to employ their manner as well as their voice, and their style as well as their pen, but also often to enlist in it all their faculties of thought and feeling. Sometimes in order to show us his divine sympathy, he has thought proper to associate their personal reminiscences, their own experiences and their pious emotions with the words which he was dictating to them. Sometimes, in order to remind us of his sovereign interference, he has preferred to dispense with this unessential concurrence of their memories, their affections and their understandings.

Such ought the word of God to be.

Like Emmanuel, full of grace and truth; at the same time in the bosom of God and in the heart of man; powerful and sympathetic, celestial and of the earth, sublime and humiliated, imposing and familiar, God and man! It does not then resemble the God of the rationalists. After having, like the disciples of Epicurus, removed the Deity very far from man and into the third heaven, they have wished the Bible to put him there too. "Philosophy," said the too celebrated Strauss of Louisburg, "employs the language of the gods; whilst religion employs the language of men." Yes, doubtless, it does; it assumes no other; it leaves to philosophers and the gods of this world, their empyrium and their language.

Studied under this aspect, and considered by this character, the word of God shows itself without a parallel; it has unequalled attractions; it offers to the men of every age, place and condition, beauties always new, a charm which does not grow old, which ever satisfies and never satiates. In direct contrast with human books, it not only pleases you, it increases in beauty, extent and elevation of meaning, in proportion as you read it more assiduously. It seems that the book, the more you study and re-study it, grows and expands, and that an invisible and benevolent Being comes daily to sew in it some new leaves! This is the reason why the souls of the learned and the unlearned,

6

who have long been nourished by it, equally hang upon it, just as those once did on the lips of Christ, who are mentioned by Luke. (Chap. xix. 48.)* They all find it incomparable; sometimes powerful as the noise of mighty waters, sometimes amiable and sweet as the voice of the bride to her bridegroom; but always "perfect, always restoring the soul, and making wise the simple."

To what book, in this respect, would you compare it? Would you place by its side, the discourses of Plato or of Seneca, of Aristotle, or St. Simon, or Rousseau? Have you read the books of Mohammed? Listen to him for one hour. Under the pressure of his piercing and monotonous voice, your ears will tingle. From the first page to the last, it is always the cry of the same trumpet, always the cornet of Medina sounding from the top of a minaret or of a war-camel; always a sybilline oracle, sharp and hard, in a continued strain of commandment and threat; whether he ordains virtue or commands murder; always one and the same voice, sharp and roaring, without compassion, without familiarity, without tears, without soul, without sympathy.

If after reading other books, you feel religious wants, open the Bible; hear it. They are sometimes indeed the songs of angels, but of angels come down among the sons of Adam.

They are the organs of the Most High; but they come to charm the heart of man and to move his concience; in the cabin of the shepherd, as in the palace; in the garrets of the poor, as in the tents of the desert.

The Bible, in fact, instructs all conditions; it brings on the stage, the humble and the great; it reveals to them equally the love of God, and exposes in them the same miseries. It addresses children; and they are often children who there show us the way to heaven, and the greatness of the Lord. It addresses herdsmen; and they are

* ὁ λαὸς ἅπας ἐξεκρέματο.

often herdsmen who there speak and reveal to us the character of God. It speaks to kings and to scribes; and they are often kings and scribes who there teach us the miseries of man, humility, confession and prayer. Domestic scenes, avowals of the conscience, secret effusions of prayer, travels, proverbs, revelations of the depths of the heart, the holy career of a child of God, weaknesses unveiled, falls, revivings, intimate experiences, parables, familiar letters, theological treatises, sacred commentaries on some ancient Scripture, national chronicles, military pageants, political censuses, descriptions of God, portraits of angels, celestial visions, practical counsels, rules of life, solutions of cases of conscience, judgments of the Lord, sacred songs, predictions of the future, accounts of the days which preceded our creation, sublime odes, inimitable poetry. All this is found in turn; and all this is there exposed to our view, in a variety full of charm, and in a whole, whose majesty is captivating as that of a temple.

It is thus the Bible must from its first page to its last, associate with its majestic unity, the indefinable charm of an instruction, human, familiar, sympathising, personal, and with a drama of forty centuries. "There are," it is said in the Bible of Desmarets, "shallows, where a lamb may wade, and deep waters, where an elephant may swim."

But mark at the same time, the peculiar unity, and the numberless and profound harmonies in this immense variety! Under all these forms it is always the same truth; always man lost, and God the Savior; always the first Adam with his race leaving Eden and losing life, and the second Adam with his people reëntering Paradise, and finding again the tree of life; always the same appeal in a thousand tones: "Oh heart of man, return to thy God; for thy God pardons. Thou art in the abyss; come up from it; a Savior has descended into it—he gives holiness and life!"

"Can a book at once so sublime and so simple, be the work of man?" inquired a too celebrated philosopher of the last century; and every page has answered; no, impossible; for, every where, through so many ages, and whichever of the sacred writers holds the pen, king or shepherd, scribe or fisherman, priest or publican, every where you recognize that the same author, at an interval of a thousand years, and that the same eternal Spirit has conceived and dictated every thing; every where, in Babylon as at Horeb, in Jerusalem as in Athens, in Rome as in Patmos, you find described the same God, the same world, the same men, the same angels, the same future, the same heaven. Every where, whether it be a historian or a poet who speaks to you, whether on the plains of the desert in the age of Pharaoh, or in the dungeon of the capitol, in the age of the Cæsars,—every where, n the world, the same ruin; in man, the same condemnation and impotence; in the angels, the same elevation, innocence and charity; in heaven, the same purity and happiness, the same meeting together of truth and mercy, the same embrace of righteousness and peace; the same designs of a God who blots out iniquity, transgression and sin, and who will yet by no means clear the guilty.

We conclude then that the abundance of humanity which is found in the Scriptures, far from compromising their Theopneusty, is but another indication of their divinity.

SECTION II.—THE TRANSLATIONS.

We come to the second objection.—You are sure, we are sometimes told, that the inspiration of the Scriptures extends even to the words of the original text; but of what use is this verbal exactness of the holy word, since after all, the greater part of Christians must use only the more or less inaccurate versions? The privilege of such an inspiration is then lost to the modern Church; for you will not go so far as to say that any translation is inspired.

We have felt at first some repugnance to presenting this objection, on account of its insignificance; but it must be noticed, since we are told that it is frequently repeated, and that it is well received among us.

The first remark to be made on this objection, is, that it is not an objection. It is not raised against the *fact* of the verbal inspiration of the Scriptures, but against its advantage. So far as respects the majority of readers, it says; "the benefit of such an interference of God would be lost, since, instead of the infallible words of the original, they can have only the fallible words of a translation. But we are not at liberty to deny a fact, because we cannot at once perceive all its advantages; and we are not permitted to reject a doctrine, merely because we cannot perceive its utility. All the expressions, for instance, and all the letters of the *ten commandments* were certainly written by the finger of God, from the *Aleph* which commences, to the *Caph* which closes them. Yet would any one dare to say that the credibility of this miraculous fact is impaired by the necessity which the majority of unlearned readers now find, of reading the decalogue in some translation? No one would dare to say it. We must then observe that this objection, without attacking directly the doctrine which we defend, brings into dispute only its advantages; they are lost as to us, it is said, by the work of the translator; they disappear in this metamorphosis.

We are going then to show how even this assertion, when reduced to its last terms, is also without foundation.

The divine word, which the Bible reveals to us, passes through four successive forms, before arriving to us in a translation. It was first, from all eternity, in the mind of God. Then, he placed it in the mind of man. Then,

6*

under the operation of the Holy Spirit, and by a mysterious translation from the mind of the Prophet into the moulds and symbols of an articulate language, it there assumed the form of words. Finally, when it had undergone this first translation, as important as inexplicable, man reproduced and transferred it by a new translation, in copying it from one human language into another. Of these four operations, the first three are divine; the fourth alone is human and fallible. Will any one say, because it is human, the divinity of the other three is to us a matter of indifference? At the same time, observe, that between the third and the fourth, I mean between the first translation of the thought by the sensible signs of a human language, and the second translation of the words by other words, the difference is immense. Between the doubts which we may entertain upon the exactness of the translations, and those which would oppress us, as to the accuracy of the original text, if it were not *literally* inspired, the distance is infinite. You say: What difference does it make to me, that the third operation is produced by the Spirit of God, if the last is effected only by the human intellect? In other words, of what avail is it to me that the primitive language is inspired, if the versions are not? But you forget, in speaking thus, that we are infinitely more assured of the exactness of the translators, than we could be of that of the original text, provided all the expressions in it were not from God.

Of this we shall be convinced by the five following considerations;

1. The operation by which the sacred writers express by words, the thought of the Holy Spirit, is itself, as we have said, a translation, not of words by other words, but of divine thoughts by sensible symbols. Now, this first translation is infinitely more delicate, more mysterious, and more exposed to error, if God does not interfere, than that

can be, by which we afterwards render a Greek word of
this primitive text by an equivalent word in French or
English. In order that a man may express exactly the
thought of God, he must, if not aided from on high in his
language, have entirely seized it in its full measure, and
in all the extent and depth of its meaning. But this is
not the case with a mere translation. The divine thought
having already become incarnate in the language of the
sacred text, the object in translating, is no longer to give it
a body, but only to change its dress; to make it say in
English or French what it said in Greek, and modestly to
replace each one of its words by an equivalent one.

It is comparatively a very inferior process, very material, without mystery, and infinitely less subject to error
than the former. It requires in fact so little spirituality,
that an honest pagan can accomplish it *perfectly*, if he possesses *perfectly* the knowledge of the two languages. The
more you reflect on this first consideration, the more the
difference of these two orders of translation must appear
incommensurable. It must not then be said; what good
can it do me that the one is divine, if the other is human?

2. A second characteristic by which we can recognise
the difference of these two operations, and by which the
work of translation will be seen to be infinitely less liable
to error than the original text would be, if uninspired, is,
that, whilst the labor of our translations is performed by a
great number of men of every tongue and country, who
have been able to consecrate to it all their time and all
their care; who have from age to age, been criticising one
another, who have mutually instructed and improved each
other; the original text, on the contrary, must have been
written *at a given moment, and by one man alone.* No
one was with that man but his God, to correct him if he
erred, to improve his expressions, if he chose those which
were imperfect. If then God has not done it, no one could

have done it. And if this man has badly expressed the thought of the Holy Spirit, he has not had, as our translators have had, friends to point out his fault, predecessors to guide him, nor successors to correct him, nor months, years, ages to revise and complete his work. It is made by one solitary man, and it is made once and forever. We see then again, by this view, how much more necessary the intervention of the Holy Spirit was to the original writers of the Bible, than to their translators.

3. A third consideration which should also lead us to the same conclusions, is, that whilst all the translators of the Scriptures have been literary men, laborious, and versed in the study of language; the sacred authors, on the contrary, were, for the most part, ignorant men, without literary cultivation, unaccustomed to write their own language, and by that alone exposed, if not guided infallibly in expressing the divine revelation, to give us a defective representation of an infallible thought.

4. A fourth consideration full of force, and which will make us feel more sensibly still, the immense difference between the sacred writers and their translators; is that, whereas the thought of God passed like a flash of lightning from heaven across the mind of the prophet; whereas this thought can no more be found any where upon the earth, except in the rapid expression which was then given it by the prophet; whereas, if he has spoken badly, you know not where to look for his prototype, that in it you may find the thought of God in its purity; whereas, if he erred, his error is forever irreparable, it must endure longer than the heaven and the earth, it has stained remedilessly the eternal book, and no human being can correct it;—it is totally otherwise with the translations. They, on the contrary, have always there, by their side, the divine text, to be corrected and re-corrected from this eternal type, until they shall become entirely conformed to it. The inspired

word does not leave us; we have not to go and seek for it in the third heavens; it is still there upon the earth, such as God primitively dictated it. You may then study it for ages, to submit to its unchangeable truth, the human work of our translation. You can to-day, correct the versions of Osterwald and Martin, after a hundred and thirty years, by bringing them more rigidly to their infallible standard; after three hundred and seventeen years, you may correct the work of Luther; after fourteen hundred and forty years, that of Jerome. The phraseology of God remaining always there, before our human versions, such as God himself dictated it, in Hebrew or in Greek, in the day of the revelation; and, our dictionaries in your hand, you can return there and examine, from age to age, the infallible expression which he was pleased to give to his divine thought, until you are assured that the language of the moderns, has truly received the exact impression of it, and has given you, for your use, the most faithful fac-simile of it. Say no more then; of what use is a divine revelation to me, if I must use a human translation? If you wanted a bust of Napoleon, would you say to the sculptor, of what use is it to me that your model has been moulded at St. Helena upon the very face of Bonaparte; since, after all, it will be but your copy?

5. Finally, that which distinguishes still the first expression of the divine thought in the words of the sacred book, from its new expression in one of our translations, is that, if you suppose the words of the one as little inspired as those of the other; yet the field of the conjectures which you might make upon their possible faults, would be, as to the original text, a boundless space, ever expanding; whereas the same field, as to the translations, is a very limited space, always diminishing as you traverse it.

If some friend, returning from the East Indies, where your father had breathed his last, far from you, should bring from him a last letter written with his own hand, or dictated by him, word for word, in the Bengalese language; would it be to you a matter of no importance that this letter was entirely his; simply because you were ignorant of that language, and because you can read it only through a translation.? Do you not know that you can multiply translations of it, until there shall remain no doubt that you comprehend it just as fully as if you yourself were a Hindoo? Do you not admit, that after each one of the new translations, your uncertainty would constantly diminish, until it vanished completely; like the fractional and convergent progressions in arithmetic, whose final terms are equivalent to zero; whereas, on the contrary, if the letter did not come from your father himself, but from some stranger, who should avow that he had only repeated his thoughts, there would be no limit to your possible suppositions; and your uncertainty, carried into new and boundless regions, would continue to increase, the more you reflected; like the ascending progressions in arithmetic, whose last terms represent infinity? Thus it is with the Bible. If I believe that God has dictated it all; my doubts, as to its translations, are shut up in a very narrow field; and in this field too, as often as you re-translate it, the limits of these doubts are always diminishing. But if I believe that God has not entirely dictated it; if, on the contrary, I am to believe that human infirmity may have had its part in the text of the Bible, where shall I stop in my supposition of errors? I do not know. TheApostles, were ignorant, I must say; they were unlettered; they were Jews; they had popular prejudices; they judaized; they platonized; . . . I know not where to stop. I should begin with Locke, and I should finish with Strauss. I should first deny the personality of Satan, as a rabbinical prejudice; and I should finish by denying that of Christ as another prejudice. Between these two terms, in consequence of the ignorance to which the Apostles were exposed, I should come, like so many others, to admit, notwithstanding the letter of the Bible, and with the Bible in my hand, that there is no corruption in man, no personality in the Holy Spirit, no Deity in Jesus Christ, no expiation in his blood, no resurrection of the body, no eternal punishment, no wrath of God, no devil, no miracles, no damned, no hell. St. Paul was orthodox, I should say, with others; but he did not rightly understand his master. Whereas, on the contrary, if every thing in the original has been dictated by God, even to the least expression, even to " an -iota and tittle;" who is the translator that could by his labor, lead me to one of these negations, and make the least of these truths disappear from my Bible?

Who does not there perceive, at what an immense distance all these considerations place the original text from the translation, in respect to the importance of verbal inspiration! Between the translation of the divine thoughts into human words, and the simple version of these words into other words, the distance is as great as that between heaven and earth. The one requires God; the other needs only man. Let no one then repeat, of what use is a verbal inspiration in the one, if we have it not in the other; since between these two terms, which some would make equivalents, there is an almost infinite distance.

Section III.—Employment of the Septuagint.

It has been said and insisted on; we agree that the fact of modern translations could not affect in the least, the question of the original inspiration of the Scriptures; but there is much more. The sacred authors of the New Testament, when they themselves quote the Old Testament, use the *Greek translation*, called the *Septuagint*, made at Alexandria, two centuries and a half before Jesus Christ. Now, no one will dare, among the moderns, to pretend, as among the ancients, that the Alexandrian interpreters were inspired. Would any one now dare to advance, that this version, still human in the days of Jesus Christ, has acquired, merely by the fact of its citation by the Apostles, a divinity which it had not originally? Would not this strange pretension resemble that of the council of Trent, declaring divine the apocryphas, which the ancient Church rejected from the canon, and which St. Jerome calls "fables, and a mixture of gold and dross;"* or declaring authentic the latin version of St. Jerome, which at first had not been, for Jerome himself, and afterwards for the church, for more than a thousand years, any thing more than a human work; respectable, without doubt, but imperfect? Would it not resemble still the absurd infallibility of Sixtus V. declaring authentic his edition of 1590; or that of his successor Clement VIII; who, finding the edition of Sixtus V. intolerably incorrect, suppressed it in 1592, to substitute for it another very different, and yet likewise authentic.†

We love to bring up this difficulty; because, like many others, examined more closely, it changes objections into arguments.

It is sufficient in fact, to study the manner in which the Apostles employed the Septuagint, in order to recognize in it a striking index of the verbal inspiration which led them to write.

---

* Caveat omnia apocrypha; sciat multa his admixta vitiosa, et grandis esse prudentiæ aurum in luto quærere. See Epis. ad Laetam. Prolog. Galeat. sive. præfat. ad lib. Regum.—Symbol. Ruffini, tom. ix., p. 186. See Lardner, vol. v. p. 18–22.

† See Kortholt: de variis, S. Scrip. editionibus, p. 110 to 251. Thomas James: Bellum papale, sive Concordia, discors Sexti V., Lond., 1600. Hamilton's Introd. to reading Scrip., p. 163 to 166.

If some modern prophet were sent by God to the churches of France, in what language, think you, he would quote the Scriptures? In French, doubtless. But in which version? Those of Osterwald and Martin being the most extensively used, he would probably make his quotations from both of these, whenever their versions should appear to him sufficiently exact. But likewise, notwithstanding our habits and his, he would take great pains to alter these two versions, and to translate in his own way, as often as the thought of the original should appear to him defectively rendered. Sometimes he would do even more. In order to make us better understand in what sense he designed to apply such or such a passage, he would paraphrase the quoted passage; and in citing it, would be confined to the letter, neither of the original text nor to that of the translations.

That is precisely what has been done in regard to the Septuagint by the writers of the New Testament.

Although the universal custom of the hellenistic Jews in all the East, was, to read in the Synagogues, and to quote in their discussions, the Septuagint version,* yet the Apostles, by the three different modes of quotation, which they used, shew us the independence of the spirit that guided them.

First. When the Alexandrian translation appeared to them exact, they did not hesitate to gratify the reminiscences of their hellenistic audiences, and to quote literally from this version.

Secondly. And this case occurs frequently; when they are not satisfied with the work of the seventy, they correct it, and quote from the original Hebrew, by retranslating it more accurately.

Thirdly. In fine, when they wished to indicate more

* The Talmud itself admits of the translation of the Scriptures, only in Greek (Talmud Megillah, fol. 86.)

clearly, the sense in which they quote such or such a declaration of the sacred Scriptures, they paraphrased it in quoting it. It is then the Holy Spirit, who, by their mouth, quotes himself in modifying the expressions which he had formerly dictated to the prophets of the ancient Jews. We may compare, for instance, Micah v. 2, with Matt. ii. 6, Mal. iii. 1, with Matt. xi. 10, Mark i. 2, with Luke, vii. 27, &c. &c.

The learned Horne, in his introduction to the Scriptures, (vol. i. p. 503), has placed in five distinct classes, the quotations from the Septuagint version of the Old Testament by writers of the New Testament. We do not here guarantee all his distinctions, nor all his figures; but our readers will comprehend the force of our argument, when we shall have told them that this writer counts eighty-eight verbal quotations conformed to the Alexandrian version: sixty-four others borrowed from it, but with some variation; thirty-seven which adopt its meaning, but change the language; sixteen which translate the Hebrew more accurately; and twenty-four in which the sacred writers have paraphrased the Old Testament, in order to make the sense in which they quoted the passage, more obvious.

These numerical data are sufficient to show the independence exercised by the Holy Spirit, when he would quote from the Old Testament, to write the New. They then not only answer the objection; they establish our doctrine.

SECTION IV.—THE VARIATIONS.

Other objectors will say, " We have no such difficulty, for it is evident that the translations have nothing to do with the question of the inspiration of the original text. But in this very text, there are numerous differences between the several ancient manuscripts consulted by our churches, and those on which the admitted editions are founded. Before the evidence of such a fact, what becomes of your verbal inspiration, and of what use can it be to us?"

The answer here too is easy. We might quote already upon the variations of the manuscripts, what we have said concerning the translations. Do not confound two kinds of facts totally distinct; that of the first inspiration of the Scriptures, and that of the present integrity of the copies made from them. If God himself dictated the letter of the sacred oracles, that is a fact accomplished, and none of the copies nor translations since made, can undo the fact of the original inspiration.

A fact once consummated, nothing that follows can erase the history of that which is past. There are then here two questions to be carefully distinguished. First, Is the whole Bible divinely inspired? The second is, Are the copies made by monks and learned men, ages afterwards, exact, or are they not? This question can in no degree affect the other. Beware then of subordinating the first to the second by a strange confusion; they are independent. A book is from God, or it is not from God. In the latter case, I should in vain transcribe it a thousand times with accuracy, I could not make it divine. And in the first case, I should in vain have made a thousand inaccurate copies; my ignorance and my unfaithfulness could not make it any less the work of God. The decalogue, we repeat once more, was entirely written by the finger of Jehovah upon two tables of stone; but if the manuscripts which now give it to me, contained some variations, this second fact, would not hinder the first. The sentences, the words and the letters of the *Ten Commandments* would have been none the less written by God. The inspiration of the first text, the integrity of the subsequent copies; these are two orders of facts absolutely different, and separated from one another by thousands of miles and thousands of years. Beware then of confounding that which logic, time and space oblige you to distinguish.

It is by a precisely parallel reasoning that we reprove the indiscreet admirers of the apocrypha. The ancient oracles of God, we say to them, were committed to the Jews, as the later oracles were afterwards to the Christians. If then the book of Maccabees was merely a human book in the days of Jesus Christ; a thousand decrees of the Christian Church could not afterwards cause, that in 1560, becoming what it never was before, it should be by transubtantiation, metamorphosed into a divine book. Did the prophets write the Bible with words which human wisdom dictated to them, or with words given by God? That is our inquiry. But have they been faithfully copied, from age to age, from manuscript to manuscript? That is, perhaps, your inquiry; it is very important undoubtedly; but it is totally different from the first. Do not then confound what God has made distinct.

It is true, without doubt, some one will say, the fidelity of a copy does not render the original divine, when it is not so; and the inaccuracy of another copy will not render it human if it is not so already. To this, therefore we have made no pretension. The fact of the inspiration of the sacred text, in the days of Moses or in those of St. John, cannot depend on the copies of them which men may have made in Europe or in Africa, two or three thousand years after them; but if the second of these facts does not destroy the first, it at least renders it illusory, in taking away its importance.

This is then the real objection. The question is now changed; we are no longer inquiring after the inspiration of the original text, but the integrity of the present text. It was at first a doctrinal inquiry: " Is it declared in the

Scriptures, that the Scriptures are inspired, even to their language ?" But it is now a question of history, or rather of criticism : " Have the copyists been accurate ? are the manuscripts faithful ?" We might then be silent upon a thesis, the defence of which is not here committed to us ; but the answer is so easy ; nay more, God has made it so triumphant, that we cannot withhold it. Besides, the faith of the uninstructed has been so often disturbed by a phantasmagoria of science, that we think it may be very useful to state the case as it is. And although the objection diverts us a little from the direct pursuit of our subject, yet it may be important to follow it.

We do not doubt that if this difficulty had been presented in the days of Anthony Collins and the Free Thinkers, we should not have been without a reply ; but we should perhaps have felt some degree of embarrassment ; because the facts were not yet completely developed, and the field of conjecture yet unexplored, remained perfectly unbounded. We remember the perplexities of the excellent Bengel on this subject ; and we know that from them proceeded, at first his laborious researches upon the sacred text, and then his admiration and devout gratitude at the wonderful preservation of that text. Of what advantage, would the objector have said to us, can the assurance be, that eighteen hundred years ago the primitive text was dictated by God, if I have no more the certain assurance that the manuscripts of our libraries present it to me now in its purity ? and if it be true (as we are assured,) that the variations of these manuscripts are at least thirty thousand ?

Such was the ancient objection ; it was specious ; but in our day it is recognised by all who have investigated it, to be but a vain pretext. The rationalists themselves have avowed that it can no longer be urged, and that it must be renounced.

The Lord has miraculously watched over his word. Facts have shown it.

In constituting for its depositories first, the Jewish, then the Christian Church, his providence must have exercised its vigilance, that by this means the oracle of God should be faithfully transmitted to us. It has done so; and to secure this result, it has employed diverse causes, of which we shall hereafter have occasion to speak. Recent scientific researches have placed this fact in a strong light. Herculean labors have been pursued during the last century, (especially in the last half, as well as during the present century,) to re-unite all the readings or *variations*, which could be furnished by the detailed examination of the manuscripts of the Holy Scripture preserved in the several libraries of Europe; by the study of the oldest versions; by a comparison of the innumerable quotations of the sacred books in all the writings of the Christian Fathers;— and this immense labor has exhibited a result admirable for its insignificance; imposing, shall I say, by its diminutiveness.

As to the Old Testament, the indefatigable investigations and the four folios of Father Houbigant, the thirty years' labor of John Henry Michaelis; above all, the great critical Bible, and the ten years' study of the famous Kennicott, (upon his five hundred and eighty-one Hebrew manuscripts,) and, finally, the collection of the six hundred and eighty manuscripts of Professor Rossi:—as to the New Testament, the not less gigantic investigations of Mill, Bengel, Wetstein, and Griesbach, (into the three hundred and thirty-five manuscripts of the Gospels alone,) the later researches of Nolan, Matthei, Lawrence, and Hug; above all, those of Scholz, (with his six hundred and seventy-four manuscripts of the Gospels, his two hundred of the Acts, his two hundred and fifty-six of Paul's Epistles, his ninety-three of the Apocalypse, without

counting his fifty-three *Lectionaria*); all these prodi-
gious labors have established, in a manner so convincing,
the astonishing preservation of this text, although copied
so many thousand times, (in Hebrew, during thirty-three
centuries, and in Greek during eighteen centuries,) that
the hopes of the enemies of religion from this quarter have
been overthrown; and that, as Michaelis * remarks, "they
have thenceforward ceased to hope anything from these
critical researches, at first earnestly recommended by them,
because from them they expected discoveries which no
one has made." The learned rationalist Eichhorn himself also acknowledges, that the different readings of the
Hebrew manuscripts collected by Kennicott, offer scarcely
sufficient compensation for the labor they have cost.† But
these very failures, and this absence of discoveries, have
been, for the Church of God, a precious discovery. She
looked for it; but she rejoices to owe it to the very labors
of her enemies, and to the labors which they designed for
the overthrow of her faith. "In truth," says a learned
man of our day, "if we except these brilliant negative
conclusions to which they have come, the direct result obtained by so many lives of men consumed in these immense researches, appears to be a nullity; and we might
say, that time, talent, and science have been foolishly
spent in arriving there." ‡ But, we repeat, this result is
immense by its nothingness, and almighty in its impotence. When we reflect that the Bible has been copied
during three thousand years, as no book of human composition has ever been, and will never be; that it has undergone all the catastrophes and all the captivities of Israel;
that it has been transported for seventy years into Babylon; that it has seen itself so often persecuted, or forgot-

* Tome ii. p. 266.   † Einleitung, 2 Th. s. 700.
‡ Wiseman, Discourse on the Relations, &c. vol. ii. disc. x.

ten, or interdicted, or burned, from the days of the Philis-
tines to those of the Seleucidæ; when we recollect, that
since the days of our Savior, it has had to traverse the first
three centuries of imperial persecutions, when they threw
to the wild beasts the men that were convicted of possess-
ing the sacred books; then the seventh, eighth, and ninth
centuries, when false books, false legends, and false decretals were everywhere multiplied; the tenth century, when
so few men could read, even among the princes; the twelfth,
thirteenth, and fourteenth centuries, when the use of the
Scriptures in the language of the people was punished
with death; when they mutilated the books of the old Fathers; when they retrenched and falsified so many ancient
traditions, and the very acts of emperors and those of councils;—then we understand how necessary it has been that
the providence of God should always have held its powerful hand outstretched, to hinder, on the one side, the Jewish Church from impairing the integrity of that word
which recounts their revolts, which predicts their ruin,
which describes Jesus Christ; and on the other, to secure
the transmission to us, in all their purity, by the Christian
churches, (the most powerful sects of which, and especially the Roman, have prohibited to the people the reading
of the Scriptures, and have in so many ways substituted
the traditions of the middle ages for the word of God,) of
those Scriptures which condemn all their traditions, their
images, their dead languages, their absolutions, their celibacy; which say of Rome, that she shall be the seat of a
frightful apostacy, where shall be seen "the man of sin
sitting as God in the temple of God, making war on the
saints, forbidding to marry, and commanding to abstain
from meats which God has made;" which say of images,
"thou shalt not worship them;" of unknown tongues,
"thou shalt not use them;" of the cup, "drink ye all of
it;" of the Virgin, "woman, what have I to do with-
thee?" and of marriage, "it is honorable in all."

Now, although all the libraries containing ancient copies of the sacred books have been called to testify ; although the elucidations given by the Fathers of all ages have been studied ; although the Arabic, Syriac, Latin, Armenian and Ethiopic versions have been collated; although all the manuscripts of all countries and ages, from the third to the sixteenth century have been collected and examined a thousand times, by innumerable critics, who sought with ardor, and as the recompense and glory of their fatiguing vigils, some new text ; although the learned men, not satisfied with the libraries of the West, have visited those of Russia, and carried their researches even to the convents of Mount Athos, of Asiatic Turkey and of Egypt, to search there for new copies of the sacred text ; —"they have discovered nothing," says a learned writer already quoted, " not even a solitary reading which could cast doubt upon any passage before considered certain. All the variations, almost without exception, leave untouched the essential thoughts of each phrase, and affect only points of secondary importance," such as the insertion or omission of an article or a conjunction, the position of an adjective before or after a substantive, the greater or less exactness of a grammatical construction.

Do we ask for a standard for the Old Testament ? The famous Indian manuscript, recently deposited in the ibrary of Cambridge, may furnish an example. It is now about thirty-three years since the pious and learned Claudius Buchanan, in visiting the western peninsula of India, saw in the hands of the black Jews of Malabar, (believed to be the remnants of the tribes scattered at Nebuchadnezzar's first invasion), an immense scroll, composed of thirty-seven skins died red ; forty-eight feet long, twenty-two inches wide, and which, in its perfect condition, must have been ninety English feet long. The Holy Scriptures had been copied on it by different hands.

There were left a hundred and seventeen columns of beautiful writing; and nothing was wanting but Leviticus and a part of Deuteronomy. Buchanan procured this ancient and precious monument, which had been used in the worship of the synagogue, and he has recently deposited it in the Cambridge library. There are features which give satisfactory evidence that it was not a copy of a copy brought there by European Jews. Now Mr. Yeates has recently examined it with great attention, and has taken the pains to compare it, word for word, letter for letter, with our Hebrew edition of Van der Hooght. He has published the results of these researches. And what has he found? Even this; that there do not exist between the text of India and that of the West, more than forty petty differences, of which not one is sufficiently serious to make the slightest change in the meaning and in the interpretation of our ancient text; and that these forty differences consist in the addition or retrenchment of an *i* or a *v*, letters, whose presence or absence in Hebrew cannot change the power of a word.* We know who were the Masorites, or teachers of tradition among the Jews; men whose whole profession consisted in copying the Scriptures; we know how far these men, learned in minutiæ, carried their respect for the letter; and when we read the rules of their profession, we understand the use which the providence of God, who had confided his oracles to the Jewish people, knew how to make of their reverence, of their rigor, and even of their superstition. They counted, in each book, the number of the verses, that of the words, that of the letters; they would have said to you, for example, that the letter A recurs forty-two thousand three hundred and seventy-seven times in

---

* See Chris. Obs. xii. p. 170.—Examin. of an Indian copy of the Pentat. p. 8.—Horne's Introd. and Append. p. 95. Edit. 1818.

the Bible; the letter B thirty-eight thousand two hundred and eighteen times, and so of the rest; they would have scrupled to change the situation of a letter evidently misplaced, they would merely have advised you of it in the margin, and have supposed that some mystery was connected with it; they could have told you the middle letter of the Pentateuch, and the middle letter of each of the books that compose it; they would never suffer an erasure to be made in their manuscripts; and if any mistake was made in copying, they would reject the papyrus or the skin which was stained, to renew their work upon another scroll; for they were equally forbidden to correct a fault, and to preserve for their sacred scroll, a parchment or a skin that had undergone any erasure.

Thus much for the Old Testament. But let it not be supposed that the Providence which watched over the holy book, and which had entrusted it to the Jews (Rom. iii. 1, 2,) has any less protected the oracles of the New Testament, committed by it to the new people of God. It has not left to them any feebler incentives to gratitude and confidence.

We would first cite here the recent experience of the authors of a version of the New Testament just published in Switzerland, and in the protracted labor of which we participated. One single fact will exhibit to every class of readers how completely insignificant are the different readings of the different manuscripts. The translators just referred to, followed without exception, the *received edition*, that is the Greek text of Elzevir 1624, so long adopted by all the French churches. But, as the original plan of their work required them to introduce into the original text the variations the most approved by the critics of the last century, they were often embarrassed by finding the impossibility of expressing even in the most literal French, the new shade introduced into the Greek by this correction. The French language, in the most scrupulous version, is not sufficiently flexible to adopt these differences, so as to exhibit them; as the moulds made on the face of a king reproduce his noble features in the brass, yet without shewing all the wrinkles and veins.

At the same time we are desirous of giving to those of our readers who are strangers to sacred criticism, two or three other more impressive proofs of this providence, which, for thirty centuries, has watched over our sacred text.

First; let us compare the two Protestant translations of Osterwald and Martin. There are few modern versions more like each other. Both made from the ancient version of the Geneva pastors, written nearly at the same time and in the same spirit, they differ so little from each other, especially in the New Testament, that our Bible Societies distribute them indiscriminately, and that it is embarrassing to state which we prefer. Yet, if you will take the trouble to notice their differences in every particular, as we have done in comparing together our four-hundred manuscripts of the New Testament, we affirm in advance (and then we think, below the truth), that these two French texts are three times, and in many chapters, ten times more distant from each other, than the Greek text of our printed editions is, we do not say, from only the *least esteemed* Greek manuscripts of our libraries, but from ALL THEIR MANUSCRIPTS TAKEN TOGETHER.——We mean to say that if some skilful and malicious man (as the unhappy Voltaire or the too celebrated Anthony Collins,) had made his selection from all the Oriental and occidental manuscripts, of the worst readings, and the most discordant variations of our received text, with the perfidious intention of composing a text the most false; such a man, we say (even in employing these variations justified by *one alone* of the four or five hundred manuscripts of our libraries,) would not be able, with all his bad intention, to produce from his labor a Testament less like ours, than that of Martin is like that of Osterwald. You might distribute it in place of the true text, with as little inconvenience as you would find in giving to the French protestants, that of Martin rather than Osterwald's or Osterwald's rather than Martin's, and with much less scruple than you feel in spreading among the members of the Romish Church, the version of Le Maître de Sacy.

It is true these latter books are only translations, whilst all the Greek manuscripts present themselves as originals ; and it must be agreed that our comparison, in this respect, is very imperfect. But it is not the less adapted to establish the friends of the word of God, in making them comprehend how utterly insignificant the variations are.

But we advance to something more direct and more precise.

In order to give all our readers some estimate, at once of the number and the innocence of the received readings in the manuscripts of our libraries, we will present two specimens. The first table contains ALL THE VARIATIONS IN ALL THE EASTERN AND WESTERN MANUSCRIPTS, in the first eight chapters of the epistle to the Romans. The second contains the entire epistle, with ALL THE CORRECTIONS which the celebrated *Griesbach*, the oracle of modern criticism, thinks ought to be introduced.

These passages have been selected promiscuously ; and we declare that no reason, relative to our argument, has made us prefer them to others.

We delight in presenting here these short documents to those persons, whose position does not call them to pursue the investigations of sacred criticism, and yet who may have been somewhat perplexed by the at once mysterious and important language so often employed on this subject, by the rationalists of the last century. To hear them, would you not have believed that modern science was about to give us a new Bible, to bring down Jesus Christ from the throne of God, to restore to man calumniated by our theology, all his titles of innocence, and to reform all the doctrines of our antiquated orthodoxy ?

As the first term of comparison, our columns present first, upon the first eight verses of the Epistle to the Romans, merely the differences of the text of Martin from that of Osterwald ; whilst the following columns, instead of comparing only one manuscript with any other one, will show the differences of *our text* from *all the manuscripts* which every critic down to Griesbach has been able to collect. This indefatigable scholar searched for the Epistle to the Romans, first, seven manuscripts in *Uncial Letters,* or Greek capitals, believed to be from thirteen to fourteen hundred years old, (the *Alexandrian* in the British Museum ; that of the *Vatican,* and that of Cardinal *Passionei,* at Rome ; that of *Ephremi* at Paris ; that of *Saint-Germain,* that of *Dresden,* and that of Cardinal *Coislin ;* and finally a hundred and ten manuscripts in *cursive* (small letters), and thirty others, mostly brought from Mount Athos, and examined by the learned Matthei, who traveled much in Russia and the East for this purpose.

For the four Evangelists, the same Griesbach has been able to consult three hundred and thirty-five.

FIRST TABLE.

EPISTLE TO THE ROMANS.

Text of Osterwald.	*Text of Martin.*
verse.	
1. *to be.*	to be.
2. which .. promised before.	the which .. before promised.
3. of the race.	of the family.
4. and who, according to the Spirit, .. was.	and who was according to the Spirit.
was declared.	was fully declared.
with power.	by power.
the Spirit of holiness.	the Spirit of sanctification.
to wit.	that is to say.
J. C. our Lord.	our Lord J. C.
5. In order to lead the Gentiles to the obedience of the faith.	in order to lead the Gentiles to believe.
6. of the number of whom you also are, you who have been called.	Among whom you also are, you who are called.
7. called and saints.	called *to be* Saints.
grace and peace *be given* to you from God our father.	may grace and peace *be* given to you by God our father.
8. Before all things.	Firstly.
in regard to you all.	concerning you all.
is celebrated.	is renowned.

These differences of the two French texts are sufficiently insignificant; and if any one should tell us that in all the verses, one or other of the two is inspired of God, our faith would receive from it a great aid. Now you will see that the variations of the Greek manuscripts are still more insignificant.

Let us now observe on the same verses, the table of the received text, compared with *all the differences*, that the *hundred and fifty Greek manuscripts* collected and examined for the Epistle to the Romans, can present.

We shall not notice here the differences presented by the ancient translations, nor those which pertain to punctuation, (this element being nearly nothing in the most ancient manuscripts.)

We shall translate the first column (that of the received text) according to Martin, who is considered more literal than Osterwald ; and we shall endeavor to translate as exactly as possible, the Greek readings of the second column.

SECOND TABLE.

The received text, (that of Elzevir, 1624.)	Variations collected from ALL the Greek manuscripts together.
1. (No difference.)	
2. By his prophets,	By the prophets. [In only one manuscript in Paris.]
3. Who was born.	Who was begotten. [In only one manuscript of Upsal, and merely by the change of two letters.]
4. Who was declared.	Who was before declared. [In only one of 22 manuscripts of the Barberini library.]
of J. C. our Lord.	of J. C. our God. [In only one manuscript of Vienna]
5 & 6. (No difference.)	
7. Who are at Rome, and dearly beloved of God, called.	Who are in the love of God, called. [One only MS. the uncial of Dresden.] Who are at Rome called, [Two MSS. only, that of St. Germain, Uncial, and one of Rome, small letters.]
of God our father.	of God the father. [Only one MS. of Upsal.]
8. First.	First. [The difference cannot be expressed. It is only in one MS.]
concerning you all.	in regard to you all. [Twelve MS.]

We see it ; these nine or ten different readings are unimportant in themselves, and moreover they have in their
favor, only one or two out of the hundred and fifty manuscripts, which have been consulted upon these eight
verses, if you except the last (" in regard to you all," instead of " concerning you all,") which counts for it
twelve manuscripts, of which four are Uncial or capital
letters.

The differences between Osterwald and Martin are
three times as numerous ; and ordinarily they have a much
more important effect upon the meaning.   This comparison, if you extend it to all the New Testament, would
possess the same character and become even more insignificant.

Yet we presume it would be agreeable to those of our
readers who are strangers to such researches, to offer them
in a third table, still a new test of the innocence of the
variations, and of the nullity of the objection drawn from
them.

This table will contain the entire collection of corrections, which the learned Griesbach, the father of sacred
criticism, has thought proper to introduce into the text of
the Epistle to the Romans, after the long researches which
he and his predecessors have made upon the manuscripts.

To appreciate fully the immensity of such labors, we
should have gone personally into this study.

At the same time we would remark to the readers of
this third table :

First, that Griesbach is, in general, accused by the
learned (such as Matthei, Nolan, Lawrence, Scholz and
others,) of being too eager to admit new readings into the
ancient text.   The temptation is explained by the habits
of the human heart.   The learned Whitby had already,
and not without reason, reproached Dr. Mill for this ;

who, however, had not admitted so many corrections as Griesbach.

Secondly :—observe again, that we show in this table, not only the corrections which the learned critic has persuaded himself to *adopt*, but those also which he himself considers as only *doubtful*, and to be preferred to the sacred text with some remaining distrust.

THIRD TABLE.

CORRECTIONS OF GRIESBACH IN THE ENTIRE EPISTLE TO THE ROMANS.

ANCIENT TEXT. (Martin's translation.)	NEW TEXT. Corrected by Griesbach, (and translated by us with the utmost possible exactness.)

CHAPTER I.

verse.

13. to gather some fruit.	To gather some fruit. [There is here only an inversion of the words.]
I am not ashamed.	I am not ashamed. [the difference cannot be expressed by by a translation.]
17. of the Gospel of Christ.	of the Gospel.
19.	[difference inexpressible.]
21.	(difference of spelling.)
24. Wherefore also.	Wherefore.
27.	(difference inexpressible)
29. Of injustice, of impurity, of wickedness.	of injustice, of wickedness.
31. Without natural affection, persons who are never pacified, without mercy.	without natural affection, without mercy.

CHAPTER II.

9. indignation and wrath.	wrath and indignation.
13.	(the article *the* omitted.)

CHAPTER III.

22. to all and upon all them
that believe.

to all them that believe.

25.

(article *the* omitted twice.)

28. We then conclude.

we conclude in fact.

29.

(difference inexpressible.)

CHAPTER IV.

1.

(order of words changed.)

Abraham our father.

Abraham our ancestor.

4.

(indefinite article omitted.)

12.

(article omitted.)

13.

(difference inexpressible.)

19. and not being weak in
faith, he looked not at
&c.

he looked not, feeble in
faith, to.

CHAPTER V.

14.

(difference of spelling.)

CHAPTER VL

1.

(pronoun omitted.)

11.

(*are* omitted.)

12.

(*it* omitted.)

14.

(*to death* omitted.)

CHAPTER VII.

6. that in which, being dead.

being dead to that in which,

10.

(difference of an accent.)

14.

(difference of a letter.)

18.

(difference of spelling.)

20.

(*I* repeated for emphasis.'

26. I render thanks to God.

thanks be to God.

CHAPTER VIII.

1.

(words omitted here, which are
transposed to the fourth verse.)

11. by his spirit (Martin says :
on account of his spirit.)

on account of his spirit.

26. to our infirmities.   to our infirmity.
                                     (another difference inexpressible.)

    prays for us with groanings.   prays with groanings.
35.   (difference cannot be expressed.)
36.   (order of the phrase changed.)

CHAPTER IX.

11.   (a difference in the order.)
15.   (a difference in the spelling.)
31. works of the law.   works.
32. for they.   they.
33. whosoever.   who.

CHAPTER X.

1. for Israel.   for them.
                                     (difference cannot be expressed.)
5.   (difference of spelling.)
15.   (difference inexpressible.)
19.   (change of the order and the spelling.)

CHAPTER XI.

2. against Israel, saying: against Israel : Lord.
   Lord.
3.   (and omitted.)
6. If it is by grace, then it is If it is by grace, it is no more
   no more of works; other-   by works; otherwise
   wise grace is no more   grace is no more grace.
   grace; but if it be of
   works, then it is no
   more grace, otherwise
   work is no more work.
7.   (difference inexpressible.)
19.   (article omitted.)
21.   (difference inexpressible.)
23.   (difference of orthography.)
30. you yourselves were.   you were.

CHAPTER XII.

                                     (a pronoun repeated.)
                                     (a pronoun omitted.)

11. serving the Lord.

serving the opportunity.
(this difference is caused by the change of one letter, and the transposition of another.)

20. If then thine enemy.

If thine enemy.

CHAPTER XIII.

1.

(difference inexpressible.)

8.

(transposition of words.)

9. Thou shalt not steal, thou shalt not bear false witness, thou shalt not covet.

Thou shalt not steal, thou shalt not covet.

CHARTER XIV.

9.

(a difference made by the addition of two letters.)

14.

(difference inexpressible.)

CHAPTER XV.

1.

(a transposition.)

2.

(the difference cannot be shown in English.)

3.

(difference inexpressible.)

7. as Christ hath also received you,

as Christ hath also received us.

8. now I say.

for I say.

19. by the power of the spirit of God.

by the power of the spirit.

24. I will go towards you, when I shall depart to go into Spain; and I hope to see you.

when I shall depart to go into Spain, I hope to see you.

29. with abundance of blessing from the Gospel of Christ.

with abundance of Christ's benediction.

CHAPTER XVI.

2.

(difference inexpressible.)

3. Priscilla.

Prisca.

5. who is the first fruits of Achaia.

who is the first fruits of Asia.

6. who has labored greatly for us.	who has labored greatly for you.
18. Our Lord Jesus Christ.	Our Lord Christ.
20.	(*amen* omitted.)
25.	(Greisbach thinks this verse ought to be at the beginning of the xvth Chapter.)

We then see clearly how insignificant those variations, are, of which so much was said at first.

Such is the astonishing preservation of the Greek manuscripts which have transmitted to us the New-Testament. After having been copied and re-copied so many times in Asia, Europe and Africa; in convents, in colleges, in palaces, or in parsonages; and that almost without interruption, for fifteen hundred years; after that, during the last three centuries, and especially the last hundred and thirty years, so many noble characters, so many ingenious minds, so many learned lives have been consumed in labors till then unrivalled in their extent, admirable in their sagacity, and scrupulous as those of the Masorites; after that all the Greek manuscripts of the New-Testament, buried in private or monastic or national libraries both eastern and western, have been searched; after that they have compared with them, not only all the ancient versions of the Scriptures, Latin, Salidic, Ethiopic, Arabic, Sclavonic, Persian, Coptic, Syriac and Gothic; but also all the ancient fathers of the Church who have cited them in their innumerable writings, both in Latin and in Greek; after so many researches; see, by our specimen, what they have been able to find.

Judge them all from this one Epistle thus put fully under your eye. It is the longest and the most important of the Epistles of the New-Testament, " the golden key of the Scriptures," " the ocean of Christian doctrine." It has four hundred and thirty-three verses; and among its four hundred and thirty-three verses, ninety-six Greek words not found elsewhere in the New-Testament. And (admitting even all the corrections adopted, or only preferred by Griesbach,) how many readings have you found in it, which change even slightly the sense of any phrase? You have found four! And what are they? We will repeat them;

1. (Chap. vi. 6.) In place of: *that in which . . . . being dead,* Griesbach reads: " *being dead to that in which.* And remark that here, the difference in the Greek is in only one letter (an *o* in place of an *e*); and that on the other hand, the greatest number of the manuscripts were so much in favor of the old text, that since Griesbach, Tittman, in his edition of 1824, has rejected this correction, and that Lachman has likewise adopted the reading of the old text in his edition of 1831; (Scholz, however, has preserved the new.)

2. Chap. xi. 6.—In place of: *if by grace, then is it no more of works, otherwise grace is no more grace ; but if it be of works, then it is no more grace, otherwise work is no more work.*

Griesbach has retrenched the latter part of the phrase.

3. Chap. xii. 11.—In place of *serving the Lord,* Griesbach reads: *serving the opportunity.*

It will be observed, that this correction is of *two letters* in one of the Greek words; and that also the number of the manuscripts does not justify the change. Again here, *Whitby* told *Mill* that more than thirty manuscripts, that all the ancient versions, that Clement of Alexandria, St. Basil, St. Jerome, all the annotators of the Greeks, and all the Latins, with the exception of Ambrose, followed the ancient text; and the two scholars we have just named, (Lachman and Tittman,) the one laboring at Berlin, the other a professor at Leipsic, have restored the ancient text, in their respective editions of the New Testament. Scholz, whom the learned world appears to prefer to all who have preceded him, has done the same in his edition of 1836.

4. Chap. vi. 16.—In place of: *whether of sin unto death, or of righteousness*—Griesbach reads: *Whether of sin, or of righteousness ;* but he marks it with his sign, which indicates merely a faint probability ; and Tittman and Lachman, in their respective editions, have also rejected this correction. Mr. Scholz has followed them.

We have omitted to re-notice the passage cut off from chap. viii. 1, because it is restored in the fourth verse.

We see, then, that such is the admirable integrity of the Epistle to the Romans. According to Griesbach, *four insignificant corrections* in the whole epistle—according to more modern critics, ONE ALONE, and that, the most unimportant of the four ;—and according to Scholz, TWO !

We repeat, that we have not chosen the Epistle to the Romans, as a specimen, for any other reason than its length and its importance. We have not taken the time to examine whether it presents more or fewer variations than any other part of the New Testament.

We have just run over, for example, in Griesbach, while re-perusing these last pages, the EPISTLE TO THE GALATIANS, written at the same time and upon the same subject as the Epistle to the Romans; and we have there found only the three following corrections which may affect the sense, or rather, the form of the meaning.

iv. 17. They would exclude us ; *say,* they would exclude you.

iv. 26. She is the mother of us all, *say :* she is mother of us.

v. 19. Adultery, fornication, impurity, *say :* fornication, impurity.

These simple tables, we think, will speak to our readers more forcibly than all our general assertions can do.

There are some truths which must be seen with our

own eyes. We have ourselves had the happy experience of this. We had unquestionably read what others have said upon the insignificancy of the different readings presented by the manuscripts; we had often studied the variations of Mill, and the severe reproaches of his opponent, Whitby;* we had examined the writings of Wetstein, of Griesbach, of Lachman, and of Tittman; but when, twice, in taking part in the labor of a new version of the New Testament, we had to correct the French text by the most esteemed variations, first to introduce and then to cut them off, and then to replace, in French, the sense of the ancient reading; then we had twice, as it were, an intuition of this astonishing preservation of the Scriptures; and we have felt ourselves penetrated with gratitude towards that admirable Providence which has ceaselessly watched over the oracles of God, to preserve their integrity so fully.

Let the objection we are answering now be weighed. Let us be shown, for instance, how three or four variations, which we have just passed in review, in the Epistle to the Romans, and which, in the opinion of the most modern critics, are reduced to one alone, or to two, could render the original inspiration an illusion to us.

We admit that, in these three or four passages, as in the other sacred books, where the genuine word of the text might be contested; there, and there alone, of the two different readings of the manuscript, one is the inspired word and not the other: we admit that you must, in these few cases, divide or suspend your confidence between two expressions; but see just how far the uncertainty extends: there it must stop, it can go no further.

It is calculated that, in the seven thousand nine hundred and fifty-nine verses of the New Testament, there are

* Examen variant. lectionum, J. Millii. Lond. 1710.

9

scarcely ten verses where these differences, which are, most frequently, merely of a word or letter, have any importance.

Thus, then, all the efforts of the enemies of inspiration, to overthrow our faith on this ground, have, in the end, only served to establish it. They have compelled the Church to follow them in their investigations, and immediately afterward to precede them in the same work; and what have we there discovered? It is, that the text is even more pure than the most pious men had dared to hope; it is, that the enemies of inspiration, and those of the orthodox doctrines, at least in Germany, have been forced to admit it. They had hoped, after the labors of Erasmus, of Stephens, and of Mill, to find, among the manuscripts of our libraries, readings more favorable to the Socinian doctrines than those which Beza and Elzevir employed. Many even imagined that the uncertainties would become such, and the discrepancies so grave, that all evangelical belief, positive, exclusive as they termed it, would be overthrown. But it is not so. It is now a process terminated; the plaintiffs are nonsuited; the inquest having been made by modern criticism, at their request; all the judges, even on the rationalist benches,* have pronounced, with entire unanimity, that it is a lost case, and that the objectors must search elsewhere for arguments and grievances.

When this question of the integrity of the original text presented itself for the first time to the excellent and learned Bengel, more than a hundred and twenty years ago, he was terrified at it; his honest and pious soul was profoundly troubled by it. Then began on his part, those labors of sacred criticism which gave a new direction to this science among the Germans. The English had pre-

* Read Michælis, tom. ii, p. 266. Eichhorn. Einleitung, 2 th. S. 700. Edit. Leips. 1824.

ceded the Germans in it, but were soon left behind them. Finally, after long researches, Bengel, in 1721, happy and confirmed, trusting and grateful, wrote to his pupil, Reuss —"Eat simply the bread of the Scriptures, such as you find it; and be not disturbed, if perchance you find here and there a little fragment of the millstone which has fallen into it. You may then dismiss all the doubts which have once so horribly tormented me. If the Holy Scriptures, which have been copied so often, and which have so often passed the imperfect hands of men always fallible, were absolutely without variations, the miracle would be so great, that faith in it would no more be faith. I am astonished, on the contrary, that there has resulted from all the transcribings, a no greater number of different readings." The Comedies alone of Terence have presented thirty thousand, and yet they are but six* in number, and have been copied a thousand times less frequently than the New Testament.

We have said enough on this great fact. We were not obliged to do more than merely to state it, in order to repel an objection; since it took us away from our subject. Our mission was, to prove a doctrine, to wit *the original inspiration* of the Holy Scriptures; and some have supposed that they could oppose us with the objection that if this were a truth, yet it would be rendered ineffectual by the alterations which this holy writing must have undergone. We found it necessary to show that these alterations were a vain and innocent phantom. We presented a doctrine, we say; but they have compelled us to make a history; we now return to the doctrine; but, before returning, we must yet once more assert, not only that the Scriptures were inspired in the day when God caused

* Archives du Christianisme, tome vii. No. 17.—Wiseman, Disc. on the Relations of Science, tome ii. p. 189.

them to be written ; but that this word, inspired eighteen hundred years ago, is now in our hands; and we can still, holding in one hand our sacred text, and in the other, all the admitted readings collected by science from seven hundred manuscripts,* exclaim with gratitude ; I hold then in my happy hand, the eternal word of my God!

SECTION V.—ERRORS OF REASONING OR OF DOCTRINE.

We leave the variations, other opponents will say, and we admit that the Sacred text may be regarded as the original language of the prophets and of the apostles ; but this very text, pure as it is, we cannot study, without perceiving the part of it which human feebleness has made. We find in it reasonings badly conducted and badly concluded, quotations badly applied, popular superstitions, prejudices and other infirmities, the inevitable tribute paid by the simplicity of the men of God to the ignorance of their time and of their condition. "Saint Paul," says Jerome himself,* " does not know how to develope a hyperbaton, nor to conclude a sentence ; and having to do with rude people, he has employed the conceptions, which, if, at the beginning, he had not taken care to announce as spoken after the manner of men, would have shocked men of good sense." Such being then the traces of infirmity which we can follow in the Scriptures, it remains impossible to recognize in such a book an inspiration that goes even to the lesser details of their language.

To these accusations against the Scriptures we have a fourfold answer.

1. We set ourselves at once, with all the energy of our conviction, against such reproaches. We maintain that a

* Scholz has cited 674 for the Evangelists alone.
* Comm. on Galatians (Bk. 11.)—Tit. (Bk. 1 on i. 1.) and Ephes.—Bk. 11. on 3. 1.)

more attentive and more serious study of the Word of God would reduce them to nothing, and we protest that they have no foundation but in the errors and precipitancy of those who advance them. We might show it in repelling, one by one, all these accusations, in every instance in which they have been rendered. It would be a task of greater length than difficulty; and this is not the place for it, because the detail is immense. There is not in fact, a reasoning, there is not a quotation, there is not a doctrine, which the adversaries of the inspiration of the Scriptures have not at some time made a subject of reproach; and every one knows well enough that the greater part of the objections which are clearly stated in three words, cannot be refuted clearly in less than three pages. In proportion then as the men of the world renew their attacks, the Church must renew her replies; and like those respectful and indefatigable servants, who in the East, watch day and night around the head of their king, she must constantly hold herself by the side of the Word of God, to repel from it those swarms of objections which are seen, just as fast as they are driven from one side, rising on the other, and incessantly returning to plant anew their sting. The experience of every age, and especially that of the latter times has sufficiently shown, that before an examination, these difficulties, which they set against the Scriptures, vanish; these obscurities are illuminated; and quickly, unexpected harmonies, beauties that until then no human eye had perceived, are revealed in the Word of God by the objections themselves. To-day, objects of doubt; to-morrow, better studied, they are incentives to faith; to-day, sources of trouble, to-morrow they are proofs.

2. In the meantime we notice all these accusations which the adversaries of the full inspiration of the Scriptures raise against this sacred book; for it is an advantage

9*

which they give us.   Yes, we shall not hesitate to say it;
in the hearing of such objections, we experience at the
same time, two opposite impressions of satisfaction and of
sadness; of sadness in seeing men who recognize the Bible
as a revelation of God, not fearing at the same time to
raise against it so hastily the gravest accusations; and of
satisfaction, in considering with what force such language
at last confirms the doctrine we defend.

In the mouth of a deist, they would be objections to
which we must reply, but in that of a Christian who ad-
vances them, it is a flagrant abandonment of his own
thesis, and an avowal of all the evil involved in such abandonment.

We would be understood: it is not before the professed infidel that we here maintain the plenary inspiration
of the Scriptures; it is before men who profess to consider the Bible as a revelation from God.   Inspiration, we
have said to them, is a doctrine taught in this sacred
book: by its own testimony, all Scripture is given of
God, it is perfect, it is pure, it is gold seven times tried
in the fire.   What reply have they made? They do not
reject, they say, such an inspiration, but in regard to the
language, the forms of speech, and the unimportant details;
otherwise they believe that a constant providence directed the minds of the sacred writers to keep them from
every grave error.   But how do they prove this thesis?
Is it to the language alone, is it to the forms of speech, is
it to insignificant details that they confine this rejection
of inspiration? alas! hear them: there are in the doctrines, superstitions; there are in the quotations, misrep-
resentations, there [are in the reasonings, infirmities!—
You see then, that in order to attack the plenary inspiration of the Scriptures, they come down thus into the
ranks of the unbelievers, who are casting stones at the
word of God; and if they do not wish, like them, to

take God from the holy Bible, they at least wish to correct God in the holy Bible. Which of the two is most
outrageous, it would be difficult to say.

We conclude then, that since the plenary inspiration
can be combatted only by accusing the word of God
of error, we must cling the more firmly to this declaration of the Scriptures, that " all Scripture is given by inspiration of God."

3. But we have something yet more serious to add.
We ask : where will you stop when you have once entered on this path ? And by what reasons will you in your
turn stop those who wish to go still beyond you ? You
dare to correct one part of the word of God ; by what
right then will you blame those who may wish to correct
the rest ? Beings of yesterday, whilst they are traversing
this earth as a shadow, with the eternal book of God in
their hands, they dare to say : This, Lord, is worthy of
thee, this is unworthy of thee ! They pretend to select
for themselves in the oracles of God, to ascribe one part of
it to the folly of man, to separate the mistakes of Isaiah or
Moses, the prejudices of Peter or of Jude, the paralogisms
of Paul, the superstitions of John from the thought of God !
Lamentable rashness ! We repeat it ; where will they
stop in this fatal work ; for they place themselves at the very
table, on the one side of which, are seated the Socinuses, the
Grimaldis, the Priestlys ; and on the other, the Rousseaus,
the Volneys, the Dupuis. Between them and Eichhorn,
between them and William Cobbett, between them and
Strauss, where is the difference ? It is in the species, not
in the genus. It is in the quantity of the imputations of
errors and of irreverent remarks ; it is not in the quality.
There is some difference in their boldness, none in their
profaneness. The one and the other have found errors
in the word of God ; they have pretended to rectify them.
But, we ask, is it less absurd, on the part of a creature, to

wish to correct in the works of God, the creation of the hyssop that cometh out of the wall, than that of the cedar of Lebanon ; to pretend to rectify the organization of a glow-worm, than to wish to shut up the light in the sun ?   By what right will ministers, who say that they see nothing but the language of Jewish prejudices in the accounts given by the Evangelists, of the demoniacs and the miracles of Jesus Christ driving out the impure spirits ; by what right will they pronounce it strange that another sees in the miracles of Saul's conversion, of the resurrection, of the multiplication of bread, or of the day of Pentecost, nothing but a discreet and useful compliance with the ignorance of a people fond of the marvellous ?   By what authority would a professor, who denies the inspiration of Paul's arguments, blame Mr. De Wette for rejecting that of the prophecies of the old Testament,[*] or of Mr. Wirgmann making his *separation of the New Testament,*[†] or Mr. Strauss changing into fable the miracles and the very person of Jesus Christ ?

Three or four years since, a young minister of Berne, put into our hands a manual of theology which, he said, had been handed him in an academy in Eastern Switzerland.   We have not retained the name of the author, nor that of his residence ; but having, at the time, taken notes of his principal arguments against the plenary inspiration of the Scriptures, we can reproduce here the quotations by which he sought to prove that the holy books, contain-

---

[*] That was his opinion some years ago. We do not know whether this professor, whose science and candor in his translation of the New Testament we admire, may not have retracted such assertions.

[†] That was the title of his book.—"He intends by it, the separation or division of the New Testament, into *Word of God,* or moral precepts, and *Word of man,* or facts of the sensible world."

ing evident errors, cannot be entirely the word of God. It will be understood that we do not mean here to reply to him. We wish only to give a specimen of his rashness.

"St. Paul says (1 Cor. v. 15,) that he had 'delivered an incestuous man to Satan.' This passage (evidently fanatical) could it be inspired!

"He says to them (1 Cor. v. 3,) that 'we shall judge the angels,'—a gnostic reverie without doubt. Could such a passage have been inspired!

"He goes on even to say to them that 'in consequence of unworthy communion many of them are sick, and some are dead,' (1 Cor. xi. 30). This passage could not be inspired!

"He says to them again, that 'all die in Adam,'—(1 Cor. xv. 22)—Jewish superstition. It is impossible that such a passage can be inspired!

"And when Saint Paul assures the Thessalonians, (1 Th. iv. 15,) and when St, James repeats (Jam. v. 8,) that 'the coming of the Lord is near,' could so manifest an error be inspired!"*

It is then in this manner that they dare to judge the eternal word! We do not yet know, we have said, whether these doctrines, professed in Switzerland, ten or twelve years since, were so, particularly at Zurich. But, if they there had currency, we must exculpate the magistrates of that city.† It was not they who called Strauss

---

* We have not thought it our duty to reply to such accusations. It would be to depart from our subject. The coming of the Lord is near to each one of us; from one instant to another, three breaths separate us from it. When a man dies, he is immediately transported into the day of Jesus Christ. As to the distance of that day relatively to this world, judge from 1 Thess. ii. 2, if the Apostle Paul was mistaken.

† Allusion is here made to the call of Strauss to the professor-

into their country, to overthrow the faith of an entire people; for Strauss was already in their professoral chairs, if such doctors as this were there giving instructions. They had seen them with great scissors in their hands, cutting out of the Scriptures the errors of the holy Apostles. What difference could they perceive between such men and him whom they were calling? A little more science, a little more boldness and consistency in his principles; with a longer and sharper instrument in his more skilful hands; but scarcely more contempt in his heart for the word of God! We see but little difference between the several judges of the Sanhedrim who struck Jesus on the face, because some struck fewer blows than others; and when sixty conspirators, in Pompey's palace, overthrew Cæsar from his golden throne in the midst of the Senate; Casca, who first slightly wounded him with his sword, was not less his murderer than Cassius cleaving his head, or than the sixty conspirators shewing him their blades on every side, and piercing him with twenty-three wounds. Is then the teacher who denies the inspiration of an argument or of a doctrine of the Scriptures, less in revolt against the God of the Scriptures, than he who rejects the inspiration of an entire book? We think he is not.

We conclude that, since in order to deny the plenary inspiration of the Scriptures, we must enter into the road of rashness, and give, by the first strokes of the sword, the signal of all opposition to the word of God; a closer attention should be paid to this declaration of the Holy Spirit: "All Scripture is given by inspiration of God." But we have yet another reflection.

4. You do not understand the divinity, the propriety,

ship of theology in the university by the magistrates; which was resisted by forty thousand of the people, and resisted successfully.

the wisdom, the utility of such or such a passage of the Scriptures, and therefore you deny its inspiration. Is that an argument of any real value, we will not say in our eyes, but in yours? Who are you? "When thou goest into the house of God," feeble child of man, "keep thy foot; be swift to hear, be slow to speak, and do not offer the sacrifice of fools; for they know not what they do. God is in heaven, and thou art upon the earth." Who art thou then, to judge the oracles of God? Has not the Bible said of itself beforehand, that it would be "a stumbling-block to some, and foolishness to others;" that "the natural man should not comprehend it, that indeed he could not, and that it is only to be known by the Spirit?"* Should you not then have expected to feel some repugnance in your mind, in your heart, even in your conscience, against its first instructions? Man must come back to his own place as an infirm, ignorant and depraved creature. He can understand God only by becoming humble. Let him bend the knee in his closet; let him pray, and he will comprehend. An argument is inconsequent because you do not apprehend it! a doctrine is a prejudice, because you do not admit it! a quotation is inaccurate, because you have not discovered its true meaning! What would remain in the world, if God should leave in it only what you can explain? The Roman emperors, being able to comprehend neither the faith nor the life of our martyrs, threw them to the wild beasts in the amphitheatre, and caused them to be dragged to the Tiber. It is thus that men throw their ignorance as a vile grapple upon the word of God, and drag to the scaffold that which they could not comprehend and which they have condemned!

We recollect, in writing these lines, an author, other-

* 1 Cor. xi. 14.

wise honorable, but imbued with the wisdom of his age, who undertook to prove that the reasonings of St. Paul are not inspired. To show it, he cited, as a convincing example, the passage in Galatians, iii. 16, in which Paul designs not to PROVE, (observe it well, all the solution is there,) not to prove, but to AFFIRM that the promise made by God to *Abraham and his posterity,* regarded not *all his descendants,* (since it was sufficiently manifest that *his descendants* by Hagar, by Keturah and by Esau, had been rejected,) but a particular posterity, elect and personal. And what does this professor, in order to establish his thesis upon this passage? He lends the apostle an argument so puerile, that the smallest child of the Galatians might have reproved him for it. Saint Paul, according to him, instead of simply affirming a fact, should have reasoned from the *singular of a collective noun* to *prove* that such a word could mean to designate only one person! "Absurd to us," he says; " this argument might have been good for Jews, or the rude Gauls of Asia Minor." We give this one example. It were easy to produce a hundred like it.

Might the author be permitted to refer in this matter to his own experience, he would recal with as much humiliation as gratitude, his first and his last impressions produced by the Epistles of St. Paul. He had already been convinced in his earliest years, that the Bible is from God; but he had not yet understood the doctrine it teaches. He wished to respect the pages of the apostle, because he had seen by other characters, that the inimitable seals of the most High God were attached to them; but a secret trouble agitated him in reading them, and turned him towards other books. St. Paul appeared to him to reason falsely; not to reach his point; to speak ambiguously and in an embarrassing manner; to make long, spiral windings around his subject; and to say the things committed

to him quite otherwise than was designed by him who
revealed them. In a word, he felt, in reading them,
as would a tender and respectful son, by the side
of a father who is declining, who has lost his memory, and
who talks stammeringly. Oh! how would he conceal
from others, and not admit it to himself, that his venerable
father is sinking, and seems no more like himself! But
as soon as Divine grace had revealed to us this doctrine of
justification by faith, which is the ardent and brilliant
flame of the Scriptures, then, each word became light,
harmony and life; the reasonings of the apostle appeared
to us as limpid as the water from the rock, his thoughts
profound and practical, all his epistles the power of God
to salvation to them that believe. We saw abundant
proofs of divinity beaming from those very passages which
had given us so long disquiet, and we could say with the
joy of a discovery, and with the gratitude of a tender adoration, as we felt vibrating within us, in unison with the
word of God, chords inimitable, and until then, untouched: "Yes, my God, all thy Scriptures are divinely inspired!"

But it is insisted that there are:

Section VI.—Errors in the Narrations; Contradic-tions in the Facts.

"We will leave, say they, if we must, all these just re-
pugnances against the reasonings or the doctrines of the
sacred writers; in admitting, that upon these points, that
which is difficult to some, may be easy to others. But if
now we appeal to facts, if we show that there are manifest contradictions in the narrations of the Bible, in its
dates, in its references to cotemporary history, in its
scriptural quotations; you may then, perhaps, reproach
us for having seen them, for not being consistent with
ourselves, and for going in that beyond our own posi-

10

tion. Notwithstanding this; those are facts which no inconsistency of reasoning can annul, and which no argument can destroy. An argument no more destroys, than creates facts. If, then, these contradictions exist, you may, indeed, convict our doctrine of insufficiency; but they rise three times as high against yours, to accuse it of error."

We will commence by admitting, that if it be true that there are, as they say there are, erroneous statements and contradictory accounts in the holy Scriptures, their plenary inspiration must be renounced. But this is not the case. These pretended errors do not exist.

We shall admit, without hesitation, that, among the numerous attacks made on the minutest details of the statements of our sacred books, there are some which, at first sight, may occasion some embarrassment; but as soon as we contemplate them more closely, these difficulties are explained and vanish. We shall give some examples, taking care to choose from among those which the opponents of plenary inspiration have appeared to regard as the most insurmountable.

We shall preface them with some observations.

1. The Scriptures have had, in every age, their enemies and their defenders, their Celsuses as well as their Origens, their Porphyrys as well as their Eusebiuses, their Castellios as well as their Calvins, their Strausses as well as their Hengstenbergs. Sixteen hundred years ago, Malchus Porphyry, that learned and malignant Syrian, who lived in Sicily under the reign of Diocletian, and whom Jerome calls *rabidum adversus Christum canem,*[*] wrote fifteen books against Christianity. In these fifteen books, the fourth of which was directed against the Pentateuch, and the thirteenth against Daniel, one of them (the first)

[*] A dog enraged against Christ.

was entirely consecrated to collecting all the contradictions (ἀντιλογίας ἐναντιοφάνῆ) which he pretended he had found in the Scriptures.* From Celsus and Porphyry, down to the English infidels of the eighteenth century; and from them to Strauss, who had done little more than copy them, according to his own avowal; they have not ceased to seek new contradictions, in comparing Scripture with Scripture, line with line, word with word, detail with detail. It was easy then to multiply them, and even to find some that are specious, in a book, eminently composed of anecdotes, where the narratives of the same events are repeated under various forms, by different historians, in different circumstances, with various objects, and with greater or less development. From that, the reader should perceive, that this fifth objection, which is composed of only detached observations, and which resolves itself into an infinitude of little details, can be refuted only in detail and by detached answers. It is, accordingly, an exhaustless subject. To each passage an objection, to each objection a reply. Our only general answer then must be; examine, and the obscurity will vanish.

Moreover it is understood by all parties that the pretended contradictions which the enemies of inspiration present, have in themselves no religious importance, and regard only dates, numbers or other very minute circumstances. But, if they cannot affect Christian doctrine directly, they do not the less tend to overthrow the plenary inspiration of the Scriptures. We must then reply to them. It is what the friends of religion in every age have done; and what has just been accomplished with such honorable success, by Mr. Hengstenberg of Berlin.

---

* Τὸν καθ'ἡμων συσκευὴν ὑπερβολῃ μισούς προβεβλήμενον, says Eusebius, in speaking of him. Euseb. Prepar. Evangel. lib. x. chap. ix.. and Euseb. Hist. Eccl. vi. 19.

It is what has been lately done by Roussel in France, by Barett, Haley, Gerard, Dick, Horne and others in England.

2. It is very easy to say in a general way and with a peremptory tone, that there are contradictions in the Bible : and it has often happened that unreflecting Christians, although pious, have not given themselves the trouble of looking more closely into the subject, and have adopted loose maxims on inspiration, before having sufficiently studied on one side, the general testimony of the Scriptures on this doctrine, and on the other, the nature of the objections which they have made. We have seen them then looking into their own minds, rather than the Bible, for a mitigated system of inspiration, which might be reconciled with the supposed existence of some errors in the Word of God. Such was the doctrine of Socinus,* of Castellio,† and of some others in the sixteenth century ; but it was then sternly rejected by all pious men. " Hoc non est causam tueri adversus atheos," said Francis Turretin‡ " sed illam turpiter prodere." " Non est eo concedendum, ad ea concilianda, ut dicamus codicem sacrum mendosum,"§ said the learned and pious Peter Martyr, the " wonder of Italy," as Calvin calls him. In our days, the respectable Pye Smith‖ in England, and the worthy Bishop of Calcutta, ¶ have indulged in expressions, which we deplore, and which probably they would correct, if they had to make them anew. And in Berlin, the learned rector of the University, Mr. Twesten, whose labors and reputation we honor in other respects, has not feared to say in his Dogmatik,** that, " all is not equally inspired

* De autorit. Scrip.   † In Dialogis.
‡ Theol. elencht ; tom. 1. p. 74.   § On 1 .Kings viii. 17.
‖ Defence of Dr. Haffner's Preface to Bible.
¶ xii Lect, on Evid. of Christianity.
** Vorlesungen über die Dogmatik. 1. 1. p. 421-429. Hamburg, 1829.

in the Bible, and that if we admit no errors in the details of the evangelical narrations, we shall be thrown into inextricable difficulties to explain them." And what examples does he give to justify, in passing, such maxims? He quotes two of the passages which we are going to exhibit; (the first, that of the blind men of Jericho, the seventh, that of the census of Cyrenius.) The reader will be able to judge of the facility with which men abandon the testimony which the Scriptures give of their own entire inspiration.

We will then present here some examples, both of these imagined contradictions, and of the causes of this precipitancy in denominating contradictory, certain passages, which require only a little reflection to reconcile them.

We have said, and we repeat it, that not being able to introduce many instances, we have taken pains to select those which the opponents have considered most embarrassing.

FIRST CAUSE OF RASHNESS.—The complement of the circumstances of two events which occurred in the East, eighteen centuries ago, remains unknown, because the sacred historians relate them to us with an admirable brevity. Yet, men have hastened, because the story does not explain the mode of reconciling two of their features, to pronounce them contradictory! Nothing is more irrational. Suppose, to give an example not in the Scriptures, that a Hindoo Pundit had just been reading three succinct, but very accurate, histories of the illustrious Napoleon. The first shall inform him that the taking of Paris, preceded by a great effusion of blood at the gates of that capital, made his abdication necessary, and that an English frigate was to transport him immediately to an island of the Mediterranean. A second relates, that this great captain, conquered by the English, who took possession of Paris with-

10*

out a blow, was transported by them to St. Helena, whither General Bertrand wished to follow him, and where he finished his days in the arms of this faithful servant. A third relates, that the fallen Emperor was accompanied in his exile by the Generals Gourgaud, Bertrand, and Montholon. All these statements are accurate, and yet, " how many flat contradictions in so few words !" exclaims the learned citizen of Benares. " St. Helena, in the Mediterranean !" Who does not know that it rises, a great rock in the Atlantic ? First contradiction : one of these books is false, it must be rejected. And again, Paris taken without a blow ; and Paris taken after a bloody combat at its gates ! Second contradiction.—And again, here one general, there three generals ! Third contradiction.

Compare now these supposed contradictions with many of the objections raised against the narratives of the Evangelists !

First Example.—Mark (xvi. 5.) tells us *that the women saw* A YOUNG MAN (one only), *seated on the right side . . . who said to them : Be not afraid . . . you seek Jesus of Nazareth who was crucified . . . he is risen again.*

And Luke relates, (xxiv. 4.), that TWO MEN *presented themselves to them . . . who said to them : Why seek ye the living among the dead ? He is not here, he is risen.*

They present these passages to us as irreconcilable ; but wherefore ? There is a difference, unquestionably ; but there is neither contradiction nor disagreement between the statements. Must they be identical in order to be true ? It is sufficient that they are true, especially in histories so admirably succinct. Does it not often happen to us, without ceasing to be exact, that we relate to two persons successively the same story in two very different ways ? And why might not the apostles do the same ? St. Luke tells us that two persons met the women, while

St. Mark speaks only of that one, who having alone rolled away the stone, was seated at the right side of the sepulchre, and who spoke to them. Thus one of Napoleon's biographers mentions three generals, whilst the other, without ceasing to be accurate, speaks of Bertrand alone. Thus Moses, after having shown us three men in the apparition of Mamre, (Genesis xviii,) immediately represents one of them speaking as if he were alone. (v. 2, 10, 17.) Thus I might relate the same event twice successively and in a very different manner, without ceasing to be true : "I met three men, who showed me the direct road. I met a man, who put me in the right way." If, then, there is, in the quoted passages, a striking difference, yet there is not even the appearance of contradiction.

Second Example.—Matthew (xx. 19,) says ; that *as Jesus was going out of Jericho, followed by a great multitude, two blind men, sitting by the way-side, hearing that Jesus was passing, cried, saying ; Have mercy on us !*

And Mark (x. 46,) tells us "as Jesus went out of Jericho with his disciples and a great number of people, blind Bartimeus sat by the way-side, begging. And when he heard that it was Jesus of Nazareth, he began to cry out, and say, Jesus, have mercy on me." Luke, also, (xviii. 35,) speaks only of one blind man.

What is there here, we still ask, of contradiction or inaccuracy ? Of these two blind men whom Jesus, in the midst of so many other works, healed at Jericho, one was more remarkable than the other, perhaps better known than the other ; and who spoke to Jesus in the name of both. Mark speaks of him alone, he even tells us his name ; but does not say that he was alone. Matthew then has named them both. The narratives of the three evangelists are equally true, without being exactly alike. What is there extraordinary in this ?

But, we are told, there is a still greater difficulty in this same narrative ; let us hear it :

It is a *third example.* Matthew and Mark inform us that the event occurred as Jesus *was going out of Jericho ;* whilst Luke tells us that it took place as Jesus *was drawing nigh to Jericho.* Palpable contradiction ! has been uttered more than once.

How can you prove that ? What do you know about it ? must be the reply. The details of this event are unknown to you, how can you show that these statements are irreconcilable ; while on the contrary, it is perfectly easy to harmonize them by a very simple supposition ?

St. Luke, as he does so often in the whole course of his gospel, has united in his narrative, two successive circumstances of the same event. Observe that it is he alone of the three historians, who mentions the first question of Bartimeus. *Having heard the multitude who were passing, he inquired what it was.* This question was proposed by the blind man *before Jesus entered* the city of Jericho. Informed then as to the character of this great prophet whom he had never known until then, he followed him, and joined the crowd, who during the repast at the house of Zaccheus, were waiting to meet Jesus as he should go out. It was *then* they told him that *Jesus of Nazareth was passing,* (these words are in St. Luke.) He followed him thus for some time ; the other blind man joined him ; and their healing was not effected until the moment when Jesus, on his way to Jerusalem, *was going out of Jericho,* where he had stopped only to visit the happy Zaccheus at his own house.

This simple explanation dissipates all the pretended contradiction of these three texts.

Fourth example.—St. Matthew (ch. xxvii. 5.) says that Judas *hung himself ;* Peter, in the Acts (i. 18,) says that *falling headlong, he burst assunder in the midst, and all his bowels gushed out.*

Some have said, that here is contradiction.

We remember, that at Geneva, in a public conference, where we were defending this very thesis with our dear friend, Professor Monod, then pastor at Lyons, he cited three analogous features of a lamentable death of which he had been almost the witness. An unhappy man in Lyons, to be more sure of his destruction, and to give himself a double death, placed himself upon the window-sill of the fourth story, and then shot himself in the mouth with a pistol. The very same narrator of this sad event might, said he, have made three different statements; and yet all the three exact. In the first, he might have described the entire occurrence; in the second, he could have said this man died by a shot; and in the third, he threw himself down from the window !

Such was also the voluntary punishment by which the wretched Judas went to his own place. He hung himself, and he fell down headlong; his body burst open, and all his entrails gushed out. The statement of only one more circumstance of this frightful death would have given us the connecting link. It has not been given us; but who would therefore venture to maintain that there is contradiction ?

ANOTHER SOURCE OF RASHNESS.—Certain reigns, as that of Nebuchadnezzar, as that of Jehoiakim, and as that of Tiberius, have had two commencements; and the dates which relate to them are pronounced irreconcilable; the first, before ascending the throne, reigned three years with his father; the second, reigned ten years with his father; the third was associated with Augustus in the government, from the 28th of August of the year II of the Christian era, and yet did not succeed Augustus until the 19th of August of the year XIV. (Velleius Paterc. ii. c. 121.)

Some examples.—2 Kings, xxiv. 8; and 2 Chron., xxxvi. 9. See also Daniel, i. 1; ii. 1; Jeremiah, xxv. 1; 2 Chron., xxxvi. 5–7. See also Luke iii. 1.

ANOTHER SOURCE OF RASHNESS.—It is frequently the case that the Holy Spirit has two very different designs in relating the same fact in two different Gospels; and yet it is demanded by these objectors, that the very same form should have been given in every case to the narrative of the same event. And when the narratives differ from each other, they pronounce them inconsistent, and, in fact, contradictory to one another!

Example.—The Holy Spirit, in the genealogy of Jesus Christ, written in Matthew (i. 1–7,) designs to shew *the Jews* that, according to the rigor of their law, Jesus Christ is the Son and heir of all the kings of Judah, by a *legal descent ;* whilst the same Holy Spirit, in the genealogy given by Luke, (iii. 23–38,) designs to show *the Gentiles,* that Jesus Christ is the Son of David by a *natural descent.* And because, with this twofold design, they give us, the one his genealogy according to *the law,* by Solomon, the son of David, and by Jacob, the father of Joseph, Mary's husband ; and the other, his genealogy by *nature,* through Nathan, another son of David, and through Eli, the father of Mary, these objectors have, in their ignorance, pronounced their narratives contradictory !*

ANOTHER SOURCE OF RASHNESS.—*A text badly translated* produces a sense contrary to reason or to history ; and immediately the sacred writer is accused of the grossest errors ! They do not examine whether, in the purity of a better translation, the difficulty would not vanish.

First example, (it is likewise one of those cited by Mr. Twesten :)—Luke, they tell us, when he has spoken (ii. 1.) of the census ordered by Cæsar Augustus, at the time of

* This difficulty is scarcely insisted on, any more. We can here only indicate its solution. Its exposition requires a development too extended for this volume. It may easily be found elsewhere.

the birth of Jesus Christ, adds these words, in the second verse; "this taxing was first made, when Cyrenius was governor of Syria."

From this it would appear, that Luke was in flat contradiction to cotemporary history; for, at the birth of Jesus Christ, Judea was governed by Herod, whilst Syria was governed by Saturninus, or rather, (from the fifth year before the Christian era,) by Quintilius Varus, who succeeded him; and during whose administration Herod the Great died. The Cyrenius, (Publius Syrius Quirinius,) under whom a second census was made, was not sent into the East until at least eleven or twelve years after the birth of Jesus Christ. The historian Josephus tells us,* in express terms, that this numbering was made in the thirty-seventh year after the defeat of Anthony; and Jesus Christ was born, at the latest, twenty-six years after that great event. It results necessarily, that St. Luke has confounded two epochs and two numberings that were separated by an interval of eleven years.

Before replying to this strange accusation, we would notice its extreme improbability, even if we regard St. Luke as an uninspired man. Can it be believed that Luke, the only one of the evangelists who was learned; Luke the physician, Luke who afterwards speaks of the census under Quirinius, in referring to that celebrated revolt under Judas the Gallilean, by which all Judea was agitated, and great numbers perished; (Acts v. 37,) Luke, writing for all nations, a book of history, of twenty-four pages; can it be believed that Luke was so far mistaken, as to place in the days of Herod the Great, an event so important, and which had occurred but thirty years before! What should we say of a physician in our day, who, even in a simple conversation, should put the battle of Auster-

* Jud. Ant. xvii. 15, xviii. 3.

litz in the days of Catherine II., and of the National Convention? And if he should publish an account, containing such an anachronism, what reception would his work meet from his cotemporaries, even the most illiterate? It has thus often occurred, that in representing the sacred writers as contradicting themselves, they are also represented to be so stupid, as to involve almost a miracle!

But we return to the passage. It is a parenthesis. According to the accent which is placed upon the first word, (ἀυτη) it becomes a demonstrative pronoun, or a pronominal adjective; and, in this alternative, the phrase must be translated *literally*, in the first case, by *this first enrolment;* and in the second case, by *the very first enrolment.* It is in this last sense that this word has been rendered by the authors of the new version, published some months since by a society of ministers in Switzerland; and this we think to be the true rendering.

There is nothing, then, in St. Luke's narrative, that is not entirely natural and exact. After having spoken, in the first verse, of an ordinance of Augustus, which began to be executed under Herod's reign, he apprises us, in the parenthesis of the second verse, that this enrolment must not be confounded with the too famous census of which all Judea still preserved such tragical recollections. *The very first enrolment,* says he, *was made while Cyrenius was yet governor of Syria.* This is the simple and literal translation of the Greek.[*]

Second example:—St. Paul, (1 Cor. xv. 44,) according to our translation, says: *there is a natural body,* (in French, *animal body,*) *and there is a spiritual body;* and

* Others, in taking πρῶτη in the sense of πρυτέρα, as the πρῶτος μοῦ ἦν of John Baptist, (John i. 15, 30.), translate it thus: " this enrolment was made." This translation would still be legitimate, although perhaps less natural, because the Greek would, in this sense, resemble less the ordinary style of St. Luke.

this expression has been sometimes condemned as contradictory. That which is corporeal, we are told, cannot be spiritual, nor that which is spiritual, corporeal. "Settle that; a spiritual body!" (says the professor of Theology in the academy of Geneva, in his treatise upon the use of reason in matters of faith.) But all the difficulty in *settling that* lies in the unfaithfulness of the translation. In the language of the Scriptures, the word so inappropriately rendered *animal* in the French, signifies *endowed with a soul, moved by a soul*, ($\gamma\acute{\epsilon}\nu o\mu\epsilon\nu o\varsigma$ $\epsilon\acute{\iota}\varsigma$ $\psi\upsilon\chi\acute{\eta}\nu$ $\zeta\tilde{\omega}\sigma\alpha\nu$;) and the word which is translated *spiritual*, signifies *moved by the Spirit, endowed by or with the Holy Spirit;* ($\pi\nu\epsilon\tilde{\upsilon}\mu\alpha$ $\ddot{\epsilon}\chi\omega\nu$,) says Jude, verse 13; ($\gamma\acute{\epsilon}\nu o\mu\epsilon\nu o\varsigma$ $\epsilon\acute{\iota}\varsigma$ $\pi\nu\epsilon\tilde{\upsilon}\mu\alpha$ $\zeta\omega o\pi o\iota o\tilde{\upsilon}\nu$,) says St. Paul. There is, then, nothing contradictory in speaking of a glorified body, endowed with the Holy Spirit and moved by the Holy Spirit.

Third example:—It has been alleged, especially in the bosom of the Romish Church, which uses the Vulgate, that the language of Elihu (Job xxxvii. 18.) is tinctured with error: "Hast thou with him spread out the sky, which is strong, and as a molten looking-glass?" We give here the exact translation from the Latin of St. Jerome—*Tu forsitan cum eo fabricatus es cœlos, qui solidissimi quasi œre fusi sunt?*

This passage, we are told, which contradicts so manifestly the truth of facts, is that which the great Galileo quoted, when defending before the court of Rome, the earth's rotary motion. And he was perfectly justifiable, in quoting it; and others are justifiable, who still quote it for the purpose of proving that we must not expect to find the language of the Scriptures always exempt from errors, when they treat of truths belonging exclusively to the order and movements of matter.

But here again, all the mistake is in the translation. It has almost as many errors as words.

11

First fault.—It is not said in the Hebrew, *as molten brass ;** but it is there : *as a brazen mirror ;* which shews that the comparison refers to the *brilliancy*, and in no wise to the *solidity* of the heavens.

Second fault.—Nor is it said in the Hebrew, *thou hast formed ;* but, *thou hast stretched, thou hast made an expanse ;* which shews that space is here referred to, and not a solid fabric.

Third fault.—In supposing (what is not true) that Elihu here speaks *of the Heavens.* This word, in the Hebrew, is not used in the objective case, but in the dative ; although the prefixed preposition ל is sometimes, it is said, taken accusatively, after the manner of the Syriac. It should then have been rendered, not *the heavens ;* but, *for the heavens.*

Fourth fault.—There is not a word said here about *the heavens.* The word of the original is not שמים, but שחקים. The lxx, who translate the first of these words four hundred and thirty-seven times by *the heavens*, have translated the latter, in this verse, by παλαιωματα, a term which has no relation to *the heavens*, and the meaning of which in this place moreover, no one has been able to comprehend.

Whatever may have been the object intended by this Hebrew expression, whose meaning is uncertain, one thing at least is certain ; it is that all idea of *solidity* is perfectly excluded here ; and that on the contrary, the expression designates that which is *most attenuated and subtile.* Buxtorf has rendered it by *res tenuissima et subtilissima ;* Kimchi : *pulvis tenuissimus, qui exsufflatus, ob tenuitatem evolat ;* and its root appears to signify : *to grind, to waste, to construct.* (The waters wear away the stones, says Job xiv. 19,)—It must then have been a

* This objection lies rather against the French, than against our English version.—*Trans.*

great mishap to make of it, a vault of the most solid brass in the heavens.   This word, in fact, is employed in Isaiah, to designate the *smallest dust* which adheres to the balance, without changing its equilibrium (Isaiah xl. 15); it is twice translated by, *the air* (ἀήρ) in the lxx.*   Eight times by *cloud* (νεφελὴ); and four times by *cloud* (νέφος)† It is rendered only once by *firmanent*, once by *the heavens*, and once by *the stars* (ἀστρα)‡, probably because God has sown the stars in space, like dust.

Fifth fault.—Finally, the Hebrew has not the superlative *very solid*, but the simple adjective *firm, fixed.*

What then must be the meaning of this passage ?   We have already said, that it is impossible to find any meaning in the translation of it by the lxx; as also nothing can authorize that of St. Jerome, on which the objection has been founded.   If then we were now permitted to hazard the translation of a sentence which has been considered very obscure, we would render it literally by these words; " hast thou made with him an expanse for the fixed stars, *pure and brilliant* as a molten mirror ?"§

Fourth Example.—St. Matthew (iv. 5,) immediately after the first temptation, says; *that* THEN *the devil led Jesus into the holy city* ; . . . and when this second temptation was ended, he adds (v. 2,) in commencing the description of the third ; *that the devil led him again upon a very high mountain, &c.* . .   St. Luke, on the contrary, (iv. 5,) immediately after the first temptation, says, that *afterward the devil led him upon a high*

* 2 Sam. xxii. 12. Ps. xviii. 12.

† Rosenmuller here renders it by : nubes, quæ, etsi solutæ et laxæ, &c. (Schol. in v. t. in Job).

‡ Jer. li. 9.

§ We adopt here the interpretation of the Chaldee paraphrase which attributes the sense of Mirror in this phrase, only to the last word מוצק, and which translates ראי by *appearance ;* " whose appearance is that of a molten mirror."

mountain ; and when this second temptation was ended, he adds in commencing the account of the third : *he led him also to Jerusalem.* . .

Here then are two Evangelists in evident disagreement as to the order of the three temptations. Necessarily one of them is wrong, in placing the last before the second. Such is the objection.

You shall see this difficulty vanish likewise, as soon as you quit the human versions, and go to the original. We might cite here many other passages, chiefly in the Epistles, where the meaning is obscured by a want of sufficiently regarding the conjunctions and adverbs, καί, δέ, γάρ, οὖν, τότε, &c.

Every one knows that St. Luke in writing his gospel, has not described events in the order of time, but of nature. Each of these methods has its own advantages, in biographical writing. Among profane writers, for example, Nepos has adopted the one, and Suetonius the other. The translators of Luke, therefore, must pay special attention to his language, and not lend him adverbs of time, order and rank, which it never entered his mind to employ, and which so awkwardly change the meaning of his discourse. Restore here the Greek conjunctions, and you will quickly perceive the contradiction of the two French texts disappear.

St. Matthew, who always follows the chronological order of facts, is careful to employ the adverbs with great exactness, in the progress of his account of the temptation : τότε, τότε, παλιν, τότε, τότε, then, then, again, then, then. But on the contrary, St. Luke, who has not intended to pursue the same course, and who had no other design than to shew us the three attacks to which the Son of God had to submit his holy humanity ; St. Luke scrupulously abstains from employing any adverb of time or order, and contents himself with connecting the facts of his narrative, ten times by the copulative, AND (και,) which our translations have so badly rendered by the adverb THEN, or AFTERWARDS.

The contradiction then does not pertain to the sacred text.

ANOTHER SOURCE OF RASHNESS.—It has not been sufficiently kept in mind, that speeches and actions, were repeated more than once during our Savior's ministry; so that some have very imprudently imagined that they observed contradictions in certain statements of two evangelists, where they found only an imperfect resemblance, and where at the same time, they imagined themselves to be reading identical facts.

Examples.—We have in the twofold miracle of the multiplication of the loaves of bread, a very striking example of the facility with which we may be led into error in this way. Twice Jesus Christ, moved with compassion for the people, nourished a starving multitude in the desert. The circumstances of both miracles have many and striking points of resemblance. If it had happened that two of the evangelists had related only the first, and two others only the second; they had not failed to cry out at the identity of the facts and the contradiction of the statements. What! in the one, five thousand men fed with five loaves; and in the other, four thousand men fed with seven loaves! In the one, twelve baskets full (κόφινους) carried away; in the other, seven baskets (σπυρίδας)! What disagreement! Happily, if St. Luke and John have mentioned only the first, Matthew and Mark have related both. But for that; what a noise had such a passage made in the school of the adversaries!

This remark may be applied to many features of the New Testament; for example, to the Lord's Prayer, which was given, at least twice to the disciples, during the ministry of our Lord.   (Matt. vi. 9; Luke xi. 2.)

See also, Matthew xii. 39, and xvi. 1, 4; Luke viii. 21, xi. 27, and Matthew xii. 49.   Luke ix. 1, x. 1, and Matthew x. 1.

We will propose yet *another example.*

It does not appear, when we look closely at it, that the Sermon on the Mount (Matt. v. vi. vii.) and that which St. Luke gives us in the latter half of his 6th chapter, were pronounced on the same occasion.*   In fact: 1. Luke omits many sentences reported by Matthew,† and he adds some others (v. 24 to 26;) 2. Matthew notifies us that the Sermon which he reports, preceded the healing of the leper (viii. 3;) and Luke, that his followed it (v. 12;) 3. Luke places Matthew among the number of those whom Jesus had already called to the apostleship, and who descended from the mountain with him before he delivered his discourse to them; while Matthew himself teaches us that the Sermon of which he speaks, preceded his vocation by many days. 4. Finally, one of the discourses was delivered *upon a mountain,* whilst Jesus was seated, with his disciples around him; the other, on the contrary, was delivered in the plain, and under other circumstances.   We pause at this remark to assure those who may have heard alleged against the doctrine of inspiration, the pretended contradiction of the sentence in which Matthew (ver. 40,) makes Jesus say; "If any man will take away thy coat, ($\chi\iota\tau\acute{\omega}\nu\alpha$) let him have thy cloak ($\iota\mu\alpha\tau\iota\upsilon\nu$) also;" to that where, according to Luke, he said; "Him that taketh away thy cloak, forbid not to take the coat also." (Luke vi. 29.)   No objection, we observe,

* See Whitby on Matt. v. 5.
† For example, Matt. v. 13–39. All the chapter vi: and vii: 6–15.

can be made from this diversity, since these two sentences were pronounced on different days.

Yet, we ought also to say, because this remark is applicable to many other objections of the same kind ; although it may have been true that these two passages had been quoted as the same fragment of the same discourse, their difference had not still caused us any kind of surprise.   We believe that the Holy Spirit, when he quotes the Holy Spirit, is not limited to the employment of the same terms, provided he preserves the same meaning.   A man of an exact mind, when he repeates himself or quotes himself, does not feel himself in the least degree bound to carry his imitation to the very words.   And we think that the Lord's commandment was *equally* represented in each of these two sentences of Luke and Matthew, (refer to what we say upon the same subject, chap. iii. sect. 2).

ANOTHER SOURCE OF RASHNESS.—Sometimes a *variation* critically respectable, which removed a difficulty, has not been noticed ; and they have preferred to impute the contradiction to the sacred writer !

Example.—According to the three first evangelists (Mark xv. 25, 33, 34 ; Matt. xxvii. 45, 46 ; Luke xxiii. 44. 54), our Savior was suspended on the cross at the third hour of the day ; that is, at nine o'clock in the morning ; the sun was darkened at the sixth hour; and Jesus gave up the ghost at the ninth hour; whereas if St. John is to be believed, (xix. 14,) the punishment could not have commenced before the *sixth hour*, (at mid-day.) Palpable contradiction !

Before replying to this difficulty, we shall present a remark quite similar to that which we have already made concerning the enrolment under Cyrenius.   Was it likely that the apostle John was ignorant of the length of time occupied by the punishment of his master ; and could he

make such a mistake as to substitute three hours for six ;
he who had remained before the cross !

But, if we consult the Greek manuscripts of St. John,
we find four in small letters, and three in uncial or capital
letters (among others, the famous manuscript of Beza preserved at Cambridge), which here read, the *third hour* instead of *the sixth hour.*   The numbers, in the Greek manuscripts, are often written in figures, that is, by simple Greek
letters ; and the 3, and the 6 being expressed by two letters easily confounded (the γάμμα and the ἐπίσημον),
many ancients have thought that the variation was caused
by this.   Griesbach who has marked this variation with a
sign of preference, quotes Severus of Antioch, and Am-
monius in Theophylact ; and adds that the chronicle of
Alexandria appealed in favor of this reading to better
copies, and even to the original autograph (ἰδιόχειρον) of
the gospel of St. John.

ANOTHER SOURCE OF RASHNESS.—The meaning of certain features of a narration is not seized ; and they rush
to the conclusion, that the writer was mistaken.

Example.—Mark xi. 11, 14. *Jesus cursed a fig tree
which had only leaves, because it was not the season of
figs.*

There is then doubtless an error there, one says: why
seek fruits out of the season when they may reasonably be
expected ?

Yet there is nothing there that is not very simple. If
it had been the season for gathering figs, this tree might
have already been stript of its fruit, and its barrenness
could not in that case have been determined simply from
the absence of fruit.

But is a tree, the objector still replies, (to say in passing,) guilty for not bearing fruit ? Why then punish it ?
We reply that in this miracle, which is a type, the tree is

no more unhappy than it is guilty ; and its suffering is no more real than its morality. The one is as completely symbolical as the other.

ANOTHER SOURCE OF RASHNESS.—This rule has not been heeded (which we love to express here in the very words of the great reformer of Italy, the excellent Peter Martyr :)* " when passages are obscure, as to their chronology, great care must be taken not to reconcile them by imputing faults to the inspired book. Wherefore, if sometimes it happens that we cannot account for the number of the years, we must simply avow our ignorance, and consider that the Scriptures are expressed with so much conciseness, that it is not possible for us always to discover at what epoch we must commence such and such a computation. It very often happens that in the histories of the kings of Judah and Israel, the respective numbers of their years cannot be easily reconciled ; but these difficulties are explained and justified in many ways.   1. The same year, commenced by one of the two, and finished by the other, is attributed to both. 2. Often the sons reigned with their fathers for several years ; which are imputed sometimes to one and sometimes to the other. 3. There were often interregnums which the Scriptures attribute sometimes to the predecessors, sometimes to the successors. 4. Finally, it sometimes happens that certain years in which oppressive and profane princes reigned, are regarded as not having existed, and are not counted."
We think that the examples which we have cited thus far, are sufficient. We shall quote no more. What we have said, may shew the real value and weight of the objections ;† for (we repeat it,) we have taken pains to ad-

---

* In his Commentary on 2 Kings xiii. 17, and 1 Kings xv. 1.
† See for greater detail, the authors we have cited, and espe-

duce those which are considered the most important.
Warned by these examples, and by so many others, let us
then learn,if hereafter any difficulties of the same kind present
themselves to us, to think as did Julius Africanus the friend
of Origen, sixteen hundred years ago ; and as have done
before and after him, all men of God. " At all events,
(said he in reading the two genealogies of Matthew and
Luke,) at all events, certainly the gospel is every where
true !"   *Τό μέντοι Εὐαγγέλιον πάντως ἀληθεύει.**

Section VII.—Errors Contrary to the Philosophy of Nature.

It will be admitted, it has been sometimes said, that
the apparent or real contradictions in the dates, the quotations and the narratives of the Scriptures, may be susceptible of solution by the resources of a more or less labored exegesis ; but there are others which you cannot
reconcile : they are all those expressions in which the
sacred writers are in manifest opposition to the laws of
nature now better understood.   At the same time (we may
add,) if this argument against the verbal inspiration of the
Scriptures, is irrefutable ; it does not compromise, in the
least, the divinity of their doctrines, any more than the
truth of the great religious facts which they relate to us.
In inspiring his apostles and his prophets, God would make
of us not scholars, but saints.   We might then, without
danger, leave the holy Scriptures to speak ignorantly of
the phenomena of the material world ; their prejudices on
such subjects are innocent, but unquestionable.   Do you
not often hear them speaking as if the earth was immovable, and the sun in motion ?   This heavenly body, accor-

cially the useful collection of Horne.   (Introduction to the Study
of the Scriptures.)
    *Eusebius Hist. Eclec. lib. 1. c. vii.

ding to them, rises and sets : " its course is from one end
of the heavens unto the other." (Ps. xix.) The moon
and stars are likewise in motion ; the sun, by the command
of Joshua, stood immovable in the mid-heaven ; it stands
still over Gibeon, and the moon in Ajalon. (Josh. x. 12.)
" The earth is founded upon the seas." (Ps. xxiv. 5.)
" Taken from the water, it exists in the water." (2 Pet.
iii. 5.) "God has laid its foundations ; it shall never be
moved." (Ps. civ. 5.) Can you admit that this is really
the language of the Creator of the heavens and the earth,
speaking to his creatures?

We shall reply to this objection ; and we rejoice to
meet it on our way, because the examination of it must
exhibit the glory of the Scriptures.

We freely admit, that if there are any physical errors,
fully proved, in the Scriptures, the Scriptures could not be
from God. But we mean to show that there are none ; and
we shall dare to challenge the adversaries, to produce one
from the entire Bible. We are going still farther ; and
we shall show, on the contrary, how much latent science
is concealed under the simplicity of its language.

We shall commence by saying something concerning
the miracle of Joshua, because it has often been adduced
for the purpose of combatting the plenary inspiration, or
even the divine mission of the men of God. We have
read the works of many infidels, who have attacked it
with their ordinary pride, and with that severe irony
which too often characterizes them. But it is easy to answer them. We do not think of discussing here the manner in which the miracle was performed ; but we wish to
show by this example, with what levity and precipitancy
they have determined, that because they did not comprehend certain passages, they must, of course, be unreason-
able.

The sun, on the day of the battle of Beth-horon, *stood*

still in the midst of the heavens, it is written in the tenth chapter of Joshua ; and, *there never was a day like it, before nor since.*

In Germany, it has been said : This phrase, taken in its natural meaning, appears to us absurd ; then it is erroneous and totally human.   Elsewhere it has been said : It is absurd ; then we must give it another meaning.   But both have reasoned from false premises.   The fact is any thing but absurd ; it is merely miraculous.

We will present the objection in the words of a professor of theology :* "The most intrepid Methodist," says he, " would be constrained to admit that, in the system of our globe, if the sun should stand still for one single instant, or if the movement of the globe were retarded, the belligerent armies, and every thing on the face of the earth, would have been swept away like the chaff before the tempest.   It is an expression which cannot be taken literally."   The enemies of inspiration produce this objection for another purpose.   The sacred historian, they say, did not know the laws of nature—he is then uninspired.

And yet, it is this very objection itself which is an error.   In fact, if the miracle, in place of arresting suddenly, in an indivisible instant, the rotation of our globe, took only the short space of a few seconds to accomplish it by a gentle and continuous action, then you have enough in this simple circumstance to assure you that such a phenomenon could not have, mechanically, any other sensible effect than to raise from west to east, the waters spread over the surface of the earth.   A child might tell you, that a coach in rapid motion, rushing against an impediment, may be dashed to pieces, because the impediment is immovable ; and all the travelers, thrown out forward, will be hurled to the ground.   But let it be stopped by a

---

* Upon the use of reason in matters of faith.—Theol. Essays of M. Chenevière, Pastor and Professor.   tome 1, p. 456.

continuous resistance, which is applied gradually, for three or four seconds: then the smallest children seated in the vehicle will remain unshaken from their seats; they will not even be aware of the impulse, which, three seconds before, they were receiving from the impetuous movement of the horses, and which, without this precaution, must have been sufficient to throw them to a great distance.

The rotation of the earth, is, at the equator, at the rate of 1426 feet a second; at Jerusalem, 1212 feet. It is the speed of a bullet at the moment of leaving the cannon, discharged by one fifth its own weight of powder. It is capable (deducting the effect of atmospheric resistance), of elevating this projectile to the extreme height of 24,000 feet; and yet a child of six years, in two-thirds of a minute, could, without danger, destroy all this force, by the elastic and continued action of its fingers. Commit to its little hands an eight pound cannon-ball for forty seconds; and during the same time, let another of the same weight fall freely through the air, and from the height of mount Himalaya. At the end of only forty seconds, the weight, after having acted *by the same impulse* upon the one and the other of these projectiles, shall merely, in regard to the first, have wearied the feeble fingers which hold it; while it shall have imparted to the other, a rapidity of motion, equal to that of the rotation of the earth impressed on the hill of Bethoron in the latitude of Jerusalem. The child does not imagine that he has been able in two thirds of a minute, to destroy, by the continued action of his little hand, a force capable of projecting a ball eight thousand feet higher than Mount Blanc, and of cutting down at an immense distance, squadrons and ramparts in the day of battle!

Thus then, if God should have employed no more than forty seconds, in the days of Joshua, to arrest by a supple

12

and successive resistance, the movement of our globe, the projecting impulse from west to east, which a mass of iron of eight pounds would have felt in the plain of Bethoron, would have been no stronger than the pressure felt to-day by the hand upon which you lay such a weight. And if the mass instead of having the form of a bullet, had had that of a quoit or of a cube, there would not have been enough of that impulse to make it overcome the resistance of friction, and change its place upon the surface of the ground.

It will perhaps be objected, that the rotation of the globe at Bethoron was twenty-seven times more rapid than the movement of a steam-carriage upon a rail-road. True; but since the retarding force necessary to exhaust a given impulse, is in inverse proportion to the time employed, suppose the miracle accomplished in eighteen minutes; take eighteen minutes instead of forty seconds, to stop entirely the movement of the terrestrial globe at the command of Joshua, and then " the contending armies instead of being swept away as by the tempest," would no more have felt what was passing, than do, at each station, the thousands of travellers who are stopped upon a rail-road!

Yet the Scriptures are reproached for having spoken upon the daily phenomena of nature, in a way that appears to show ignorance, and which is incompatible with a plenary inspiration. According to the sacred writers, the sun rises, the sun sets, the sun stops, the earth remains firm! It has been demanded that the Creator, in speaking to us through a book which he has inspired, should have showed us more clearly, that the Spirit who directed the sacred historians, knew before we did, the rotary motion of our globe, its periodical revolution, and the relative immobility of the Sun.

Let us still farther examine this reproach.

We will first inquire of those who make it, if they would have had the Bible speak like Isaac Newton. Would they forget, that if God should speak about scenes of nature,—I do not say only, as he sees it, but as the scientific men of future ages will see it,—then the great Newton himself had understood nothing of it? Besides, even the most advanced language of science is not yet, and never will be, after all, any thing more than the language of appearances. The visible world is, much more than you imagine, a figure which passes, a scene of illusions and of phantoms. That which you there call reality, is still in itself only an appearance relatively to a more elevated reality, and a more profound analysis. In our ignorant mouth, the word *reality* has nothing absolute ; it is a term totally relative, and employed in proportion as we think we have reached a new round on the ladder by which we come up from the depths of our ignorance. The human eye sees objects only under two dimensions, and projects them all upon the same canvass, until the touch and some experience have rendered to them the reality of depth, or a third dimension. Colors are accidents, and belong only by reflection, and by illusion to the objects which present them to you. The very impenetrability of bodies, their solidity, their extension, are after all, only an appearance, and present themselves to us as a reality only in expectation of a profounder science, which shall substitute another for it. Who may tell us where this analysis is to stop ; and what would be our language concerning beings which are the most familiar to us, if we were only endowed with one more sense ; with antennæ, for example, like the ants and the bugs ? The expression of appearances, provided it be exact, is then among men, a language philosophically correct ; and is that which the Scriptures ought to adopt. Would you have the Bible speak to us of the scenes of nature otherwise

than as we speak of them to one another in our social or
domestic intercourse; otherwise even than the learned
themselves speak of them to one another? When Sir
John Herschell asks his servants to send some one to
awake him exactly at midnight, for the passage of some
star over his meridian lens; does he think himself obliged
to speak to them of the earth, of her rotation, and of the
moment when she shall have brought their nadir into
the plane of her orbit? I think not. And if you ever
heard him converse, in the Observatory of Greenwich,
with the learned Ayrie, you would see that even in this
sanctuary of science, the habitual language of these as-
tronomers is still just like that of the Scriptures. For them,
the stars rise, the equinoxes recede, the planets advance and
are accelerated, stop and retrograde. Would you then
have Moses speak to all the generations of men, in a language more scientific than that of La Place, of Arago and
Newton?

But still farther; we adduce two general facts which
shine with a great light, when they are studied; and which
betray quickly in the Scriptures, the pen of the Almighty
God. Here, as everywhere else, the objections when contemplated more closely, return back on the objector, are
recanted triumphantly, and become arguments.

These two facts are analogous to that which you may
observe in the words of a learned astronomer, conversing
with his young children, and showing them with his finger, the earth and the heavens. If you followed him in
these interviews, when his tenderness stooping to their
level, presents to their new-born intelligence, images and
words which it can comprehend, you would then quickly
remark his respect for truth, by a two-fold sign. First,
he would never tell them any thing that was not true;
and secondly, there would be in his words many indications that he knows more than he sees fit to communicate

to them. He doubtless would not pretend to teach them science; but on the one hand, nothing in his discourse would contradict its principles; and on the other, many of his words would already indicate, that although silent upon them, he comprehended them. Afterward, when his children, having become men, shall review his words; not only will they find them exempt from all error, but they will also recognize that, skilfully chosen, they were already in preëstablished harmony with science, and presented it to them in its germ, although they could not comprehend it. In proportion as their own knowledge shall increase, they will see with admiration, under the reserve and the simplicity of his language, concealed wisdom, learned exactness, turns of phraseology, and forms of expression, which were in harmony with facts, then unknown to them, but long known by him.

Such then is likewise the double observation that every attentive reader can make of the language of the Scriptures. They speak poetically, but precisely, the true language of appearances. We there hear a father who condescends to speak to the smallest of his children, but in such a manner that the elder can never discover a single word of his conversation contrary to the true position of the things which he has made, and in such a manner too, that often he drops without affectation, words enough to show them that all that which they have learned of his works for four thousand years, he knew before them, and better than they now do. It is thus, that in the Bible, eternal wisdom addresses its children. In proportion as they grow, they see the Scriptures made for their age, adapted to their developments, appearing to grow with them, and always presenting to them the two facts which we have noticed; on the one hand, absence of all error; on the other, indirect indications, but incontestable, of a science which preceded all that of man.

12*

First fact.   There is no physical error in the word of
God.   If there were, we have said, this book could not
be from God.   God is not a man that he should lie, nor the
son of man that he should mistake.   In order to be understood by us, he must, unquestionably, stoop to our feebleness; yet to stoop to it, is not to partake of it; and his
language will always attest his condescension, never his
ignorance.

This remark is more important than it at first appears
to be.   It becomes brilliant when surveyed more closely.

Examine all the false theologies of the ancients and
moderns; read, in Homer or Hesiod, the religious codes
of the Greeks; study those of the Budhists, those of the
Brahmins, those of the Mohammedans: you will there find,
not only systems revolting in their views of the Deity, but
you will there meet the grossest errors concerning the
material world; their theology will doubtless be revolting
to you; but their natural philosophy too and their astronomy, always bound to their religion, will present the
most absurd notions.

Read in the Shaster, in the Pouran, in the four books of
the Vedham, or law of the Hindoos, their shocking Cosmogony,—the moon is 50,000 leagues higher than the
sun; it shines by its own light; it animates our body.
The night is formed by the descent of the sun behind the
Someyra mountains, situated in the middle of the globe,
and many thousand leagues high.   Our earth is flat and
triangular, composed of seven stories, each of which has
its own degree of beauty, its inhabitants and its sea.   The
first is of honey, the other is of sugar, the other of
butter, the other of wine; and finally all the mass is carried
on the heads of innumerable elephants who, in shaking
themselves, cause the earthquakes.   In a word, they have
placed the whole history of their gods in the most fan-
tastical, and yet the most indissoluble relations to the phy-

sical world, and all the phenomena of the universe. The missionaries to India too, have often declared that a telescope, silently placed in the midst of the holy Benares or the antient Ava, would be a battery powerful as thunder, to overthrow all the system of Bramah and that of Budh.

Read again the philosophers of Greek and Roman antiquity, Aristotle, Seneca, Pliny, Plutarch, Cicero. How many sentences do you find, of which one alone would suffice to compromise all our doctrine of inspiration, if it should be found in any book of the Bible? Read the Koran of Mohammed, representing mountains as being made, to hinder the earth from being moved, and representing it as held by anchors and cords. What do I say? Read even the cosmogony of Buffon, or some of the ironies of Voltaire upon the doctrine of a deluge, or upon the fossil animals of a primitive world. We will go still farther. Read again, we say, not the absurd reasonings of the Pagans, of Lucretius, of Pliny, or of Plutarch, against the theory of antipodes, but even the fathers of the Christian church. Hear the theological indignation of the admirable Augustine, who said that it was opposed to the Scriptures; and the scientific eloquence of Lactantius, who believes it to be contrary to good sense. "*Num aliquid loquuntur !*" exclaims he; is any one so simple as to believe that there are men with their feet above their heads, trees having fruits hanging upward, rain, snow, and hail falling upward! "To answer you," he says, "they pretend that the earth is a globe?" "*Quid dicam de iis nescio, qui, cum semel aberraverint, constanter in stultitiâ perseverant, et vanis vana defendunt !* One knows not what to say of such men, who once in an error, engulf themselves in their folly, and maintain absurdity by absurdity !"*

* Of false wisdom, liv. iii. chap. 24.

Hear too Boniface the legate, representing Virgilius to the Pope as a heretic, for his views on this subject; hear Pope Zachary treating this unfortunate bishop as *homo malignus*: "If it be proved," writes *he*, "that Virgilius maintains, that there are other men under this earth; assemble a council, condemn him, drive him from the church, and despose him from the priesthood!" Still later, hear the higher clergy of Spain, and especially the imposing council of Salamanca, indignant at the geographical system by which Christopher Columbus was seeking a world. Hear, at the epoch of Newton's birth, the great Galileo, "who mounted, says Kepler, "upon the highest walls of the universe," and who vindicated by his genius as well as by his telescope, the unknown and condemned system of Copernicus; see him, groaning, at the age of eighty years, in the prisons of Rome, for having discovered the movement of the earth, after having been compelled to pronounce these words, ten years before (the 28th of June, 1633), before their highnesses in the palace of the holy office: "I, Galileo, in the seventieth year of my age, on bended knees before your eminences, having before my eyes, and touching with my own hands the holy Scriptures, I adjure, I curse, and I detest the error of the earth's movement."

What should we not have been justified in saying of the Scriptures, if they had spoken of the phenomena of nature as all the ancient sages did? if they had referred every thing to four elements, as was done for so long a time? if they had called the stars crystal, as Philolaus of Crotona; and if, as Empedocles, they had enlightened the two hemispheres of our globe with two suns? if they had said, as Leucippus, that the fixed stars, heated by the quickness of their diurnal motion around the earth, enkindled the sun with their fires? if they had formed the heavens and the earth, as Diodorus Siculus and all the

Egyptian sages, by the motion of air and the ascension of fire? or if they had said, as Philolaus, that the sun has only a borrowed light, and that it is only a mirror which reflects back on us the light of the celestial spheres? if they had made it, as Anaxagoras, a mass of iron larger than Peloponnesus, and the earth a mountain, whose roots go infinitely deep? if they had spoken of the heavens as a solid sphere to which the fixed stars are attached, as have done, with Aristotle, almost all the ancients? if they had called the celestial vault a *firmanentum* or a στεϱέωμα, as their interpreters, both Latin, Greek and English have done? if they had spoken, as has been recently done among a Christian people, of the influence of the movements of the heavens upon the elements of this lower world, upon the characters of men and upon the course of human affairs? Such is the natural propensity of all people to this superstition, that, in spite of their religion, the ancient Jews, and the Christians themselves, have alike fallen into it. The modern Greeks, says D'Alembert,[*] have carried it to excess; scarcely is there found one of their authors, who, on every occasion, does not speak of predictions by the stars, of horoscopes, of talismans; so that there was scarcely a house in Constantinople and in all Greece, which was not built according to rules of *apotelesmatic astrology.* The French historians observe, that astrology was so in vogue under Catharine de Medici, that nothing important could be undertaken without consulting the stars; and under Henry III., and even Henry IV., in the conversations of the court of France, inquiry was made of nothing but the predictions of astrologers. We have seen, toward the close of the last century, says Ph. Giulani,[†] an Italian send to Pope

* Encycl. on Dict. rais. des Sciences, etc. tome 1, p. 663, (Lucques 1758).

† Encyc. on Dict. rais. des Sciences, &c. tome 1, p. 664.

Innocent XI., a prediction in the form of a horoscope, concerning Vienna, then beseiged by the Turks, and which was very well received. And in our days, the count Boulainvilliers has written quite seriously on this subject.

But now, open the Bible; study its fifty sacred authors, from that admirable Moses, who held the pen in the desert, four hundred years before the Trojan war, even to that fisherman, the son of Zebedee, who wrote fifteen hundred years afterwards in Ephesus and Patmos, under the reign of Domitian; open the Bible, and search if you can there find any thing like this.—No.—None of these mistakes which the science of every age discovers in the books of the preceding ages; none of those absurdities especially, which modern astronomy discovers in such great numbers in the writings of the ancients, in their sacred codes, in their philosophies, and in the most admirable pages of even the Christian fathers, none of those errors can be found in any one of our sacred books; nothing there will ever contradict that which, after so many ages, the investigations of the scientific world have revealed to us as sure, concerning the state of our globe and of the heavens. Go carefully through the Scriptures, from one end to the other, seeking for such spots; and whilst you give yourself up to this examination, remember that it is a book which speaks of everything, which describes nature, which recounts its grandeurs, which narrates its creation, which tells us of the formation of the heavens, that of the light, that of the waters, that of the atmosphere, that of the mountains, that of the animals and of the plants; it is a book which teaches us the first revolutions of the world, and which also predicts to us its last; it is a book which relates them in circumstantial histories, which exalts them in a sublime poetry, and which sings them in fervent hymns; it is a book full of oriental imagination, of elevation, of variety and of boldness; it is a book which speaks of the celestial and invisible world, and at the same time of the earth and of things visible; it is a book to which nearly fifty writers of every degree of cultivation, of every state, of every condition, and separated by fifteen hundred years from one another, have successively contributed; it is a book written first in the centre of Asia, in the sands of Arabia, or in the deserts of Judea, or in the courts of the Jewish temple, or in the rustic schools of the prophets of Bethel and of Jericho, or in the sumptuous palaces of Babylon, or upon the idolatrous banks of Chebar; and afterwards, in the centre of western civilization, in the midst of the Jews and of their ignorance, in the midst of Polytheism and its idols, as in the bosom of Pantheism, and of its sad philosophy; it is a book whose first writer had been for forty years, the pupil of those Egyptian magicians, for whom the sun, the stars and the elements, being endowed with intelligence, reäcted upon the elements, and governed the world by continual effluvia; it is a book whose first writer preceded, by more than nine centuries, the most ancient philosophers of ancient Greece and of Asia, Thales and Pythagoras, Zaleucus, Xenophon, Confucius; it is a book which carries its descriptions even to the plains of the invisible world, even to the hierarchies of angels, even to the most remote periods of the future, and to the glorious scenes of the last day; now, seek in its 50 authors, seek in its 66 books, seek in its 1,189 chapters, and its 31,173 verses. . . Seek one alone of those thousand errors with which the ancients and the moderns are filled, when they speak either of heaven or of earth, or of their revolutions, or of their elements; seek, you will not find.

Its language is unconstrained, open; it speaks of every thing, and in every strain; it is the prototype, it has been the inaccessible model, nay, the inspirer of all the most elevated productions of poetry. Ask Milton, the two Racines, Young, Klopstock. They will tell you, that this divine poetry is of all the most lyric, the boldest, the most sublime; it rides on a cherub, it flies upon the wings of the wind. And yet this book never does violence to the facts nor to the principles of a sound philosophy of nature. Never will you find a single sentence in opposition to the just notions which science has imparted to us, concerning the form of our globe, its magnitude and its geology; upon the void and upon space; upon the inert and obedient materiality of the stars; upon the planets, upon their masses, their courses, their dimensions or their influences; upon the suns which people the depths of space, upon their number, their nature, their immensity. So too in speaking of the invisible world, and of the subject of angels, so new, so unknown, so delicate, this book will not present you a solitary one of its authors, who, in the course of one thousand five hundred and sixty years of their writing, has varied in describing the character of charity, humility, fervor and purity which pertains to these mysterious beings; so too, in speaking of the relations of the celestial world to God, never has one of these fifty writers, neither in the Old nor the New Testament, written one single word favorable to this incessant pantheism of the Gentile philosophy;—thus also you shall not find one alone of the authors of the Bible who has, in speaking of the visible world, let fall from his pen one only of those sentences which, in other books, contradict the reality of facts; none who makes the heavens a firmament, as do the Seventy, St. Jerome, and all the Fathers of the Church; none who makes of the world, as Plato, an intelligent animal; none who reduces every thing below, to the four physical elements of the ancients; none who thinks with the Jews, with the Latins and the Greeks, with the better spirits of antiquity, with the great Tacitus among the ancients, with the great De Thou among the moderns, with the sceptical Michel Montaigne, that " the stars have dominion and power, not only over our lives and fortunes, but our very inclinations, our discourses, our wills; that they govern, impel and agitate them at the mercy of their influences; and that (as our reason teaches us and finds it), all this lower world is agitated by the slightest movement of the heavenly bodies. *Facta etenim et vitas hominum suspendit ab astris ;*"* not one who has spoken of the mountains as Mohammed did, of the cosmogony as Buffon, of the antipodes as Lucretius, as Plutarch, as Pliny, as Lactantius, as St. Augustine, as the Pope Zachary. Surely if there was found in the Bible one alone of those errors which abound in the philosophers, ancient as well as modern, our faith in the plenary inspiration of the Scriptures would be more than exposed; we should have to admit that there are errors in the word of God, and that these erroneous sentences appertain to a fallible writer, and not to the Holy Spirit; for God is not a man that he should lie; there is in him no variableness, nor shadow of turning; and he to whom lying lips are an abomination, cannot contradict himself, nor dictate that which is false.

There is, then, no physical error in the Scriptures; and this great fact, which becomes always more admirable, in proportion as it is more closely contemplated, is a striking proof of the inspiration which has dictated to their writers, even in the choice of the least expression. But there is still another fact.

Not only has the Bible admitted no false sentence or expression, but it has also employed words which make us recognize, in a way that cannot be mistaken, the science of the Almighty. His great object, doubtless, was, to reveal to us the eternal grandeurs of the invisible world,

---

* Essais, liv. ii. ch. 12.

and not the barren secrets of that which perishes. Yet it often happens that his language, when it is attentively regarded, gives a glimpse of knowledge which it is not aiming to teach, but of which he cannot be ignorant, *since knowledge is in him a profound abyss.* Not only does he never say any thing false to us, even incidentally ; but also, you will often light upon words which shall betray to you the voice of the world's Creator. You will often remark there, a wisdom, a prudence, an exactness, of which the past ages had never a suspicion, and which the discoveries alone of the telescope, of modern calculation and modern science, have enabled us to appreciate ; so that its language will carry, in these features, the evident characters of the most entire inspiration. The discreet and unusual choice of its expressions, the nature of certain details, whose perfect propriety and divine harmony with facts were not revealed until three thousand years afterward, the reserve in the use of words, sometimes its very boldness and its strangeness at the time when it was written ;—all these signs will shew you the learned one *par excellence,* the Ancient of days, who is addressing children unquestionably, but who speaks like the father, and who knows all his house.

When the Scriptures speak of the form of the earth, they make it A GLOBE !* When they speak of the position of this globe in the bosom of the universe, *they suspend it upon nothing ;* (על בלימה).† When they speak of its age, not only do they put its creation, as well as those of the heavens, *at the beginning,* that is, before the ages, which they cannot or will not number ; but they are also careful to place before the breaking up of chaos and the creation of man, the creation of the angels, of the archangels, of

---

* Isa. xl. 22. Job xxvi. 10. Prov. viii.

† Job xxvi. 7. κριμαζων γην επι ουδενος, say the LXX.

the principalities, and of the powers; their trial; the fall of some, and their ruin; the perseverance of others, and their glory. When they speak afterward of the origin of our continents, and of the later creation of the plants, of animals, and of men, they give then to this new world, and to our proud race, an age so young, that the men of every period and nation, and even our modern schools, have foolishly revolted from it; but an age to which they have had to consent, since the labors of De Luc, of Cuvier, and of Buckland, have so fully demonstrated that the surface of the globe, as well as the monuments of history, and those of science, were about to command for it the assent of the learned as well as the vulgar. When they speak of the heavens, they employ, to designate and to define them, the most philosophic and the most elegant expression; an expression which the Greeks, in the Septuagint, the Latins, in the Vulgate, and all the Christian Fathers, in their discourses, have pretended to improve, and which they have distorted, because it seemed to them opposed to the science of their day. The heavens, in the Bible, are *the expanse;* (רקיע)* they are the vacant space, or ether, or immensity, and not the *firmamentum* of St. Jerome; nor the στερέωμα of the Alexandrian interpreters; nor the *eighth heaven,* firm, solid, crystalline, and incorruptible, of Aristotle and of all the ancients. And although the Hebrew term, so remarkable, recurs seventeen times in the Old Testament, and the Seventy have rendered it seventeen times by στερέωμα, (firmament,) never have the Scriptures in the New Testament, used this expression of the Greek interpreters in this sense.† When they speak of the light, they present it to us as an element independent of the sun, and as anterior, by three epochs, to the period

* Gen. i. 6. Ps. xix. 7.

† They have used it once, but to designate something totally different from the heavens.

in which that great luminary was formed.* When they speak of the creation of the plants, they make them vegetate, grow, and bear seed, before the appearing of the sun, and under conditions of light, moisture, and heat quite different from those by which the vegetables of our day are nourished ;† and it is thus that they reveal to us, for many thousands of years, an order of things which the fossil botany of our day has just declared incontestable, and of which the necessity is attested by the gigantic forms of vegetables recently discovered in Canada and in Baffin's Bay—some, as Mr. Marcel de Serres, ‡ resorting, to explain it, to a terrestrial magnetism at that time more intense, or to auroræ boreales more luminous; the others, as M. de Candollè,§ to a great inclination of the ecliptic (although in reality, according to the famous theorem of La Grange, the Mécanique Céleste confines this variation of the planetary orbits within very narrow limits).‖ When they speak of the air, the gravity of which was unknown before Galileo ; they tell us that at the creation, " God gave to the air ITS WEIGHT (משקל), and to the waters their just measure."¶ When they speak of our atmosphere and of the upper waters ;** they give them an importance which modern science alone has justified ;†† since, from their calculations, the force annually employed by nature, for the formation of the clouds, is equivalent to an amount of labor which the entire human race could not accomplish in 200,000 years.‡‡ And when they separate the inferior from the

* Gen. i. 4, 14.　　　　　† Gen. i. 12.

‡ Memoires de Marcel de Serres.

§ Biblioth. Universelle, lviii. 1835.

‖ The oscillations of the Ecliptic on both sides of its mean position, cannot be more than 1¼°.

¶ Job xxviii. 25.　　　** Gen. i. 7.

†† See the calculations of Leslie.

‡‡ Annuaire du bur. des longit, 1835, p. 196. Arago, in this calculation, supposes that 800,000,000 form the population of the globe, and that only the half of this number are able to work.

superior waters, it is by *an expanse,* and not by a solid
sphere, as their translators would have it. When they
speak of the mountains, they distinguish them as primary
and secondary ; they represent them as being born ; they
make them rise ; they make them melt like wax ; they
abase the valleys ; in a word, they speak as a geological
poet of our day would do. " The mountains were lifted
up, O Lord, and the valleys were abased in the place
which thou hadst assigned them !"* When they speak of
the human races, of every tribe, color and language, they
give them one only and the same origin, although the philosophy of every age has so often revolted against this
truth, and while that of the moderns finds itself compelled
to acknowledge it.† When they speak of the interior
state of our globe, they declare two great facts long unknown to the learned, but rendered incontestable by recent discoveries ; the one, relating to its solid crust, the
other to the great waters which it covers. In speaking of
its solid covering, they teach us that, while its surface
gives us bread ; beneath, (תחתיה) it is ON FIRE ;‡ elsewhere, that it is reserved unto fire, and that it will be
burned in the last times, with all the works which are
found therein.§ And when they speak of the waters that
our globe contains, they refer to them as the only cause, at
least in this relation, of the immense inundations which have
(according to the learned themselves) completely and for a

* Ps. xc. 2; xcvii, 5; civ. 6, 8, 9; cxliv. 5.—Prov. viii. 25.—
Gen. ii. 14; vi. 4;—Zech. xiv. 4, 8;—Ezek. xlvii.

† See Sumner: The Records of the Creation, vol. 1, p. 286; also Prof. Zimmerman; Geographical history of man. Wiseman's
3d Discourse on the natural history of the human race, vol. 1, p.
419.

‡ Job, xxviii. 5; literally: " beneath, it is overturned, and as
on fire."

§ 2 Peter, iii. 7–10.

13*

long time submerged it, at different periods. And while the learned tell us of the shallowness of the seas ; while they assure us that an elevation of the land, only 656 feet, or less than twice the height of the tower of Strasburg would suffice to cause the Baltic Sea, the North Sea, St. George's Channel and the British Channel to disappear ; and that Mount Blanc, removed into the depth of the Pacific Ocean, would be sufficiently high, to appear there as an island ; whilst La Place has thought we may infer from the elevation of the tides, that the mean depth of the ocean does not exceed 3280 feet, (the height of the Salene or Heckla); while they thus prove to us how insufficient the seas are for the immense inundations our globe has undergone— the Scriptures teach us, that " the earth is standing out of the water and in the water,"* and that its solid crust covers a GREAT ABYSS (תהום רבה), whose waters broke out (יבקעו) with violent dashings,† at the epoch of the deluge, as at that of the chaos and of the numberless ages which had preceded it.

When they speak of the deluge, they suppose an internal fire, which raising the temperature of the seas and of the deep waters, caused on the one side, an enormous evaporation and impetuous rains, as if the flood-gates of heaven were opened ; and on the other, an irresistible dilation, which not only raised the waters from their depths, broke up the fountains of the GREAT ABYSS, and raised its powerful waves to the level of the highest mountains,‡ but which caused immense stratifications of calcareous carbonate, under the double action of a great heat and a pressure equivalent to 8000 atmospheres. When they would describe the state of our globe at the period preceding the breaking up of its chaos, they suppose an internal heat,

---

* 2 Peter, iii. 5.   † Gen. vii. 2:

‡ The water is dilated 1–23, in passing from the temperature of ice-melting to that of water-boiling. An elevation of from 16 to

and cover it entirely with waters in a state of liquidity.* When they tell us of the creation of the birds and of the fishes, they give them a common origin ; and it is known that modern naturalists have established between these two classes of animals, intimate relations, imperceptible to the eye, but revealed by anatomy, even in the microscopic form of the globules of their blood.† When they arrest the sun, that is to say, the rotation of the earth, in the days of Joshua, the son of Nun ; the moon must also stay her progress in the same degree and for the same cause as the sun ; a precaution, says Chaubard,‡ that an astronomy ignorant of our diurnal motion would never have imagined ; since after all, the purpose of this miracle was but to prolong the day.§ When they represent the Lord as coming like the lightning, in the twinkling of an eye, at the

17 degrees Rèaumur will then increase its volume 1–111. Now we find by an easy calculation, that the quantity of water necessary to submerge the earth to the height of 1–1000 of the radius of our globe is equal to 1–333 of its entire volume, or 1–111 of its third. If then we suppose that the third of the terrestial globe is metallic (at the mean specific gravity of 12 1–2) ; that the second third is solid (at the weight of 2 1–2) ; and that the remaining 1–3 is water ; then, 1st, the mean specific gravity of the entire globe will be equal to 5 1–2 (agreeably to the conclusions of Maskeline and of Cavendish) ; and 2dly, it will have been sufficient for the submersion of the earth to the height of 6,368 metres, or 1546 metres above Mount Blanc ; that the temperature of the mass of the water in the days of the deluge should have risen to 16 degrees of Rèaumur. This was very nearly the hypothesis of Sir Henry Englefield.

* Gen. i. 2. † Memoirs of Dr. J. L. Provost at Geneva.

‡ Elements of Geology by Chaubard, vol. i. 8vo. Paris. The author there establishes by numerous arguments, the chronological coincidence of the miracle of Joshua with the deluges of Ogyges and of Deucalion. He remarks that these two inundations refer to the same epoch, last the same period of time, are accompanied by the same catastrophes, and produce currents in the sea from west to east.

§ Josh. x. 12.

last day, they again bear testimony to the rotation of the earth, and to the existence of the antipodes; for at this solemn hour it will be, say they, day for one portion of mankind, and at the same time night for another portion.* When they describe the past and future wealth of the land of Canaan, to which a wonderful fertility of vegetation is promised for the latter times, they term it rich, not only in springs, but in subterraneous waters; and seem to anticipate the excavations by which the moderns have learned to fertilize a sterile country.† When they speak of the languages of men, they give them a primitive unity that seems to contradict our first study of the different idioms of nations, but which a more profound examination confirms. When they describe the deliverance of Noah, they give to the ark dimensions which at first sight we pronounce too limited. Had we been charged with the narrative, we should have increased them a hundred fold; but a study of the subject has proved them sufficient. When they speak of the number of the stars, instead of supposing a thousand (1026) as does the catalogue of Hipparchus or of Ptolemy; while in the two united hemispheres the most practised eye can see but 5000; while the human eye, before the invention of the telescope, could perceive but 1000 in the clearest night; the Scriptures pronounce them INNUMERABLE; and like Herschel, they compare them to the sand of the sea; they tell us, that with his own hand and in infinite space, God has sown them like the dust; and that notwithstanding their number, "he calls them all by their names." When they speak of this immensity, listen with what learned and sublime wisdom they depict it; how prudent they are in their noble

---

* Luke, xvii. 31, 34, Mat. xx. 3.

† Deut. viii. 7. " A land of brooks of water, of fountains and deeps that spring out of valleys and hills; (תהמת) See also Isa. xxxvi. 6. Ez. xxxi. 4. Ps. lxxviii. 16.

poetry, how philosophical in their sublimity; "the heavens declare the glory of God; the expanse showeth his handy-work; there is no speech nor language where their voice is not heard." When they speak of the relation of the stars to this sublunary world; instead, like the ancients, of supposing them animated, instead of ever attributing to them an influence over human events, as did, for so long a time, the Christian people of Italy and of France, even to the period of the reformation; they are, say they, inert matter, brilliant, without doubt, but disposed and guided by a creating hand: the heavens, even the heaven of heavens move with the order, the entireness and the unity of an army advancing to battle. "Lift up your eyes on high, and behold who hath created these things, that bringeth out their host by number; he calleth them all by names, by the greatness of his might, for that he is strong in power, not one faileth." "Why sayest thou, oh Jacob, and speakest, oh Israel; my way is hid from the Lord, and my judgment is passed over from my God?"* When they describe the heavens, they are careful to distinguish them; first, the heaven of the birds, of the tempests, of the powers of the air, and of evil spirits; then the heaven of the stars; and lastly, the third heaven, *even the heaven of heavens*. But when they speak of the God of all that; how beautiful their language, and at the same time, how tender! "The voice of his thunder is in the heavens," say they, (Ps. lxxvii. 19,)—"but the heavens, even the heaven of heavens, cannot contain Him." (1 Kings, viii. 27.) "To whom then, will ye liken Him? or what likeness will ye compare unto Him? He has set his glory above the heavens. Who humbleth himself to behold the things that are in heaven. Whither shall I go from thy Spirit, or

---

* Isaiah xl. 26, 27.

whither shall I flee from thy presence?"* But when they seem to have said enough of all these visible grandeurs; these are yet, say they, but the beginning of his ways; and how little a portion of Him is known! And lastly, when they seem to have told all the grandeurs of the Creator of all these immensities, listen yet again: "He counts the number of the stars, and calls them all by name; at the same time that He healeth the broken in heart, and bindeth up their wounds.† He puts your tears into his bottle; the sparrow falls not to the ground without his care; even the hairs of your head are numbered.‡ The eternal God is thy refuge, and underneath are the everlasting arms.§ Oh, my God, how manifold are thy works; how excellent are they, but thou hast put thy mercy above all thy name. Open thou mine eyes that I may behold wondrous things out of thy law."‖ Again; in the midst of all these grandeurs—"Whence then cometh wisdom? And where is the place of understanding? The depth saith; it is not in me. God understandeth the way thereof and he knoweth the place thereof; for he looketh to the ends of the earth, and seeth the whole heavens; to make the weight for the winds; and he weigheth the waters by measure. When he made a decree for rain and a way for the lightning of the thunder, then did he see it and declare it; he declared it; yea, and searched it out. And unto man he said; behold the fear of the Lord, that is wisdom, and to depart from evil is understanding."¶

Such then is the inspiration of the Holy Scriptures; thus then we see beams of light reflected from heaven, when we had thought to detect only error. If with deferential touch you draw the obscure veil, with which

* Isaiah xl. 18. Ps. viii. 1-10; cxiii. 6; cxxxix. 7.
† Ps. cxlvii.　　　　　　　　‡ Ps. lvi. 9. Matt. x. 29-30.
§ Deut. xxxiii. 26, 27.　　　‖ Ps. xxxviii. 2; cxix. 18.
¶ Job xxviii.

they are sometimes covered for your sake, you will behold there a majestic light; for, like Moses, they descend from the sacred mount, and bring to you the tables of testimony in their hands! There, where you feared darkness, you have found light; there, where an objection has been started, God produces a fresh witness of the truth; where a doubt had existed, he puts an assurance.

So far as this seventh objection is concerned, we find difficulties converted into proofs of the inspiration of the sacred volume ; and we see in the light of this and of many other facts, that every page gives evidence that the entire Bible is the word of God.

Let us listen to another and the last objection.

SECTION VIII.—THE VERY ACKNOWLEDGMENT OF ST. PAUL.

We are sometimes told, that it would be superfluous to dispute the fact of the partial and interrupted inspiration of the Scriptures, since even the Apostle Paul has plainly decided the question. Has he not been ever careful to distinguish between those passages which he uttered by inspiration, and those advanced in his own name, as a Christian ? Does he not, in his first epistle to the Corinthians, express very clearly, three several times, this distinction, in answer to different questions addressed to him on the subject of marriage ?

And first, in the 25th verse of the 7th chapter, when he says; "Now concerning virgins, I have NO COMMANDMENT OF THE LORD; yet I give my JUDGMENT, as one that hath obtained mercy of the Lord to be faithful." Then in the 10th verse, where he writes; " unto the married *I* command, (YET NOT I, BUT THE LORD ;) let not the wife depart from her husband, and let not the husband put away his wife." And finally, in the 12th verse he adds ; " but to the rest speak I, NOT THE LORD; if any brother hath a wife that believeth not, and she be pleased to dwell with him; let him not put her away," &c. It is then easily seen by these three sentences, that there are passages in the epistle of this apostle, that are of Paul, and other passages which are of God; that is to say, *inspired passages, and passages uninspired.*

The answer is obvious. When the objectionable passages are more closely examined, it will be found that they cannot be adduced as proof against the doctrine of a full inspiration.

Far from limiting the divinity of apostolic language, these verses, on the contrary, speak as only the fullest and most sovereign inspiration could authorize. St. Paul could speak thus, only by placing his epistles, if I may so say, as St. Peter has done (2 Peter iii. 6,) ON THE LEVEL with THE OTHER sacred writings: nay, we must say; ABOVE THEM, (inasmuch as we there hear a more recent and binding expression of the will of our Lord.) Let us examine this point. What does the apostle of Jesus Christ seek in this chapter? He there treats of three cases of conscience; concerning one of them, God has commanded nothing and interdicted nothing. "So then he that giveth her in marriage, doth well. I speak this by PERMISSION, and *not of commandment*, but as an apostle I give from the Lord, merely *counsel;* and he is careful to add in the fortieth verse; " I think also that I have the Spirit of the Lord." The Lord would leave you free herein, says the apostle; he will place no snare in your path; and if you care not to follow the general advice that is given to you, you violate no commandment, and commit no sin; only, " he that marrieth, doeth well; he that marrieth not, doeth better."

In regard to the other case however, be careful; FOR HERE IS A COMMANDMENT OF THE LORD. He has already made known his will (Matt. v. 31, 32; Mal. ii. 24,) and I have nothing new to declare unto you. But the Old Testament and Jesus Christ have spoken. It is NOT therefore *I*, the Apostle of Jesus Christ, it is the LORD, who already has made known his will unto you. "And unto the married I command, yet not I, but the Lord; let not the wife depart from her husband, and let not the husband put away his wife." (v. 10, 11.)

For the third case, that of the brother who finds himself bound to an unbelieving wife; you had a commandment from the Lord in the Old Testament. I come to revoke it, and I think also that *I have the spirit of the Lord.* I abolish then the former commandment, and am charged to replace it by a contrary order. It is not the Lord (v. 12) who forbids you to put away an unbelieving wife; it is "*I*, Paul an Apostle, not of men, neither by man, but by Jesus Christ and God the Father, who raised him from the dead."

We see then, with the clearness of noon-day :—the Apostle instead of appealing to the ancient word of the Lord, revokes it, to replace it by a contrary order; so that this passage, very far from weakening the inspiration, confirms it strongly; since it would have been nothing less than an outrageous blasphemy, if the Apostle had not felt, that in using this language, he was the mouth of God; and if he had dared to say by his own authority—" It is not the Lord, *it is I. I*, myself tell you, and not the Lord: if any man have an unbelieving wife, let him not send her away." The Lord had given a contrary commandment. (Deut. viii. 3; 1 Kings xi. 2.)

We must then acknowledge that these verses of St. Paul, far from authorizing the supposition of any mingling of human wisdom in the Scriptures of the New Testament; are there to attest that, in their epistles and in the most familiar details of their epistles, the Apostles were the mouth of God, and ranked themselves not only as successors of Moses and the ancient Prophets, but even above them; as a second message from God must supersede that which was before it, and as the New Testament must surpass the Old, if not in excellence, at least in authority.

We have heard some oppose our doctrine yet again, by citing as an acknowledgment of the intermission and imperfection of his inspiration, those words of St. Paul; in which, after having related to the Corinthians his rapture to the third heaven, he adds: " whether in the body or out of the body, I cannot tell, God knoweth."* Can it be supposed, say they, that the Holy Spirit was ignorant how this miracle was accomplished? Such a passage must be from Paul, and not from God.

We answer that, although the Holy Spirit was not ignorant of it, Paul was; and that the Holy Spirit chose that Paul should inform us of his own ignorance. Shall we forget that God has always employed the personality of the Sacred writers, in the Sacred Scriptures, to reveal himself to us; and it is thus that he has ever chosen to instruct his Church? When David speaking by the Spirit, cries in the Psalms, that he knows his transgressions, that his sin is continually before him,—and that he was conceived in sin; it is surely not the Holy Spirit who knows his own transgressions, and whose sin is continually before him; but it is the Holy Spirit who for our sakes, has put the language of repentance in the heart and on the lips of his humiliated prophet. It is in a sense analogous to this, that he made St. Paul say: " whether it were in the body, I know not; God knows."

We have not yet examined all these objections. Three now remain, which we would rather call *evasions;* because instead of resting as do the others, on some argument or facts; they are rather systems, by which a portion of the Scriptures is withdrawn from the divine influence of Theopneusty. It remains for us to investigate them.

* 2 Cor. xii. 4.

CHAPTER III.

EXAMINATION OF THE EVASIONS.

SEVERAL systems of exceptions have been proposed. Some, while they admit that the thoughts of the Scriptures have been given by God; maintain notwithstanding, that the style and the expressions are human;—others have excluded from inspiration, the purely historical books;—others again have wished to exclude certain details, which to them appear too vulgar and too unedifying to be attributed to the Holy Spirit.

SECTION I.—COULD INSPIRATION REGARD THE THOUGHTS, WITHOUT EXTENDING ALSO TO THE LANGUAGE ?

The prophets and apostles, say some, in writing their sacred books, were inspired in thought, without doubt; but we must believe that they were then left to themselves in the choice of language; the ideas were given by God, and the expression by man.

The task of the sacred writers, resembles somewhat that of a man, to whom very highly colored pictures are presented in quick succession; while he is bidden to describe them, just so far as his eye may have rested on them. It is thus that the Holy Spirit may have presented sacred truths to the minds of the evangelists and prophets, leaving them only the care of expressing them; and this manner of conceiving of their labor, it is added, will account satisfactorily for the diversities of style that their writings present.

We reply;

1. That this theory is directly contrary to the testimony of the Scriptures. The Bible declares to us, that it has been written, "not in the words which man's wisdom teacheth, but which the Holy Ghost teacheth." They call themselves; "the word of God, the words of God, the voice of God, the oracles of God, the Holy Scriptures, the Scripture of God." A scripture or writing is composed of letters and of words, and not of invisible thoughts only: now "all Scripture is given by inspiration of God," we are told. That which is WRITTEN, is then inspired of God ($\theta\varepsilon\acute{o}\pi\nu\varepsilon\upsilon\sigma\tau\sigma\varsigma$); and that which is inspired of God, is the WHOLE SCRIPTURE, that is, all that is written ($\pi\tilde{\alpha}\sigma\alpha\ \gamma\varrho\alpha\varphi\acute{\eta}$).

2. If this theory is anti-biblical, it is also very irrational.

The thoughts of our fellow-men clothe themselves in words. Spirits are revealed to us only in their fleshly tabernacles. You learn their character, you know their will and experiences, you even suspect their existence, and you enter into relation with them, only when they are clothed with flesh, and have received organs by which they manifest themselves to you. My most intimate friend is known to me, only by the language of his person, voice, and actions. If he had not these, in vain might he dwell beside me for twenty years; he would be to me as if he were not.

To pursue this thought; such is to us the inevitable dependence of the soul on its organs, and of ideas on words, that we not only learn the existence of the one by the language of the other; but even after hearing their voice, we perceive their true character, only just so far as we have the assurance, that the organ is a faithful interpreter of the mind, that the word is the exact image of the idea, and the proposition that of the thought. So

long as a fear may be admitted, that language has not
been the obedient and competent servant of the will, we
can have no confidence that we may not be mistaken.
Although we should know that God himself has breathed
the purest thoughts of heaven into the soul of a writer,
in order that we might have a sure revelation of them by
his words; yet must he always give us the assurance that
these words are well chosen, that they reflect the divine
thoughts with exactness, and that they reproduce without
change, all the objects deposited in the secret places of
the writer's soul.

Language is then the wonderful mirror that reflects to
us the depths of the mind.

Suppose you were a son in affliction, and that God, to
comfort you, should present you for some moments, in a
glass, the ever-loved features of your mother; would it
satisfy you that he caused it to approach very near to you,
and in such a position that the light from the object
should reach your eyes abundantly? Certainly not, if the
mirror has a curve, a flaw, or a stain. Uneven and faith-
less in its reflection, how would it console you? You
would, it is true, have near you, the smiling features of a
mother, her heart would seem to beat near yours, with
lively emotions; her inimitable look would convey to
you the ardent expression of her maternal wishes and her
august blessing; but all would be in vain; you would
see only the eye of a stranger, perhaps only a hideous
expression, only a deformed being and a revolting expression. Oh, my good mother, this is not then thyself! you
would exclaim.

These reflections will suffice to show us, how irrational
is the idea of receiving with exactness and certainty, the
thoughts of others, while their language is inaccurate and
uncertain. Can you arrive at their idea in any other
way, than by their words? And without the words of

God, how are you confident that you possess the thoughts of God?

3. This theory of a divine revelation, wherein you have the inspiration of thought and not of language, is necessarily so irrational, that it cannot be sincere, and very soon deceives those themselves who have received it; before they are aware of it, it leads them down much lower in their argument, than their first thesis had seemed to indicate. Listen to them. If the words are of man, say they; the thoughts are of God.

And how do they prove this to you? Alas! yet again, by attributing to this word of God, contradictions, mistakes, ignorance. Is it then to the words only that they refer; and are not these pretended errors in the thoughts, much more than in the language? So true is it that we cannot separate the one from the other, and that a revelation of the mind of God demands always an inspiration of the word of God.

4. This theory is not only anti-biblical, irrational, and hurtful; it is also arbitrarily assumed; it is but a gratuitous hypothesis.

5. Again,—it is very useless, for it proves nothing. You find it difficult, you say, to conceive how the Holy Spirit can dictate the words of the sacred Scriptures; but can you better explain how he has suggested the thoughts? Can you, for example, more readily explain how God revealed to Moses the knowledge of all the scenes of creation, or to St. John, that of all the scenes of the latter day; than to imagine how he dictated to them the narrative of it; whether in the Hebrew or the Greek tongue?

6. Bear with us still.—The extreme inconsistency of this theory must strike every attentive mind; since even they who maintain it the most earnestly, are often compelled to admit, that the largest portion of the Scriptures require the inspiration of God, EVEN TO THEIR VERY WORDS.

Suppose that the Holy Spirit should now command you to go out on the public square, and proclaim there in Russ, or Tamul, "the wonderful things of God;" what would be your position, if he were to inspire only the thoughts, without giving you the words? You would have before your eyes, the third heaven, and in your heart, the transports of archangels; yet must you remain mute and stupid before this multitude of men. To render your inspiration useful to them, the periods, sentences and smallest words of your discourse must all be given you. What do I say? Your own thoughts might well be dispensed with, provided you could utter, even without fully comprehending them, the thoughts of God in the words of God. Let us carry this supposition back to Jerusalem and to the persons of the Apostles. When the fishermen of Capernaum and Bethsaida, assembled in their upper chamber on the day of Pentecost, received command to descend, that they might go and publish to this people, assembled from every nation under heaven, "the wonderful things of God," in Latin, in Parthian, Persian, Chaldaic, Coptic, Arabic; was it not needful that the words should be given them? What could they have done with the thoughts, without the words? Nothing; yet with the inspired words, they could convert the world!

At a later period, when, in the Corinthian Church, the saints who had received miraculous powers, spake in the midst of assembled multitudes, in strange languages, and called to their aid another faithful brother to whom the gift of interpretation had been granted, that their unknown language might be received and understood by their hearers, was it not equally necessary that the words and all the sentences should be wholly dictated to them! (1 Cor. xiv.) when all the Prophets, after having written the sacred pages, applied themselves to meditate upon them, with such respect and care, as they would have shewed to the oracles of a *strange* prophet ; when they meditated upon them night and day ; "searching what or what manner of time the Spirit of Christ which was in them, did signify, when it testified beforehand the sufferings of Christ and the glory that should follow ;" was it not also necessary that all the words should be given them ?   When Moses describes the creation of the world and the breaking up of chaos ; when Solomon describes eternal wisdom, when David repeats, a thousand years in advance, the prayer of the Son of God on the cross ; when Daniel gives in detail, and without a full comprehension of it himself, the future and far off destiny of the world and of the church ; and when at last, St. John continues in his own prophecy, the revelations of the prophet Daniel, must not the smallest word have been given them ? And in reading them, do not all interpreters acknowledge that the smallest word substituted for another ; the tense of a verb chosen incorrectly, or a particle imprudently placed, might make an utter perversion of the truth ?

We must then determine, that since so large a portion of the Scriptures, is of necessity inspired, even in the language ; the theory of an inspiration of thoughts, and not of language, is supremely inconsistent.   There are not two kinds of divine words in the Holy Scriptures ; there are not two kinds of oracles of God.   If "the holy men of God spake as they were moved by the Spirit," all the sacred letters were divinely inspired, and that which is divinely inspired in the holy letters, is " ALL THE SCRIPTURE."

But these last reflections carry us back to a point, at once more simple and more important.   Let us examine it carefully ; for the question has been displaced.   It has been said that the sacred writers were inspired of God ; and it has been asked, in what degree were they so inspired ?   This was not however the object that should have been sought.

7. We have said, that our investigation refers to the book, and not to the writers. You believe that God always gave them the thoughts, and not always the words; but on the other hand, the Scripture says that God gave them always the words, and not always the thoughts. While they were writing, God could inspire their thoughts with more or less life, vividness, purity, elevation; this excites my love, but does not exercise my faith. This is to me the all important fact; the Scriptures, which they have transmitted to me, without comprehending their meaning, at least without ever comprehending them fully; the Scriptures are inspired.

St. Paul may have been under a mistake, when appearing before the council of priests, and not recognising the high priest of God, he dared to say to him: "God shall smite thee, thou whited wall." It matters little, however, since I know that WHEN HE WRITES THE WORD OF GOD, it is Jesus Christ that speaks in him.*

St. Peter may have been deceived in his thoughts, when, refusing to believe that God could send him to the heathen, he remembered not, "that in every nation, those that serve God, are accepted of him." It is possible he was in a still greater error, when in Antioch he compelled St. Paul to withstand him face to face, in the presence of all, because he was to be blamed, and walked not in the faith of the Gospel.† But what matters this, I again repeat, at least in connection with my faith? It cares not to know at what time, or in what degree, Paul, John, Mark, James, were inspired in their minds, or sanctified in their hearts. What interests it, before all other considerations, is, to know that all the sacred pages were divinely inspired; that their written words were the words of God; and that in giving them to us, they spake "not in the

* 2 Cor. xiii, 3.   1 Cor. vii. 17.   † Gal. ii, 14.

words which man's wisdom teacheth, but which the Holy Ghost teacheth."* (οὐκ ἐν διδακτοῖς ανθρωπίνης σοφίας λόγοις); that it WAS NOT THEN THEY who spake, but the Holy Ghost;† in a word, that GOD, hath spoken BY THE MOUTH of all his Holy Prophets, since the world began.‡

The sacred writers were SOMETIMES inspired, but the Holy Scriptures were ALWAYS inspired. The time, the extent, the degree, the interruptions of the inspiration of the men of God are not for us, objects of faith; but this is an object of faith, that the Scripture is divinely inspired, and that the whole Scripture is divinely inspired. "Not a tittle of it must pass away."

There is doubtless an inspiration of the thoughts, and also an inspiration of the words. The first makes the CHRISTIAN, the second the PROPHET.

A true Christian is inspired in his thoughts; "the Spirit reveals to him the deep things of God.§ Flesh and blood have not revealed to him the counsels of God and the glories of Jesus Christ; it is God the Father;‖ for the Holy Spirit guides him into all truth;¶ and no man can say, Jesus is the Lord but by the Holy Ghost."** Every true believer is then inspired in his thoughts, but not in his words. He is a Christian, but not a prophet. The most sacred words of Cyprian, of Augustine, of Bernard, of Luther, Calvin, Beza, Leighton, are only the words of men on truths of God; venerable, precious, powerful words they are, without doubt, and worthy of our attention, on account of the wisdom that has been given them, and the abundant expressions of the mind of God which they contain; but after all, they are human words, they are sermons, not revelations. With the Prophet, it is far otherwise. He may have, or he may not have the thoughts

---

* 1 Cor. ii, 13.   † Mark xiii, 2.
‡ Acts iii, 21, Luke i, 70.   § 1 Cor. ii, 10.
‖ Matt. xvi, 17.   ¶ John xvi, 13.   ** 1 Cor. xii, 3.

of God in his thoughts; but so LONG AS HE SPEAKS AS A PROPHET, so long will he have the WORDS OF GOD ON HIS LIPS.

"The spirit of the Lord will speak by him, and his word will be on his tongue."* He will be the mouth of God; whether an intelligent or an unintelligent mouth, whether voluntary or involuntary; it matters little, if from it fall the oracles of God, and I receive from it the mind of my God clothed in the language of my God.

In a word, one may be a Christian, without having on his lips the words of God; and one can be a prophet, without having either in his heart or mind, the thoughts of God; but one cannot be a Christian, without having in his heart the thoughts of God; and one cannot be a prophet, without having on his lips the very words of God.

We shall presently establish the point, that in the language of the Bible, a prophet is a man, to whose lips God conveys for a time, those words he will have uttered on earth. Such an one prophesies only by intervals, "as the spirit gives him utterance."† Like Saul, he might be a prophet but twice during life; or like his soldiers, but once.‡ Then might he pronounce the words of God, either understanding or *not understanding them;* often even without *knowing* beforehand *that he was* to pro-phecy, and sometimes even without *wishing* it.

Daniel tells us that when he wrote his last pages, he did not himself know what the spirit had caused him to write.§ When Caiaphas uttered prophetic words, "*he spake not of himself.*" *He had the will,* but neither the *knowledge* nor *understanding* of what God made him speak.‖ When Balaam went three times to the summit of the rock, to curse Israel; and three times, words of blessing proceeded from his lips, in spite of himself, "because the most High had met him, and put these words in his mouth;"¶ he

---

* II Sam. xxiii, 1, 2. † Acts ii, 4. ‡ 1 Sam. x. 19.
§ Dan. xii, 8, 9. ‖ John xi, 51. ¶ Num. xiii, 16.

had the *consciousness* of it, but he had neither the full *knowledge* of the meaning of the words, nor a cordial *will* in uttering them. When the armed men of Saul had sought David in Rama, and the Holy Spirit had so come upon them, that they likewise prophesied; and when Saul thrice sent others of them, who also thrice prophesied, and when the wicked Saul repaired thither himself, even to the great well on his way to Najoth; and God (to show forth his power, and the better to manifest to us what a prophet is and what his word is); caused his Holy Spirit to come upon this unbelieving man; when he continued thus on his way, prophesying; when the word of God was on those profane lips, and he prophesied day and night before Samuel, " what then happened to the Son of Kish?"*—" Was Saul indeed then among the prophets?" —yes;—and Saul had also the consciousness of his state, and of the part he acted as prophet; but he had neither *foreseen* it nor *willed* it, nor probably had he a full *understanding* of what he uttered.

When the old prophet was seated amicably at table with the man of God, whom he had just turned from his path, by an unbelieving and carnal good-will; and when on a sudden, by a power from above, loud and menacing words proceeded from his lips against his imprudent and guilty host;† he prophesied with a *consciousness* of what he did, but he prophesied without *willing* it. What do I say? Did not God utter his voice in the air, before Moses and all the people on Mount Sinai? Has he not caused it to be heard on the pillow of a child, in the tabernacle of Siloh; in the ears of the three Apostles and the two saints recalled from the invisible world, upon Mount Tabor; in the ears of John the Baptist and all the people on the banks of the Jordan? Let it then be well understood,

---

* 1 Sam. xix, 23, 24.   † 1 Kings, xiii., 21.

these are the *holy writings* (τά ἱερα γράμματα) ; *all that is written*, both the phrases and the words are divinely inspired ; they are θεόπνευςτοι. We inquire then concerning the *word*, and not the men who have written it. Their state is comparatively unimportant in this investigation. The Spirit could associate in a greater or less degree, their individuality, their consciousness. their memories, their affections with what he made them say ; and you are in no wise obliged to know any thing of this ; but that which is most needful for you to know is, as St. Peter hath it, "that *no* PROPHETIC WRITING came by *the will of man*, but that holy men of God spake as they were moved by the *Holy Ghost.*" So at the supper of Belshazzar, they were little anxious to know what was passing in the fingers of that terrible hand projected from the wall by the side of the chandelier ; while on the contrary, every thought of the guests was directed to the words that it traced on the plaistering of the wall : "*Mene, Mene, Tekel Upharsin*" ; because they well knew that these words were of God ; so it matters little to you, as an object of faith, to know what was passing in the mind of Mark, of Luke, of John, and of Matthew, while they were writing the scroll of the Gospels. Rather let every look be turned to those words which they have written, because you know that these words are of God. Whether the prophet be holy as Moses, or wise as Daniel, hostile to his God as Caiaphas, ignorant of God when he speaks to men, as the prophets of Corinth, unholy as Balaam ; what do I say ? insensible as the hand on the wall of the palace in Babylon ; without form, without body, without soul, as the open air in which was heard the voice of God on Sinai, on the banks of the Jordan, or on Tabor — little matters it, yet again we say, except in those cases when even their personality might form an essential part of their revelation.

15

Thy thought, oh! my God; thy thought and thy words,
they concern me.

SECTION II.—SHOULD THE HISTORICAL BOOKS BE EXCLUDED FROM THE INSPIRED PORTIONS OF THE BIBLE?

We admit, it is said, that inspiration may have reached
even to the choice of expressions, wherever this miraculous work was necessary; to state doctrines, for instance,
to declare a history of the past more ancient than the birth
of the mountains, or to announce a future which none but
God can know. But should we go so far as to maintain
that cotemporary men had need of the Holy Spirit, for
stating facts of which they themselves had been witnesses,
or which they had heard others relate; to tell us, for example, of the humble marriage of Ruth in the village of
Bethlehem, or the emotions of Esther in the palace of
Shushan, or the catalogue of the Kings of Israel and of Judah, their reigns, their lives, their deaths, their genealogies? Luke, for example, who from Troas, had accompanied the Apostle to Jerusalem, to Cæsarea, to the island
of Malta, and even to Rome; had he not recollections
enough to tell us how Paul was seized in the portico of
the temple, how his nephew warned him in the fortress,
of the conspiracy of forty Jews; how the captain led the
lad to the Tribune, and how the Tribune taking him by
the hand, led him aside and asked him what he knew.
Did he then need for facts so simple, and so familiar to
him, a continual intervention of power from above? We
think not; and we maintain, that it is not necessary, nor
even reasonable to believe, that all the historical passages
of the New Testament are inspired.

To such objections, our first answer is always very simple; "all Scripture is given by inspiration of God;"
"thou hast known, Timothy, the holy books; but, all

these holy books are given by the breath of God."* We have not heard the Holy Spirit make a single exception any where to these declarations; and we do not acknowledge in any man, nor in any angel, the right of hazarding one.

But still further. If it were permitted to put one book of God before another; if we must select in the firmament of the Scriptures, the more glorious constellations and stars of the first magnitude, we should certainly give the preference to the historical books. In fact:

1. It is to the historical books, that the most brilliant and the most respectful testimony is rendered by the prophets in the Old Testament, and by the apostles in the New. Which book of the Old Testament is holier than the Pentateuch; and what is grander in the New, than the four Gospels! Is it not of the historical books alone that it is written; "the law of the Lord is perfect, converting the soul; the testimonies of the Lord are sure, making wise the simple; they are pure, more to be desired than gold; the words of the Lord are pure words, as silver tried in the furnace, seven times refined? Happy then is he, who takes pleasure in them and meditates therein night and day."†

2. Remark, too, with what respect our Lord himself quotes them; and how, in quoting them, he is pleased to show that divine decrees lie couched in their minutest details, and sometimes even in the employment of a single word.

3. The histories of the Bible have not been given, merely to transmit to future ages the memory of events already past; they are presented to the Church of all ages, to exhibit to her the character of God by facts; they are there like a mirror of Providence and of Grace; they are destined to reveal to her the thoughts of God, the designs

* 2 Tim. iii. 14, 16. † Psalm cxix. 96–126.

of God, the invisible things of God, his heaven, his glory, his angels, and those mysteries which "the angels desire to look into." * But all that requires the most entire Theopneusty.

4. But still farther: the historical Scriptures are given to reveal to us the deep things of man. It has been said of the word of God, that "it is quick and powerful, and sharper than any two-edged sword, piercing even to the dividing asunder of the soul and of the spirit, and of the joints and marrow, and is a discerner of the thoughts and intents of the heart." That is true of the written word, as of the personal Word of God, because the one is the language of the other; but it is emphatically true of the historical word. Do you not see that this word, in its narrations, is a two-edged sword, and that it searches the conscience? And just as it describes to you that which took place on our globe in the days of chaos, when the Holy Spirit moved on the face of the deep; so it still tells you the things which pass in the depths of the human heart, the mysteries of the invisible world, and the secret interference of the angels of God in the affairs of men; it reveals to you secret motives, hidden faults, and human thoughts, which, without it, had not been known until that last day, in whose light every thing shall be revealed. Is it thus that men relate events?

5. But this is not all. See again how, even without the knowledge of the authors themselves, the Bible histories are full of the future. While relating to us past events, "they are types for us who should live in the latter times." † They relate, it is true, national or domestic scenes; but, whilst they are relating, Jesus Christ is there incessantly and prophetically portrayed in all his manifestations and in all his characters. See the history of

* 1 Pet. i. 12.　　　† 1 Cor. x. 6—11.

Adam, of Noah, of Abraham, of Isaac, of Joseph, of Moses, of the immolated Lamb, of the deliverance from Egypt, of the column of fire, of the manna, of the Rock, which was Christ, (1 Cor. x. 4.) of the goat Azazel, of all the sacrifices, of Joshua, of David, of Solomon, of Jonah, of Zerubbabel. The entire history must be adduced, to render justice to this truth. Read again, in order to appreciate it, the pages of St. Paul upon Hagar, Sarah, Aaron, or Melchisedec.

A little reflection will excite our admiration at the constant presence and power of inspiration in every part of these Scriptures; and it will convince us that if there are any pages of the Bible which needed to be inspired in every line and every word, they are those of the historical books. They preach, they reveal, they teach, they legislate, they prophesy.

Do not, then, compare them to other histories; they have altogether another end, totally another rank.

This plenary inspiration was indispensable to them, that they might state, without any error, facts beyond the range of human knowledge. They needed it, in describing the creation of the universe, the breaking up of chaos, the birth of light, the establishing of mountains, the ministration of angels, the secret counsels of God, the thoughts of the human heart and its unknown faults. They needed it when they prefigured Christ by a thousand types, unperceived by the writer himself; they needed it for exhibiting thus, even in their narrations of the past, the characteristic features of the Messiah, his sufferings, his death, and the glories which were to follow. They needed it to speak suitably of the events which were known to them; to suppress some, to present others, to distinguish them, to judge them; and thus to show, in them, the mind of God. They needed it to describe with accuracy, and in the precise measure, of this mind of God, and of the

15*

Church's future necessity, the national or domestic scenes, which were to convey in themselves the types of redemption, to prefigure the latter days, and to possess a great significancy, thousands of years after their occurrence. They needed it for the degree of their communicativeness, for that of their reserve, for the discreet employment of their expressions, and for that admirable circumspection which they have been enabled uniformly to observe.

6. Probably their divine brevity has not been sufficiently remarked nor admired. If you would appreciate the Scriptures in this respect, compare them with the biographies written by men, or with the codes of doctrines which they give us, when they are uninspired. See, for example, the modern Jewish or the Latin Church. Whilst the former have identified their two Talmuds with the Scriptures, by ascribing to them the same divine authority; the one of which, (that of Jerusalem,) makes a large folio volume; and the other, (that of Babylon,) which is the most popular, and which all their teachers are required to study, is a work of twelve folio volumes;* and whilst the Romish Church, in her Council of Trent, has declared that " she receives with the same affection and reverence as she gives the Scriptures, her traditions concerning faith and practice;" that is to say, the immense repository of her synodical acts, of her decretals, of her bulls, of her canons, and of the writings of the holy Fathers; †—See what the Holy Spirit has done in the Bible; and admire there the celestial wisdom of its inimitable brevity.

---

* The last edition of Amsterdam. Maimonides has made a learned extract from it in his *Yad Hachazaka.* See Prideaux' *Hist. of the Jews.* Amsterdam, vol. ii. page 130.

† Council of Trent, session 4, first and second decrees, published, Ap. 28th, 1546.—Bellarmine *de verbo Dei.* lib. 4, cap. 3, 5, 6.—Coton. lib. ii. cap. 24, 34, 35.—Baile, traité I. Du Perron against Silenus.

Who of us could have been, for three years and a half, the constant witness, the intimate friend, of such a man as Jesus Christ; and could have put, in sixteen or twenty short chapters, or in eight hundred lines, the history of all that life, of his birth, of his youth, of his miracles, of his ministry, of his preachings, of his sufferings, of his death, of his resurrection, and of his ascension into the heavens? Who of us could have recounted so much goodness, without a reflection; so many sublime thoughts, without an emphasis; so many sufferings, without complaints; so much injustice, without bitterness; so many innocent infirmities of the master, or so many culpable infirmities of the disciples, without the least concealment; so much ingratitude in their base abandonment of him, so much resistance, so much hardness of heart, without an apology and without a comment? Is it thus that men relate events or describe character?

Who of us, again, could have distinguished that which must be cursorily presented, from that which must be related in detail? Who of us, for instance, would have thought that the whole creation of the world must be told in one chapter of thirty-one verses; then the trial, the fall and condemnation of our race in another chapter of twenty-four verses; whilst so many chapters and pages must be devoted to the construction of the Tabernacle and its furniture, because in it was contained for future ages, a continual and typical picture of Jesus Christ and his redemption? Who of us, for the same reason, would have employed the fifth part of Genesis in relating the history of only one of Jacob's twelve sons, whilst two chapters would have appeared to him sufficient to make nearly seventeen hundred years, from the fall of Adam to the deluge? Who of us, after having shared for ten years in the labors of St. Paul, his dangers, his imprisonments, his preachings and his prophetic gifts, could have related

twenty-two years of such a life, without saying one word
of himself, and without showing to other men, except by
the mere change of the personal pronoun, (Acts xvi. 10,)
that from Troas to Jerusalem and Cæsarea, and that from
Jerusalem and Cæsarea, even to Malta and to Rome, he
had been his suffering companion, faithful and indefatigable? To discover who this was, we must learn from
Paul, who, in his last prison wrote to Timothy; "in my
first defence, no man stood by me, all forsook me; Luke
alone was with me." (2 Tim. iv. 16, 11,) Holy and celestial reserve; humble and noble silence! The Divine
Spirit alone could have taught him!

Where would you find, among all the inspired historians, a man who could have written like St. Luke, the
Acts of the Apostles; who could have related in thirty
pages, the ecclesiastical history of thirty of the most brilliant years of Christianity, from the ascension of the Son
of Man above the clouds of heaven, to the imprisonment
of St. Paul in the capital of the Roman world? Incomparable history; at once short and grand! What do we
not find there? Preachings to the Jews, to the Greeks,
before the tribunals, before the Areopagus, and before the
Sanhedrim, in public places and before a pro-consul, before synagogues and before kings; admirable descriptions
of the primitive church; miraculous and dramatic scenes
in its bosom; interventions of angels to deliver, to warn
and to punish; controversies and divisions in Christian
assemblies; new institutions in the church; the history of
her first council and its synodical epistle; commentaries
on the Scriptures; accounts of heresies; judgments of
God, solemn and terrible; apparitions of the Lord, by the
way, in the temple and in the prison; detailed conver-
sions, often miraculous, and singularly varied; that of
Æneas, that of the Eunuch, that of the captain Cornelius,
that of the Roman jailor, that of the pro-consul, that of

Lydia, that of Apollos, that of a numerous people at Jeru-
sulem ; without speaking of those that were merely commenced, as in the emotions of King Agrippa, in the trou-
bles of Festus, in the professions of Simon of Samaria, in
the anguish of Pilate's wife, in the terrors of Felix, in the
kindness of the captain Julius ; missionary journies, diverse solutions of cases of conscience ; permanent divisions upon external things, between Christians of different
classes ; mutual prejudices, disputes between brethren and
between apostles ; bursts of passion ; explanations, and at
the same time, triumph of the spirit of charity over obstacles ; communications from one military officer to another,
from pro-consul to pro-consul ; resurrections ; revelations
made to the church to hasten the calling of the Gentiles ;
collections for the poor of one church by those of another ;
prophesies ; national scenes ; punishments inflicted or
prepared ; arraignments before Jewish tribunals or Roman
municipal authorities, before governors and kings ; Christian meetings from house to house ; their emotions, their
prayers, their charity, their doubts ; a persecuting king
smitten by an angel and consumed of worms, at the very
moment when, to repeat the gratification he had given the
people by the murder of one apostle, that of another was
now prepared by his orders ; persecutions in every form,
by synagogues, by princes, by municipal officers, by Jews
or by mobs ; deliverances of godly men, now by a child,
now by an angel, now by a Roman tribune, now by a
sea-captain, by Pagan magistrates, or by idolatrous soldiers ; tempests and shipwrecks, which by the accuracy of
their nautical details (we have witnessed it,) still charm
the seamen of our day. And all that, in thirty pages, or
twenty-eight short chapters. Admirable brevity! Did
not this conciseness require the Holy Spirit of God, this
choice of details, this style, so pious, so varied, so brief,
so richly significant, which employs so few words, while it

teaches so many things? Fullness, conciseness, clearness, simplicity, elevation, practical richness; behold the book of ecclesiastical history which the people of God needed!

It is true; yet we repeat, it is not thus that men write history.

Could you find upon the earth, a man capable of relating the assassination of his mother, with the calmness, the sobriety, the self-possession, the apparent want of passion, which distinguish that four-fold history of the Evangelists relating the punishment of that Jesus, whom they loved more than any mother is loved, more than life is loved; of that Jesus whom they adored; of that Jesus whom they had seen prostrate in Gethsemane; then betrayed, forsaken, led to Jerusalem with his hands bound, and finally nailed naked upon the cross, while the sun withdrew his light, while the earth was rent, and while he who was raising the dead, was himself reduced to the state of the dead! Was it not necessary that each line, each word of such a history, should be written under the guidance of the Holy Spirit, that a suitable selection might be made amidst a world and an age of reminiscences?

7. This entire guidance was also necessary for that prophetic reserve which the sacred historians have been able to exercise in so many respects, and for that prudence altogether divine, which manifests itself not only in their teachings, but in their silence; not only in the terms which they employ, but in those which they avoid.

See them, for example, when they speak of the mother of Jesus. What divine foresight, what prophetic wisdom, both in their narrations and in their expressions! How easy it was in their ardent adorations of the son, to have expressed themselves concerning the mother, in terms too respectful! Would not one single word, which might so easily have escaped in the imprudence of their first emotions, have forever authorized that idolatry of future ages towards Mary, and the crime of that worship which is now rendered her? But that word they have never uttered. But have they not merely gone so far as to call her the mother of God? No, not even that; although he was to them Emmanuel, the Man-God, the Word who was in the beginning with God, who was God, and who was made flesh. Hear them; what will they say of her, after the death and resurrection of the Savior? One single sentence; and then perpetual silence! "All those continued in prayer with the women, and with the mother of Jesus and with his brethren. (Hi omnes erant perseverantes in oratione cum mulierbus, et Mariâ matre Jesu et fratribus ejus.") They mention her there, neither the first nor the last; she appears there, as the mother of Jesus, among the brothers of Jesus and the Gallilean women. And what will they say of her before the death of Christ? Remark it, for it is not thus that men relate. Among all the words which Jesus may have said to his mother from the opening of his mission, they have selected but three to report to us. This is the first: "Woman," (when she interfered with his ministry just commenced, and asked him to perform a miracle), "woman, (woman!) what have I to do with thee?" (John ii. 14,) When afterwards a woman in the crowd, exclaimed in her enthusiasm, "Happy the womb that bare thee!" "Say rather, said he, happy is he who heareth the word of God, and keepeth it." (Luke xi. 27). That is the second. Now hear the third; his mother and brethren were shaken in their faith; they had been heard to say; he is beside himself, (dicebant enim: quoniam in furorem versus est); and one came and said: "Thy mother and thy brothers are without, desiring to speak with thee." "Who is my mother?" replied he: and stretching his hand towards his disciples said, "Behold my mother. Every woman who shall do the will of my Father in heaven, the same is my mother. Ecce mater mea." And when; finally, he saw her from his cross, he no more called her mother; but he bequeathed her to the disciple whom he loved, saying: "Woman, behold thy son; John, behold thy mother; and from that hour, that disciple received her to his house," not to adore her, but to protect her, as a feeble and suffering being whose soul a sword had pierced.

Is it then thus, we again ask, that men write history; and must it not be that the prophetic Spirit was the sole narrator of all these facts?

We should love to quote other examples; they present themselves in a throng before our eyes at this moment, and it is a sacrifice to us to withhold them; for the more closely these historical books are studied, the more the prophetic wisdom of the Spirit of God which has dictated them, there reveals itself in the details at first the most unperceived. We should love to signalize among others, the altogether prophetic wisdom with which the Holy Spirit often, when he relates an important fact more than once, takes care to vary his expressions, in order to prevent false interpretations which might be given to his words, and to condemn beforehand, the errors which in after times might be attributed to them. We would cite, for example, the remarkable and unanticipated manner in which the tenth precept of the decalogue is repeated in Deuteronomy (Deut. v. 21, Exod. xx. 17, Luke viii. 25), with a remarkable transposition of its first terms; the Holy Spirit wishing thus to confound prophetically the artifice by which the teachers of the church of Rome should see fit, fifteen centuries afterwards, to divide this commandment into two, thus to conceal their nefarious abduction of the second commandment: "thou shalt not make unto thee any images . . . thou shalt not bow down to them nor serve them." We should love to show again the varied expressions by which the Holy Spirit has showed to us the divine institution of the Lord's Supper, and has often paraphrased it, in order to make us the better understand what Christ intended by it, and to condemn in advance, the carnal sense which men should afterwards give to the words: "THIS IS my blood, this CUP IS the new COVENANT in my blood;" and he has also said: "this cup is the COMMUNION or COMMUNICATION of the blood of the New Testament." We could wish to point out the prophetic wisdom, by which, in order to confound those who should pretend in future times, that Judas did not take part in the last supper (and that he went out before it, or did not come in until after it), *the* Holy Spirit has taken care to inform us by Mark and ~~the~~ Matthew (Matt. xxvi. 21, 26, Mark, xiv. 19, 23,) that Jesus announced the treason of Judas, Judas being present; and by Luke, that he announced it after the communion, Judas being present. (Luke xxii. 19, 23). We should love to show among all the writers of the New Testament, the constant sobriety of their words, when the relation of pastors to their churches is spoken of; and that admirable prudence with which they have always abstained from applying, even in one single instance, to the ministers of the Christian church, the name of *priest;* and have merely appropriated to them the title of *elders*, which was given to the laity of Israel, to distinguish them always from the sacerdotal race (that represented Jesus Christ, and that was to cease when the true and only priest should have appeared). We should love too, to point out that prudence with which they avoid leading a soul to any other *pastor*, or any other director ($\varkappa\alpha\theta\eta\gamma\eta\tau\eta\varsigma$), (Matt. xxiii. 8, 10,) than Jesus Christ; and with which, in recommending deference to their spiritual guides, they have taken care to name them always in the plural, in order never to authorize from the Scripture this idea so natural to the pastor and

16

to the flock, that every soul must have *its pastor* among men.   What precaution, what reserve in the narrations, in order never to give too much to man, and to recount the great things which "God had done by the apostles," (Acts xiv. 27, Rom. xv. 18, 1 Cor. iii. 6), so that each one should be abased before God, and all the glory be ascribed to him, and that every servant of the Lord might learn to say with the last prophet of the Old Testament and the first of the New: "he must increase but I must decrease."

We repeat, that it is almost doing violence to ourselves, to have the Bible before us, and quote no more of it.

From all these features reunited, we must then conclude, that if all Scripture is divinely inspired; the historical books exhibit this divine intervention more strongly than all the others; they show the necessity of it more clearly; they attest that for such pages, it was indispensable that the invisible and powerful hand of the Holy Spirit be placed upon that of the sacred writer, and that he guide it from the first line even to the last; more than men was required, more than learned men, more than holy men, more than minds enlightened and superintended, more than angels, more than archangels;   God must do it.

We will say then with Origen: "The sacred volumes breathe the plenitude of the Spirit; and there is nothing, either in the prophets, in the law, in the gospels, or in the apostles, which does not come from the plenitude of the majesty of God;"* And with St. Ambrose: "utrumque poculum bibe veteris et Novi Testamenti, quia ex utroque Christum bibis.   Bibe Christum, ut bibas sanguinem quo redemptus es; bibe Christum, ut bibas sermones ejus.— Bibitur Scriptura sacra, et devoratur Scriptura divina,

---

* Homil. II. in Jerm. cap. L.

cum in venas mentis ac vires animi succus verbi descendit eterni."†

But what then, it has sometimes been said; must we believe that the letter of the Pagan Lysias, or the harangue of Gamaliel the Jew, or the discourses of Job's severe friends were inspired words?—Surely, no; no more than those of Cain or Lamech—of Rabshakeh or Satan. But the sacred writers were as really led by God to transmit them to us, as to report to us the song of Mary in the hill-country, or that of the seraphim in the year of king Uzziah's death, or that of the celestial army at Bethlehem. The Holy Spirit is not always the author of the words which he relates; but he is always their historian.

But there is still another evasion, which is adopted in order to separate one part of the scriptures from the Theopneusty. If it is not the most serious objection, it is at least one of those the most frequently repeated.

SECTION III.—WOULD THE APPARENT INSIGNIFICANCE OF CERTAIN DETAILS OF THE BIBLE, JUSTIFY US IN SEPARATING THEM FROM THE INSPIRED PORTION.

Does it comport with the dignity of inspiration to accompany the thought of the Apostle Paul, even into those vulgar details into which we see him descend in some of his letters? Would the Holy Spirit condescend to dictate to him those public salutations which terminate his epistles;—or those hygienic counsels to Timothy concerning his stomach and his often infirmities;—or those commissions with which he charges him, with regard to his parchments and a certain cloak which he had left at the house of Carpus at Troas, when he was leaving Asia?

The reader will suffer us to beseech him to be cautious

† Ambrose in Psalm I. Enarratio.

of this objection, when, holding the Bible in his hands, he happens not to recognize on the first perusal, the signs of God's hand in such or such a passage of the word. Let those imprudent hands not cast one verse of it out of the temple of the Scriptures. They hold an eternal book, all of whose authors have said with St. Paul: "And I think that I too have the Spirit of the Lord!" If then, he does not yet see any thing divine in such or such a passage, the fault is in him, and not in the passage. Let him rather say with Jacob: "Surely the Lord is in this place, and I knew it not!"* This book can sustain the light of science; for it will bear that of the last day. The heavens and the earth shall pass; but none of its words shall fail, not even to the least letter. God declares to every one that heareth the words of this prophecy; that if any one shall take away from the words of this book, God will take away his part from the book of life.†

Let us examine more closely the alleged passages. St. Paul from the depths of his prison, sends for his cloak. He has left it at the house of Carpus, in Troas, and he entreats Timothy to hasten before winter, and not forget to bring it to him. This domestic detail, so many thousand times objected against the inspiration of the Scriptures, from the days of the Anomians of whom St. Jerome speaks: ‡ this detail seems to you too trivial for an apostolic book, or at least too insignificant and too foreign from all practical utility, for the dignity of inspiration. Unhappy, however, is he who does not perceive its pathetic grandeur.

Jesus Christ also, on the day of his death, spoke of his cloak and of his vesture. Would you have this passage taken away from the inspired volume? It was after a night of fatigue and anguish. They had led him about

* Gen. viii. 16. † Rev. xxi, 18, 19.
‡ See Proemium in Epit. ad Philem.

the streets of Jerusalem for seven successive hours, by the light of torches, from street to street, from tribunal to tribunal, buffeting him, covering him with a veil, striking his head with staves. The morrow's sun was not yet risen, before they had bound his hands with cords, to lead him again from the high priest's house to Pilate's Prætorium. There, lacerated with rods, bathed in his own blood, then delivered for the last punishment, to ferocious soldiers, he had seen his garments all stripped off, that they might clothe him in a scarlet robe, whilst they bowed the knee before him, placed the reed in his hands, and spit upon his face. Then, before laying his cross upon his bruised frame, they had replaced his garments upon his wounds, to lead him to Calvary ; but, when they were about to proceed to the execution, they took them away for the third time ; and it is then that, stripped of every thing, first his cloak, then his coat, then of even his underdress, he must die naked upon the malefactor's gibbet, in the view of an immense multitude. Was there ever seen under heaven, a man, who has not found these details, touching, sublime, inimitable ? And was one ever seen, who, from the account of this death, thought of retrenching as useless or too vulgar, the history of these garments which they divided among them, — or of this cloak for which they cast lots ? Has not infidelity itself said in speaking of it ; that the majesty of the Scriptures astonished it, that their simplicity spoke to its heart ; that the death of Socrates was that of a sage, but Jesus Christ's, that of a God !*—and if the divine inspiration was reserved for a mere portion of the holy books, would it not be for these very details ? Would it not be for the history of that love, which, after having lived upon the earth poorer than the birds of the air and the foxes of the field, was

* J. J. Rousseau.

16*

willing to die still poorer, deprived of all, even to its cloak and its under-garments, and fastened naked to the male-factor's gibbet with the arms extended and nailed to the wood? Ah! be not solicitous for the Holy Spirit; he has not derogated from his own majesty; and so far from thinking that he was stooping too low, in announcing these facts to the world, he had hastened to recount them to it; and that too, a thousand years in advance. At the period of the Trojan war he already was singing them upon the harp of David: "They have pierced my hands and my feet," said he, "they look and stare upon me, they part my garments among them, and cast lots upon my vesture." (Psalm, xxii. 18, 19. John, xix. 23, 24.)

But it is the same Spirit who would show us St. Paul writing to Timothy, and requesting him to bring his cloak. Hear him; he too is stripped of every thing. In his youth, he was already eminent, a favorite of princes, admired of all; but now he has left every thing for Christ. It is now thirty years and more, that he has been poor, in labors more than the others, in wounds, more than they, in pri-son oftener; five times he had received of the Jews forty stripes save one; thrice was he beaten with rods; once he was stoned; thrice he has suffered shipwreck; often in journeyings; in perils upon the sea, in perils in the city, in perils in the desert; in watchings oft, in hunger and in thirst, in cold and nakedness (we quote his own words). Hear him now; behold him advanced in age; he is in his last prison; he is at Rome; he is expecting his sentence of death; he has fought the good fight; he has finished his course, he has kept the faith; but he is cold, winter is coming on, and he is poorly clad! Buried in a dungeon of the Mamertine prisons, he is so much despised, that all the very Christians of Rome are ashamed of him, and that at his first appearing, no man was willing to befriend him. Yet, he had received, ten years before, while a prisoner at

Rome, and loaded with chains, at least some money from the Philippians; who, knowing his sufferings, united together in their indigence, to send him some succor. But now, behold him forsaken; no one but St. Luke is with him; all have abandoned him; winter is approaching. He would need a cloak; he has left his own, two hundred leagues off, at the house of Carpus in Troas; and no one in the cold prisons of Rome would lend him one. Has he not then left every thing, with joy, for Christ; has he not esteemed all the glory of this world as dross that he might win Christ; and does he not suffer all things cheerfully for the elect's sake? (Phil. iii. 8. 2 Tim. ii. 10.) We were ourselves at Rome, last year, in a hotel, on a rainy day, in the beginning of November. Chilled by the piercing dampness of the cold evening air, we had a vivid conception of the holy apostle in the subterranean dungeons of the capitol, dictating the last of his letters, regretting the absence of his cloak, and entreating Timothy to bring it to him before the winter!

Who would then take from the inspired Epistles so striking and pathetic a feature? Does not the Holy Spirit carry you to the prison of Paul, to astonish you with this tender self-renunciation and this sublime poverty; just too, as he shewed you with your own eyes, his charity, sometime before, when he made him write in his letter to the Philippians: "I weep in writing to you, because there are many among you, who mind earthly things, whose end is destruction?" Do you not seem to see him in his prison, loaded with chains, while he is writing, and tears are falling upon his parchment? And does it not seem to you that you behold that poor body, to-day miserably clothed, suffering and benumbed; to-morrow beheaded and dragged to the Tiber, in expectation of the day when the earth shall give up her dead, and the sea the dead which are in it; and when Christ shall transform our

vile bodies, to make them like unto his own glorious body?
And if these details are beautiful, think you they are not
also useful? And if they are already useful to him who
reads them as a simple historical truth, what will they not
become to him who believes in their Theopneusty, and
who says to himself: oh my soul, these words are written
by Paul; but it is thy God who addresses them to thee?
Who can tell the force and consolation, which, by their
very familiarity and naturalness, they have for eighteen
centuries, conveyed into dungeons and huts! Who can
count the poor and the martyrs, to whom such passages
have given encouragement, example and joy? We just
now remember, in Switzerland, the pastor Juvet, to whom
a coverlet was refused, twenty years ago, in the prisons of
the Canton de Vaud. We remember that Jerome of Pra-
gue, shut up for three hundred and forty days in the dungeons of Constance, at the bottom of a dark and loathsome
tower, and going out only to appear before his murderers.
Nor have we forgotten the holy Bishop Hooper, quitting his
dark and dismal dungeon, with wretched clothes and a
borrowed cloak, to go to the scaffold, supported upon a
staff, and bowed by the sciatica. Venerable brethren, happy martyrs; doubtless you then remembered your brother
Paul, shut up in the prison of Rome, suffering from cold
and nakedness, asking for his cloak! Ah! unfortunate he,
who does not see the sublime humanity, the tender grandeur, the fore-seeing and divine sympathy, the depth and the
charm of such a mode of teaching! But still more unfortunate perhaps he, who declares it human, because he
does not comprehend it. We would here quote the beautiful remarks of the respectable Haldane on this verse of
St. Paul. " This passage, if you consider the place it occupies in this Epistle, and in the solemn farewells of Paul
to his disciples, presents this Apostle to our view, in the situation most calculated to affect us. He has just been before

the Emperor; he is about to finish his days by martyrdom; his departure is at hand, the crown of righteousness is reserved for him; behold him on the confines of two worlds; in this which he is about to leave, ready to be beheaded, as a malefactor, by the orders of Nero; in that which he is going to enter, crowned as a just man by the Lord of lords; in this, abandoned of men; in that, welcomed by angels; in this, needing a poor cloak to cover him; in that, covered with the righteousness of the saints; clothed upon with his heavenly tabernacle of light and joy; so that mortality is swallowed up of life."

Ah, rather than object to such a passage, thereby to deprive the Scriptures of their infallibility, we should there recognize that wisdom of God, which, so often by one single touch, has given us instructions, for which, without that, many pages would have been necessary. We should adore that tender condescension, which, stooping even to our weakness, is pleased, not only to reveal to us the highest thoughts of heaven in the simplest language of earth, but also to offer them to us under forms so living, so dramatic, so penetrating, often compressing them in order to render them more intelligible, within the narrow space of a single verse.

It is then thus that St. Paul, by these words thrown at hazard even into the last commission of a familiar letter, casts for us a rapid flood of light over his ministry, and discovers to us by a word, the entire life of an Apostle; as a single flash of lightning in the evening, illuminates in an instant, all the tops of our Alps; and as persons sometimes show you all their soul by a single look.

How many striking examples of this could we quote. They present themselves in crowds; but we are obliged to restrain ourselves; and we should in fact rather confine ourselves to the very passages which the objector selects.

Yet we must say before going any farther; we almost

blush to defend the word of God under this form; and we feel, for this species of apology, a kind of conscientious disgust. Is it entirely proper; and can we give ourselves to it without irreverence? Care must be taken at all times, as to the manner of defending the things of God; lest we imitate the imprudence of Uzzah, who reached out his hand to hold up the ark of God, because the oxen had slipped. The wrath of God, we are told, burned against his indiscretion (2 Sam. vi. 6, 7). If it is well understood on both sides, that a word is in the canon of the oracles of God, why defend it as worthy of him, by human reasons? You might, without doubt, defend it against unbelievers; but with men who recognize the divinity of the Scriptures, is it not to wrong this word; is it not to take a false position, and touch the ark as Uzzah did? If this word should present itself to our eyes as a root out of a dry ground; were it without any charm; were there neither form nor comeliness, nor any thing in it to make it desirable; still ought you to venerate it and expect every thing for it, from him who has given it. Is it not then to fail of your duty to him; to attempt when he speaks, to prove by argument, the respect which is his due? Should I not be ashamed, when my Savior and my God has been showed me, rising from supper, taking a basin, girding himself with a napkin, and coming to wash the feet of his disciples; should I not be ashamed to set myself to proving, that, in spite of all that, he is still the Christ! Ah; I would rather adore him more than ever! But it is so; the majesty of the Scriptures will stoop even to us. Do you see it there rising from the table, laying aside its robe, putting on the dress of a servant, and kneeling before sinners to wash their feet? "If I do not wash thee, thou hast no part with me." Is it not then, in this very humiliation that it reveals itself with the greatest charm, as the voice of the humiliated Word? Could we mistake it, and could we rank ourselves for an instant by the side of those who do not know it ?

It seems to us, that there is no arrogance comparable to that of a man, who, recognising the Bible as a book of God, pretends after all, to assay it with his hand; to separate the pure from its impure, the inspired from the uninspired, God from man. It is to overthrow all the foundations of faith; it is to make it no more a belief in God, but a belief in man. It ought then to be enough for us that a chapter or a word makes part of the Scriptures, to induce us to believe it divinely good; for God has pronounced upon it, as upon the creation: "I have seen every thing that I have made, and behold, all is good." We will never then say, I find this word admirable, therefore it is of God; and still less, I do not see its utility, therefore it is of man. God preserve us from it! But we will say, it is in the Scriptures; then it is from God. It is from God; then it is useful, it is wise, it is admirable; if I do not see it such yet, the fault is in me alone.

We regard as utterly misapplied, this protection which the wisdom of man would extend to that of God; we hold as an outrage, this gross stamp with which it pretends to legalize the Holy Scriptures, and this absurd signature with which it dares to authorize their passages.

If then we here proceed to prove the divine wisdom of certain passages which some have dared to pronounce human, it is not to found their divinity upon the judgments of man's better informed wisdom, nor preposterously to make them respected, merely on account of the beauty which is there revealed. Our respect has preceded; it was founded upon the fact that the passage is written in the oracles of God. From that time, before having seen, we have believed. We then intend to refute the objection, merely by presenting some examples of its rashness.

Let us hear yet two or three passages to which some have pretended to refuse the honors of inspiration, because, on a superficial examination, they have thought them to be without spiritual bearing. We can here quote only a very small number. A sentence may be pronounced useless or vulgar in four words; but to show that the objection is founded in misapprehension, pages would be requisite.

One of the passages which we have frequently placed in the front, when they would justify a distinction between that which is inspired and that which is uninspired in the word of God, is the recommendation of St. Paul to Timothy, on account of his bad digestion, and the maladies under which this young disciple was suffering: "drink no more water, but a little wine, for thy stomach's sake and thine often infirmities." (1 Tim. v. 23.)

At the same time, if you examine this passage more closely, what an admirable and living revelation will you find, of the greatness of the Apostolic vocation and of the amiableness of the Christian character. Remark first, that it was pronounced as in the temple of God; for, immediately before, you have these solemn words: "I charge thee before God and the Lord Jesus Christ, and the elect angels, that thou observe these things without preferring one before another, doing nothing by partiality. Lay hands suddenly on no man; neither be partakers of other men's sins: keep thyself pure. Drink no more only water." We see that it is in the presence of their common Master and of the holy angels, that St. Paul would speak to his disciple. Entering then into the same temple, to understand him, and placing ourselves at the same height, in arraigning ourselves as he did, "before the Lord Jesus and his holy angels"; then we shall quickly recognize how many beauties these passages reveal in the ministry of the Apostles, and in the ways of the Lord towards his own. The celebrated Chrysostom had well understood it, when preaching upon these very words, he observed with so much feeling, how little the most ardent and the most useful servants of God ought to be surprised, if it ever happens that the Lord sees proper to try them, as Timothy was tried, by infirmities in their lungs or in their head, or in their stomach; if he puts some thorn in their flesh, and if he thus buffets them by some angel of Satan, in order to increase on the one hand their sympathy, their meekness, their tenderness of heart, their cordial affections, their tender compassions; and on the other, their patience, self-renunciation, self-denial, and above all, their spirit of prayer. Reperuse seriously, and as in the light of the last day, this beautiful passage of the Apostle ; and immediately in the narrow space of this single verse, you shall admire the many precious instructions the Holy Spirit would here give us, besides those which the pious bishop of Constantinople has remarked. How many words and almost chapters would have been necessary to say so much under another form ! You will again learn there, for example, the sobriety of this young and ardent Timothy: he had wished, like St. Paul, to "keep his body under"; he drank only water—he abstained entirely from wine. You will there see in the third place, with what tender and paternal delicacy the Apostle reproved him, either for his imprudence, or for an austerity which he carried too far. You will there see again, with what wisdom the Lord authorizes and invites by these words, the men of God to take the necessary care of their health, at the same time however, that he has thought best to diminish it by sickness. You will there see, in the fifth place, with what prophetic foresight this word placed in the mouth of an apostle, condemns in advance, the human traditions which, in future days were to forbid to the faithful, the use of wine as an impurity. You will there see, in the sixth

17

place, with what tender solicitude, what sympathy,
what paternal vigilance, the Apostle Paul, in the midst
of his high functions, and despite the "care of all the
churches from Jerusalem to Illyrium, and of those
from Illyrium even to Spain," which came upon him,
was still not undmindful of the personal circumstances of his beloved disciple, of his health, of the infirmities of his stomach, of his frequent maladies and of
his imprudent habits of daily regimen. You will there
learn again, an historical fact which will cast for you a
useful light upon the nature of the miraculous gifts. In
spite of the interest of St. Paul for the ailments of his
disciple, it was not possible for him to restore Timothy,
even for him who had so often healed the sick, and even
raised the dead; because the apostles, (and we learn it
too by this verse, as by the sickness of Epaphroditus*)
had not received the continual gift of miraculous power,
any more than that of theopneusty; and that this virtue
must be renewed to them for every special occasion.

But if all these lessons of the apostle are important, and
if we receive them all thus in one single verse, and in the
manner most calculated to affect us; oh! how beautiful
they become, and how penetrating they are, for a simple
and Christian heart, as soon as it is assured that this is not
merely the word of a good man; that it is not even that
of an apostle merely; but that it is the voice of its God,
who will teach it in so affecting a manner, sobriety,
fraternal affection, tender interest for the health of others,
the usefulness of afflictions and of infirmities for the most
zealous servants of God; and who, to give us all these
precious lessons, deigns to address us by the mouth of a
simple creature! For, the Lord is good; he has placed
his tender compassions above all his works; the heavens

* Philip ii, 27.

are his throne, and the earth is his footstool; he counts the stars; he heals the broken-hearted, and he treasures our tears in his phials.

The salutations of St. Paul at the close of his epistles, are often objected to, which are, they say, only the ordinary compliments that we all employ in closing a letter. There is nothing unworthy of an apostle, it has been admitted; nor is there any thing there inspired. The Holy Spirit has let the pen of Paul run on there, in order that he might give free course to his personal affections, as we ourselves should allow a secretary to terminate alone, by the usual compliments, a letter, whose first pages we had dictated to him. Consult, for instance the last chapter of the Epistle to the Romans. Is it not sufficiently evident that the apostle there abandons himself during sixteen verses, to the entirely personal reminiscences of his friendship? Had this dry nomenclature of all these persons need of the Holy Spirit? The Apostle points out eighteen of them by name, without counting all those who were to be saluted collectively in the house of Aquilas, in that of Narcissus, as in that of Aristobulus. These verses do not require inspiration; and it would at the most, have been sufficient, in order to have them written, that the Holy Spirit should have exercised that 'superintendence, under which they wrote when left to their personality.

We fear not to avow it; we take pleasure in recollecting here those sixteen verses so often objected to; for they are, on the contrary, of the number of those passages, the divine wisdom of which commends itself; and if you look closely at them, you will immediately admire with us, the fecundity, the condescension, and the elevation of this mode of instruction; you will there find under the most practical and natural form, a living picture of a primitive church. You will there discover with lively interest, the relations of the members to one another; and you will there see to what height even the most ignorant and the most feeble members were raised in its bosom.

Hear first with what tender interest, the Apostle recommends to the charity of the Church in Rome, that humble woman who, was making, as it appears, a journey from Corinth into Italy, for her temporal affairs. She was a beloved sister, who had given herself to the service of the saints, and who had not feared to open her house to a great number of the faithful, and to Paul himself, notwithstanding the perils of this hospitality. She was the servant of the Church of Cenchrea. It was necessary then that the brethren who were at Rome, should welcome her in the Lord, and that they should administer to her wants. See again, the example which the apostle furnishes us, in a few words, of that Christian urbanity which should characterize all the mutual relations of the children of God. Admire how, while he passes so rapidly in review, the brethren and the sisters of the Church of Rome, he can spread, even over this nomenclature that is called arid, the sweet unction of his charity. He has some words of encouragement and tender esteem for each one of them, he there recalls the generous hospitality of Phebe, the dangers of death which Aquilas and his wife had braved for him ; the honor of Epinetus as having been the first of the Achaians converted to Christ ; the great labors of Mary, of Andronica and of Junias, who had even preceded him in the faith ; his christian love for Amplias ; the evangelical works of Urbanus, the tried fidelity of Apelles ; the multiplied labors of Tryphena and Tryphosa in the Lord, and those of the beloved Persis. What an appeal again to the conscience of every serious reader, is this rapid catalogue ! See then, ought he to say to himself, the character of the faithful whom he wished to be saluted in the Church of Rome ! And if the same apostle was writing a letter to the Church, in which I myself occupy a place, what would he say of me? Would my name be found there? Could he there add, that I receive as Phebe, the saints into my house; that I hold, as Aquila and Priscilla, christian meetings under my happy roof? that I have, as Mary, taken much pains for the ministers of the Lord; that I have suffered for Jesus Christ, as Andronica and Junias; that I am a man approved in Christ, as Apelles; that I am elect in our Lord, as Rufus; that I am, as Urbanus, his companion in work; that I labor in our Lord, as Tryphena and Tryphosa; and that I even labor much, as the beloved Persis?

But see above all, what a lesson for Christian women, is contained in these admirable verses. In the simple familiarity of the salutations which terminate this letter, how he shows them the elevation of their calling! What an important part is there assigned them in the church, and what a place in heaven! Without having yet seen the city of Rome, Paul mentions there, by their own name, and as his companions in labor, as many as nine or ten women. There is first, besides Phebe, that admirable Priscilla, that happy wife of the happy Aquila, who had even exposed herself to punishment for the apostle, and to whom all the churches of the Gentiles were grateful. Then came a woman named Mary, who had, says he, labored much for the apostles; there was Tryphena and Tryphosa, who labored still in the Lord; there was Persis, who was particularly dear to him, and who had labored much in the Lord; there was Julia, there was the sister of Marcus; there was perhaps Olympia;* there was finally the venerable mother of Rufus. And observe, in passing, with what respect he names this woman, and with what delicacy he salutes her by the endearing name of mother. Is not that the christian politeness which he

---

* This may be a woman's name, but more probably it is a man's.

recommended to these same Romans in the 12th chapter of this letter: "Salute Rufus, elect in the Lord, writes he, and his mother who IS ALSO MINE!"—What a touching model too do these same verses propose to husbands and wives, in the persons of Aquila and Priscilla!—You see them here in Rome; you may have seen them, five years before, driven from Italy by the Emperor Claudius, arriving at Corinth, and receiving the apostle Paul into their house; then, eighteen months afterwards, departing with him for Asia, and living at Ephesus, where they had already a church in their house,* and where they welcomed with so much success, the young and brilliant Apollos, who, notwithstanding his talents, found himself happy in placing himself in the school of their christian conversation and charity. Now that Claudius had just died and given place to Nero, you see them, scarcely returned to Rome, already consecrating their new dwelling to the church of God. It is at their house they assemble; and you here learn again, as in passing, that these two had not hesitated to expose together their lives for that of St. Paul.

But, besides all these lessons which, in these sixteen little verses, are offered to our consciences, you may likewise learn from them, two facts of great importance in the history of the Church. And first you see there, with the simplest and fullest evidence, that at that day, no one in Rome thought of such a thing as the episcopacy, nor popeship, nor primacy, nor even of the presence of Peter. Do you not recognize a prophetic foresight in the care which the Holy Spirit has taken to introduce into this epistle to the Romans, that which he has done for no other of the fourteen letters of St. Paul, and to terminate it thus by a long catalogue of the women and the men most

---

* 1 Cor. xi. 9.

esteemed at that time in all the Church of Rome? Behold then the Apostle of the Gentiles, who, twenty years after his conversion, in writing to them, salutes at least twenty-eight of their number by their names, and many others besides, by collective designations, and who says not one word to them of the Prince of the Apostles, as he is called, of the vicar of Jesus Christ, of his superior, the chief of the universal Church, of the founder of the Romish Church! St. Peter was the Apostle of the Circumcision, and not of the Gentiles:* his place was in Jerusalem; it is there we must look for him, and it is there St. Paul had always found him. In his first journey, three years after his conversion, Paul visits him there, and remains fifteen days in his house.† In his second journey, for the first council, he meets him there again. In his third journey, in the year 44, at the epoch of the death of Herod Agrippa, St. Peter is still living at Jerusalem.‡ In his fourth journey, seventeen years after his conversion,§ St. Paul again finds him there, in the capacity, mark it well, of Apostle, not to the Gentiles, but to the Circumcision. And when at last he is on his way for his fifth and final journey, he writes to the Romans and to the Galatians; and then, that all the Church might fully understand that Peter is not at Rome, and that he has never been there, Paul shall take pains to salute by their names, all of the most distinguished Christians of Rome, even of the women. What bishop is there of our day, in the Latin sect, who would dare to write a letter in sixteen chapters to the Church of Rome, without uttering a word in it, either of St. Peter, or of him whom they call the Vicar of Jesus Christ?‖

* Gal. ii. 7, 8, 9. † Gal. i.18.
‡ Acts, xii. 1, 3. § Gal. i. 7.
‖ See on this subject, the excellent dissertation of the Rev. Mr. Bost; "Du pouvoir de St. Pierre dans l'Eglise." Geneva, 1833:

But there is another historical fact, still more interesting, to the knowledge of which, these sixteen verses which have been called useless, lead us by the most striking features. See, in the very details of these short salutations, by what humble instruments, and yet with what expansion, the gospel had in so short a time, established itself in the mighty Rome. No apostle had put his foot there,[*] and yet see what had been already the progress of the word of God, through the labors of merely travelers, artisans, merchants, women, slaves and freed men who happened to be at Rome! Already had Jesus Christ disciples there, even in the palaces of the Jewish princes who resided near the imperial court, and even among the pagans who served nearest the person of Nero. St. Paul requests that among other Christians, they would salute from him, first, "those of the household of Aristobulus," and secondly, "those of the household of Narcissus, who were in the Lord." Now, the first of these great personages was the brother of Agrippa the great, and of the impure Herodias; the second was the powerful favorite of the emperor Claudius. Agrippina did not cause his death, until the close of the year 54.

Ah! let every one who calls himself a Christian, renounce for ever, those rash systems, in which man lifts himself against the words of the Scriptures, to dispute their propriety; in which he dares to take away from God's Bible such a passage, such a sentence, to make of it (as least as to that passage or that sentence), a human Bible; and in which he makes himself responsible likewise for all the rashness of the boldest scholars, who imitate in respect to a whole book, his treatment of a single verse. What idea has he of the sacred writers, when he imagines them capable of the gross folly of mingling

* Rom. i. 11, 13, 14, 15; xv. 20.

their own oracles with the oracles of the Almighty ?   We recollect an insane man, a pensioner of our hospitals, whose hand-writing was still so good, that a minister of Geneva employed him to transcribe his sermons.   Conceive of the confusion of the minister, when in receiving his manuscripts, he found that this unfortunate man had imagined he could enrich every page by adding his own thoughts.   Yet the distance between a lunatic and a minister, be he holy as Daniel, and sublime as Isaiah, is less than between Daniel or Isaiah and Eternal Wisdom !

Arrived then, thus far, we would, before proceeding any farther, recommend to our readers, to observe in using sacred criticism, three precautions, the importance and necessity of which, the doctrine of inspiration should make them feel.

CHAPTER IV.

OF THE USE OF SACRED CRITICISM, IN ITS RELATIONS TO THEOPNEUSTY.

We would be understood. Far from us be the thought of casting the least disparagement on the labors of this useful science! We honor them, on the contrary; we call them necessary; we study them; we consider all the ministers of the gospel bound to know them, and we believe that the Christian church owes them the highest gratitude. Sacred criticism is a noble science. It is so by its object: to study the history of the sacred text, its canons, its manuscripts, its versions, its witnesses and its innumerable quoters;—it is so by its services: how many triumphs gained over infidelity, how many objections put to silence, how many miserable doubts for ever dissipated! —it is so by its history: how many eminent men have consecrated to it either the devotion of a pious life, or the powers of the finest genius! it is so, finally, by its immense labors which no one perhaps can estimate, if he has not studied it.

God preserve us then from ever opposing faith to science; faith, which lives upon the truth, to science which seeks it; faith, which goes directly to the hand of God to seize it, to science which seeks it more indirectly elsewhere, and which often finds it! Every thing that is true in one place, is in preëstablished harmony with that which is true in another and higher place. Faith knows then at once, and before having seen any thing, that every truth will render it testimony. If then, every true science, whatever, is always the friend of faith, sacred criticism is more than its friend; it is almost its relative. But if it is honorable, useful, necessary, it is all that, only so long as it remains true and keeps its place. So far as it does not abandon the sphere assigned it, it is worthy of our respect; but as soon as it does wander, it must be restrained; it is then no more a science, it is a crazy divination. Now, as it has three temptations to quit this sphere, we therefore desire to recommend here three precautions to the young men who study it.

Section I.—Sacred Criticism is a Scholar, and not a Judge.

In the first place, critical science is no longer in its own place, when, instead of being a scholar, it wishes to be a judge; when, in place of collecting the divine oracles, it composes them, decomposes them, canonizes them, uncanonizes them; and when it makes itself oracular! Then it tends to nothing less than to overthrow faith from its foundation. This we are going to show.

Employ your reason, your time and all the resources of your genius to assure yourself if the book which is put into your hands, under the name of the Bible, contains in fact the very oracles of God, whose first deposite was confided, under the divine providence, to the Jews*, and of which the second deposite, under the same guardianship, was remitted to the universal church from the apostolic times. Assure yourselves then, whether this book is authentic, and whether the copyists have not altered it. All this labor is legitimate, rational, honorable; it has been

---

* Romans iii. 1, 2.

abundantly done by others before you ; but if the investigations of others have not satisfied you, resume them, peruse them, instruct us ; and all the churches of God will thank you for it.   But after all this labor, but when you have well established that the Bible is an authentic book, but when science and reason have clearly showed you that the unquestionable seals of the Almighty God are attached to it, and that He has there placed his divine signature, then hear what science and reason loudly proclaim to us ; then, sons of men, hear God ; then, *sursùm oculi, flexi poplites, sursùm corda !* then, bow the knee ! lift the heart on high, in reverence, and in humiliation !   Then science and reason have no longer to judge, but to receive ; no longer to pronounce sentence, but to comprehend.   It is still a task, and it is a science, if you please ; but it is no more the same ; it is the science of comprehending and of submitting.

But if, on the contrary, after receiving the Bible as an authentic book, your wisdom pretends to constitute itself the judge of its contents ; if, from this book, which calls itself inspired, and which declares that it will judge you yourself at the last day, it dares to retrench any thing ; if, sitting, as the angels in the last judgment,* to draw up the book of God on the banks of science, to gather the good into its vessels, and to cast away the bad, it pretends there to distinguish the thought of God from that of man ; if, for example, to cite only one case of a thousand, it dares to deny, with Michaëlis, that the two first chapters of Saint Matthew are from God, because it does not approve their Scriptural quotations ; then, to deny the inspiration of Mark, and that of Luke, because it has found them, it says, contradictory to St. Matthew ;* in a word, if it thinks it

* Matthew xiii. 48.

† Introduction to N. T. by Michaëlis, t. 2, p. 17 ; t. 1, p. 206 to 214.

can submit the book, recognized as authentic, to the outrageous control of its ignorance and of its carnal sense; then, we must reprove it; it is in revolt, it judges God. Then, it is an enormity, reproved as much by reason as by faith. It is no longer science, it is enchantment; it is no more progress, it is obscuration.

' Let us compare to the wretched labors of theologians upon the word of God, the more reasonable course pursued by the naturalists in their studies upon his works. Here, at least, we claim in advance as an axiom, that all the objects of creation have ends full of wisdom and harmony. Here, science applies itself, not to contesting these ends, this wisdom, these harmonies; but to discover them. Here, what is called progress in science, is not the temerity of controlling the works of God; it is the happiness of having investigated them, of having better recognised their wonders, of having been able to propose them under some new aspects to the admiration of the world, and of having thus found new inducements again to cry:

> What grandeur infinite!
> What divine harmony
> Results from their accordance!

Why then should not Christians treat the works of God in redemption, as naturalists do the works of God in creation? why, if, among the pagans themselves, a physician, the great Galen, could say: "that in describing the different' parts of the human body, he was composing a hymn in honor of the Creator of the body," why should not the, Christian comprehend, that to describe with truth, the different parts of the word of God, would be always "to compose a hymn in honor of him who had made it?" Thus thought the apostolic Fathers; thus, for example, the pious Irenæus, disciple of Polycarp, the pupil of St. John: "The Scriptures," said he, "are perfect. In the Scriptures let God ever teach; and let man ever learn!

18

it is thus that from the bosom of the *polyphony* of their instructions, an admirable *symphony* is heard in us all, praising in hymns the God who made all things."*

If some one should come to tell us that there exists a very studious nation, among whom the science of nature, taking a new direction, has commenced immense labors, for the purpose of showing that there are mistakes in creation ; plants badly constructed, animals badly contrived, organs badly adapted ; . . . what would you think of this people and of its great labors ? Would you believe that science was advancing there ? would you not rather say that they were obscuring it, degrading it, and that they were there wearying themselves, learnedly to discover the art of being ignorant. Inexplicable as the anatomists have found the use of the liver in the human body, or of the antennæ in that of the insects, they have not therefore blamed nature ; they have accused only their own ignorance in regard to it ; and they have waited. Why then, when you do not yet discover the use of a word in the Scriptures, would you blame any other than yourself, and why do you not wait ?

This thought is not new ; a pious man expressed it, better than we, sixteen hundred years ago, and preached it with unction to the men of his time. We have found ourselves happy, whilst we were writing it, to meet it in Origen, (it is in the thirty-ninth of his homilies), " If ever says he, in reading the Scriptures,† thou happenest to strike against a thought which becomes to thee a stone of stumbling and a rock of offence, accuse only thyself

---

*" Sic, per dictionum multas voces, una consonans melodia in nobis sentietur, laudans hymnis Deum qui fecit omnia." According to the Greek preserved by John Damascenus ; διά τῆς των λέξεῶν πολυφωνίας, ἐν σύμφωνον μέλος ἐν ἡμιν ἀίσθησεται. (Adv. Hæreses, lib. ii. 2. 47.)

† Origenes adamantius, Hom xxxix, in Jeremiah xliv. 22.

(αιτιῶ σεαυτόν) ; do not doubt that this stumbling-stone and this rock of offence has a great meaning (ἔχειν νοήματα), and is to accomplish this promise: 'he that believeth in me, shall not be confounded.' Commence then by believing, and quickly thou shalt find, in this imaginary stumbling-block, *an abundant and holy utility.** If we are commanded not to speak idle words, because we must give account of them at the last day, how much more should we think in regard to the prophets of God, that every word proceeding from their mouth, had its work to do and its use !† I believe then that for those who know how to use the excellence of Scripture, each one of the letters written in the oracles of God, has its end and its work (εργαζεται), even to an iota, or tittle . . . and as among plants, there is not one without its virtue ; and as at the same time it pertains only to those who have acquired the science of botany, to be able to tell us how each one ought to be applied and prepared, in order to become useful ; so also, whoever is *a holy and spiritual botanist of the word of God* (τις βοτανικός ἔστιν ὁ ἅγιος καὶ πνευματικός,) he, collecting each iota and each element, shall find the virtue of this word, and shall recognise that nothing in that which was written, is superfluous (ὅτι οὐδέν παρέλκει). Will you have another comparison? Each member of our body has its function, for which it has been placed in its position by the great Architect. Yet it does not pertain to every one to know their uses and their powers, but only to those physicians who have studied anatomy . . . I consider then the Scriptures as ' *the collection of the plants of the word,*' or as ' *the perfect body of the word.*' But if you are neither a botanist of the Scriptures, nor an anatomist of the prophetic words, do not imagine there is in them any thing super-

---

* Πολλήν ὤφελει αν ἁγιαν.   † Ἐργατικον ἦν.

fluous; and when you cannot find the reason for what is
written, do not blame the holy letters; blame not them,
but yourself alone for it."*   Thus spake Origen; but we
could find similar thoughts in the other Fathers, and
particularly in Bishop Irenæus, nearer yet to the apostolic
times.†

At the same time we must again remark, this pretension
to judge the word of God, overthrows all the foundations
of faith.   It would indeed render faith impossible in the
hearts of all those who have the least degree of consistency.
This is but too easily proved.

That a soul may receive life, it must receive faith;
that it may have faith, it must believe God; that it may
believe God, it must begin by renouncing the prejudices
of its own wisdom concerning sin, the future, judgment,
grace, itself, the world, God, every thing.   Has he not
written; that "the natural man receiveth not the things of
the Spirit of God; for they are foolishness unto him:
neither can he know them because they are spiritually
discerned."‡   The gospel then will shock either his
reason or his conscience, or both.   And yet he must
submit to it upon the testimony of God alone; and it is
only after having thus received it, that he will recognize
it as being "the wisdom of God and the power of God to
every one that believeth."   You see that we must believe
without seeing; that is to say, that the gospel, before it
has been comprehended, must confound our own wisdom,
abase our pride, and condemn our self-righteousness.
How then could you ever make it acceptable to men who
might be so unfortunate as to imitate you, and who would,
as you, wait to have every thing approved, in order to

* And he adds: Τοῦτο μοι τὸ προοίμιον εἴρηται καθόλικῖως, χρήσιμον
εἶναι δυναμένον εἰς ὅλην τὴν γράφην, ἵνα προτράπωσιν οἱ θελοντες προσέχειν
τῇ ἀναγνώσει, μηδὲν παραπέμπεσθαι ἀναξετάστον καί ἀνεξερεύνητον γράμμα.

† Irenæus, Adv. Hæres, book ii, c. 47.   ‡ 1 Cor. ii. 14, i. 23.

receive every thing? Imbued with your principles, they
will impute to man every thing in the scriptures which
shocks their carnal sense. They will believe that they
must reject the apostle's prejudice, concerning the consequences of Adam's sin, the Trinity, expiation, eternal
punishment, the resurrection of the body, the doctrine of
demons, election, the gratuitous justification of the sinner
by faith, perhaps also those concerning miracles. How
then, if he has the misfortune of doing as you do, will a
man ever find life, peace and joy, by means of faith? How
could he, like Abraham, hope against hope? How could
he, a miserable sinner, ever believe himself saved? He
must pass his days in doctrines, vague, vaporous, uncertain;
and his life, his peace, his love, his obedience must remain,
even unto death, such as his doctrines! We conclude then
with this first counsel: make the science of criticism a
scholar; do not make it a judge.

SECTION II.—LET SACRED CRITICISM BE A HISTORIAN, AND NOT A CONJURER.

There is, in regard to the inspiration of the Scriptures,
another precaution, no less important for us in employing
this science.

The work of sacred criticism is to gather facts concerning the Scriptures; do not permit it to lead you into vain
hypotheses. It would thus do you much harm. It ought
to be a historian; do not make it a prophet. When it
divines, do not listen to it, turn the back upon it, for it
would make you lose your time and more than your time.
Now, the safeguard of the faithful, here, is again, the
doctrine of inspiration, such as we have described it; I
mean, the inspiration not of the men, but of the book.

All Scripture is given by inspiration of God: thus the
authentic book of the Scriptures declares to us. But what
was passing in the understanding and conscience of the

sacred writer? On that the Bible is silent, and that we shall never be required to know. The misunderstanding of this great principle has occasioned an immense loss both of time and of words. The Scriptures are inspired, whether the author had or had not the previous knowledge of that which God was about to cause him to write. Let any one then, have studied, in each book of the Bible, the peculiarities of its style, of its language, of its reasonings, and all the circumstances of its sacred writer; we could see nothing but good in these researches; they are useful, legitimate, respectful; and that is truly science. Let him there have sought, by these very characters, to fix their date; and determine the occasion of their being written; we should yet see only that which is instructive and proper in such a study. It may be useful, for example, to know that it was under Nero that Paul wrote to the Jews;* "Let every soul be subject unto the higher powers." It may be well to know that St. Peter had been married more than twenty-three years, when St. Paul reminded the Corinthians,† that this apostle (the first of the popes, as some call him,) was still leading his wife about with him in all his apostolical journeys, and that the other apostles, and that even St. James (reputed the first of the pillars of the church‡), was doing the same thing. All this is still science. We value highly, for the church of God, every labor which makes her understand a passage better, yes, were it only one passage, one single word of the holy Scriptures. But when you pass on to crude hypotheses; when you embrace a thousand conjectures concerning the sacred writers, to make their word depend on the hazard of their presumed circumstances, instead of regarding their circumstances as prepared and chosen of God for their instruction; when you subordinate the nature, the

* Rom. xiii. 1.   † 1 Cor. ix. 5.   ‡ Gal. ii. 9.

SACRED CRITICISM A HISTORIAN.

abundance or brevity of these instructions to the more or less fortunate concurrence of their ignorance or of their recollections; this is to degrade inspiration, and to bring down the character of the word of God; it is to lay deep the foundations of infidelity; it is to forget that " men of God spake as they were moved ($\varphi\varepsilon\varrho o\mu\varepsilon\nu o\iota$) by the Holy Ghost, not in the words which man's wisdom teacheth, but which the Holy Ghost teacheth."[*]

It has been asked; did the Evangelists read each other's writings? And what is that to me, if they were all "moved by the Holy Ghost;" and if, like the Thessalonians, I receive their book, "not as the word of man, but as it is, in truth, the word of God." Let this question be proposed in its place, it may be entirely innocent; but it is so no longer when it is discussed as it has been, and when so much importance is attached to it. Can the solution of it throw light on one single passage of the sacred books, and establish its truths more firmly? We do not believe that it can.

When we hear it asked, (as Dr. Mill [†] and Professor Hug [‡] do, and as Dr. Lardner [§] and Professor Michaëlis [||] do not ask;) whether St. John had read the Gospels of the other three; if St. Mark and St. Luke had read the Gospel of St. Matthew before writing their own; when we hear it asked, whether the Evangelists did anything more than transcribe, with discernment, the most important portions of oral traditions, (as Dr. Gieseler does; [¶]) when we see great volumes written upon these questions, to attack or defend these systems, as if faith and even sci-

---

[*] 1 Cor. ii. 13. 1 Pet. i. 21.

[†] Millii Proleg. § 108.

[‡] Einleitung in die Schriften des N. Testam. Stutgart, 1821.

[§] Vol. vi. pages 220, 250.

[||] Introd. &c., tom. 1. p. 112, 129.

[¶] Historisch-Kritischer Versuch, &c. Minden, 1818.

ence were truly interested in it, and as if the answers were
very important to the Christian Church; when we hear
it affirmed that the first three Evangelists had consulted
some original document now lost; Greek, according to
some; Hebrew, according to others; (as John Le Clerc at
first dreamed, and as Kopp, Michaëlis, Lessing, Niemeger,
Eichhorn, and others,* have imagined sixty years after
him;) when we see men plunging still farther into this
romantic field; when we see them reaching the complicated drama of the Bishop of Landaff,† with his first Hebrew historical document, his second Hebrew dogmatic
document, his third Greek document, (a translation of the
first); then his documents of the second class, formed by
the translation of Luke, and Mark, and Matthew, which
finally reduces the sources to seven, without counting
three others, peculiar to St. Luke and St. Mark; or even,
again, when we see Mr. Veysie, ‡ in England, and Dr.
Gieseler, in Germany, deriving either the first three Gospels, or the four Gospels, from apocryphal histories previ-
ously circulated among the Christian churches; when we
see the first of these Doctors determining, that Mark has
copied them with a more literal exactness than Luke, on
account, they say, of his ignorance of the Greek; while
Matthew's Gospel, written at first in Hebrew, must, doubtless, have been translated afterward into Greek, by a person who modified it, to make it correspond with Mark
and Luke, and, finally, gave it to us as we have it; when
we see these systems exhibited, not in a few phrases, in
the indulgence of a light curiosity, but so many and such
great volumes written upon them, as if they involved the
interests of the kingdom of God, oh! we must say it, we
feel, in the view of all such science, a sentiment profound-

* Horne's Introduction, vol. ii. p. 443. edit. 1818.
† Bishop Marsh's *Michaëlis*, vol. iii. part ii. p. 361.
‡ Veysie's Examination, p. 56.

ly painful. But, after all, is that science? Is judicial astrology a science? No; and these men are no longer philosophers: they have abandoned facts; they prophesy the history of the past; they are, alas! the astrologers of theology. It is believed, in astronomy, that a book of observations upon the feeblest satellite discovered near Uranus, or upon the discovery of a second parallax found accompanying some star, or upon a simple spot on the moon, is a precious acquisition to science; whereas, all the writings of Count Boulainvilliers, and three hundred volumes upon the barbaric sphere, upon the influences, the aspects, or the horoscopes of the seven planetary bodies, can be for it, only folly and a vain encumbrance. Thus we shall esteem very highly, in the studies of sacred criticism, everything which can throw any additional light upon the least passage of the Scriptures; but what good can these crude hypotheses ever effect? They turn you from the luminous roads of science as well as of faith; the mind, in pursuing them, is wearied in the chase of vanity! Vain and boisterous labor of vaporous conjectures borne upon the clouds! No good can come of these wretched studies, which teach us to doubt, where God teaches us to believe! " Who is he, saith the Lord, that darkeneth the counsels of the Most High, by words without knowledge ?"

In fact, would to God that there were nothing more in these studies than vain phantasies and an enormous loss of time! But it is worse than the dissipation of time: faith is engulfed in them; the mental eye is fascinated by them, and they turn away our studious youth from hearing the first and great author of the Scriptures. It is evident that these idle researches can proceed only from a want of faith in the inspiration of the Scriptures. Admit inspiration for a moment; admit that Jesus Christ has given his apostles the $\pi\tilde{\omega}\varsigma$ $\varkappa\alpha\acute{\iota}$ $\tau\iota$, *the what and the how* of that which they were to write; admit that God has made his apostles recount the life of Jesus Christ, as he has made them describe his session at the right hand of God; and immediately you will perceive that all these hypotheses are reduced to nothing. Not only do they teach you nothing, and can teach you nothing; but they change the very exercise of your faith; they sap by degrees the doctrine of inspiration; they indirectly enfeeble the testimony of God, its certainty, its perfection; they turn your pious thoughts from their true direction, they mislead our youth who were seeking the living waters at the well of the Scriptures, and leave them thirsting in the sandy deserts, far from the fountains that spring up to life eternal. What do they find there after all? Broken cisterns, clouds without water; or at least perhaps, those fantastic streams which the sun of vain glory will paint for a few days, like a deceitful mirage in the deserts of this world.

What should we think of a theologian who should pretend that he was going to seek in the instructions of Joseph the carpenter, or in the lessons of the schools of Nazareth, the origin of the discourses of Jesus Christ, of his doctrines and of his parables? Idle and pernicious, you would exclaim.—But, the same must be said of all those conjuring systems which wish to account to us for the construction of the Scriptures, without supernatural aid. Idle and pernicious; say we,—admit inspiration, and all this labor vanishes as a foolish fantasy. The Scriptures are the word of God; they are dictated by him; and we know that " prophecy came not in old time by the will of man; but holy men of God spake as they were moved by the Holy Ghost."* The history of the nephew of St. Paul warning his uncle in the prison of Antonias, is inspired of God, although Luke may have heard it twenty

* 1 Peter i. 21.

times from the mouth of the apostle, before having received it from that of the Holy Spirit; this history is as fully inspired as that of the invisible angel, who was sent from God to smite the king of the Jews upon his throne, in the city of Cæsarea. The history of the striped and spotted sheep of Jacob is as much dictated by God, as the history of the creation of the heavens and of the earth. The history of the fall of Ananias and of Sapphira is as inspired as that of Satan and his angels.

Yes; without doubt, the apostles consulted one common document; but this document, as bishop Gleig has well expressed it,* " is no other than the very preaching and life of our divine Savior." Behold their prototype.

When therefore you hear it asked, from what documents Matthew could have drawn his history of the birth of Jesus Christ, Luke that of his first years, Paul that of the apparition of the Savior to James, or the words of the Savior upon the blessedness of giving, Hosea the tears of Jacob, and Jude the prophecy of Enoch, or the contention of Michael for the body of Moses, answer: they have drawn them from the same source whence Moses learned the creation of the heavens and the earth. "The Holy Spirit," says the illustrious Claude, "has employed the pen of the evangelist and apostles, of Moses and the prophets; he has furnished the occasions of writing; he has given these both the will and the power to do so; the matter, the order, the arrangement, the expressions are by his immediate inspiration, and by his direction."

We have just said that a sound doctrine of inspiration would shelter our studious youth from the excessive aberrations of modern criticism, at the same time that they would draw from this noble science, all the benefits that

---

* Remarks on Michaëlis, Introd. to N. T. p. 32, and following: —Horne's introd. ii. p. 458, ed. 1818.

it can impart.   The first of these errors, we have already
said, is to pretend to judge the Scriptures, after having
received the collection as authentic.   The second is, to
surrender ourselves to dangerous speculations concerning
the sacred books.   But a third reflection still remains to
be made on the relation of science to the great question
which occupies us.

SECTION III.—SACRED CRITICISM IS NOT THE GOD, BUT THE DOOR-KEEPER OF THE TEMPLE.

This reflection presents itself at once under the form
of advice and of argument; we shall indulge in the advice,
only as it leads to the argument; for we do not forget
that our task, in this book, is to establish Divine inspiration, and not to preach it.

First; the counsel.

Science is a door-keeper, who conducts you to the
temple of the Scriptures; never forget then, that she is
not their God, and that her dwelling-house is not the
temple.   In other terms, beware, in studying sacred criticism, of resting there ever in reference to science; it will
leave you in the street, whereas you must enter.

Now the argument.   If you really enter into the temple of the Scriptures, then will you not only find written
there with the hand of God, upon all the walls, that God
fills it, and that he is universally there; but you will also
find the proof of it in your own experience; you will
then see it in every part; you will then feel it throughout.   In other words; when we read the oracles of God
with care, we find there, not only frequent declarations
of their entire theopneusty, but we also receive in our
understanding and in our heart, by unexpected flashes,
often from a single verse, or by the power of a single
word, a profound conviction of the divinity which is
imprinted on every part of them.

As to the counsel, it must not be imagined that we have given it for the purpose of discrediting the investigations of science; we offer it, on the contrary, for their advancement and perfection. In fact, it too often happens, that the prolonged study of the externals of the sacred book, of its history, of its manuscripts, of its versions, of its language, so absorbs the attention of those who yield themselves to it, that they become inattentive to its most intimate characteristics, to its sense, to its design, to the moral power which it developes, to the beauties revealed in it, to the life diffused through it. And as there existed at the time, necessary relations between these characteristics and the exterior forms, two great evils result from these studies, to him who pursues them.

As man, he stifles his spiritual life, and compromises his eternal life by them. But it is not of this evil that we speak in these pages. As a scholar, he compromises his science, and renders himself incapable of a sound appreciation of the very objects of that science, by these studies. It remains incoherent, lame, and consequently straitened and groveling. Can he know the temple? He has seen but its stones; he knows nothing of the Shecinah! Can he then comprehend the types? He does not conceive of their antetype; he has seen nothing but altars, sheep, knives, utensils, blood, fire, incense, costumes and ceremonies; he has not seen the redemption of the world; the future, the heaven, the glory of Jesus Christ! And in this condition, he has not been able to seize even the relations which these external objects bear to one another; because he has not understood their harmony with the whole.

A learned man without faith, in the days of Noah, who might have studied the structure of the ark, would not only have perished in the deluge, but he would also have

remained in ignorance of a great portion of the very objects which he pretended to understand.

Imagine a Roman traveler in the days of Pompey the Great,
attempting to describe Jerusalem and the temple. Having
arrived in the city on the Sabbath, he goes directly to the holy place with his guide ; he walks around it ; he admires its
enormous stones ; he measures its porticoes; makes inquiries
about its antiquity, its architects; he passes its gigantic
gates, opened every day at sunrise, and shut at mid-day by
two hundred men ; he sees the Levites and the singers in
thousands, proceeding to the temple in order, arrayed in
their linen garments. In the interior, the sons of Aaron
clothed in their sacred robes, are performing their rites ;
while the psalms of the royal prophet resound under the
vaulted ceiling, and thousands of singers, accompanied by
instruments, respond to each other in their sublime anti-
phonies ; whilst the law is read, the word is preached, and
the souls who wait for the consolation of Israel, soar with
delight to the invisible grandeurs, and thrill at the thought of
that God, with whom is abundant redemption ; whilst the
aged Simeons lift their thoughts to that glorious salvation
constantly longed for ; whilst more than one publican is
smiting his breast, and returning to his house justified ;
whilst more than one young heart is consecrating itself to
God, like Nathanael ; and whilst more than one poor wid-
ow, under the impulse of holy zeal, is casting her two
mites into the treasury of God ; whilst so many prayers,
invisible but ardent, are mounting towards heaven, ...
what is this traveler doing ?—he is counting the columns,
admiring the pavements, measuring the courts, examining
the assembly, drawing the altar of incense, the candlestick,
the table of shew-bread, the golden censer ; he then goes
out, mounts to the battlements of the fortress, descends to
the Xystus or to the Cedron, traverses the walls, all the
while, counting his steps, returns to his hotel, to digest his

observations and prepare his book. He may boast, indeed, of having seen the people, the worship and the temple of the Hebrews ; he will publish his volume ; and his numerous readers will open it for information ; and yet even in relation to the very information he wished to impart, how many false judgments will he have made ; how many errors will those who are worshipping in the temple, be able to detect in it !

Listen then to our counsel, in regard to the interests of your own science merely. On account of the indispensable relations which exist between the eternal ends of the word of God and its external forms, you cannot form a solid judgment of the latter, without taking cognizance of the former.

If you desired to learn the character of a physician, you would do well to inform yourself of his country, of his studies, of the universities which he has attended, and of his certificates of recommendation ; but, if on the first visit, he should at once tell you all your complaints ; if he should awaken impressions and a sense of miseries, until then vaguely felt, but whose secret reality you should recognise, the moment he defined them ; and if, above all, he should finally make you take the only remedy which ever could have relieved you ; oh ! then would not such an experience tell you much more about him, than his diploma ?

This then, is the counsel which we venture to give, to all those of our readers who have paid any attention to sacred criticism. Read the Bible, study the Bible in itself and for itself ; ask it, if you please, where it took its degrees, and in what school its writers studied ; but come to its consultations, like a patient longing to be healed ; bestow as much care upon acquiring the experience of its words as you have given to the study of its diplomas, of its language and of its history ; then you shall be not only healed (which does not concern our present investigation),

but you shall be enlightened. "He that healed me, the
same said unto me, take up thy bed and walk. Whether
he be a sinner, I know not; only one thing I know; that
whereas I was blind, I now see."

The author would here relate, what a thirst he had for
apologetic writings, during the early stages of his studies;
how Abbadie, Leslie, Huet, Turretin, Grotius, Littleton,
Jennings, Reinhardt and Chalmers, were his habitual reading; and how, harassed by a thousand doubts, he found
no relief, no conviction nor satisfaction in any thing but
the Bible itself. It bears witness to itself, not only by its
assertions, but by its effects; as the light, as the heat, as
life, as health; for it carries in its beams, health, life, heat,
light. You might prove to me, by sound calculations,
that at this moment the sun should be upon the horizon;
but what need have I of your proofs, when my eye be-
holds it, and its rays are bathing and quickening me?

Read the Bible then; complete your science, arrange it.
It shall convince you; it shall tell you whether the Bible
comes from God. And when you shall have heard it in
a voice which casts down with power, or which lifts up
with tenderness, a voice sometimes more powerful than
the sound of mighty waters, sometimes sweet and gentle, as
that which Elijah heard whispering; "the Lord God, merci-
ful and gracious, long-suffering, slow to anger, the God of
consolation, the God forgiving iniquity, transgression and
sin." Oh then, we venture to predict, you will feel that
the single perusal of a psalm, of a narrative, of a precept,
of a verse, of a word in a verse, will instantly prove to you
more powerfully the divine inspiration of all the Scriptures,
than all the most eloquent and most solid reasonings of
learned men or of books have before done. Then you
shall see, you shall hear, you shall feel that God is there
in every part; then you will not ask it any more, whether it is all inspired; for you will feel it to be the power-

ful and efficacious discerner of the thoughts and intents of the heart, sharper than any two-edged sword, piercing even to the dividing asunder of the soul and the spirit, and the joints and the marrow; bringing up your tears from a deep and unknown fountain, casting you down with a resistless power, and raising you with a tenderness and with sympathies which are found only in God.

Thus far we have only given you advice; but we mean to show you in what respect these considerations can at the same time be presented, if not as a proof, at least as a powerful presumption in favor of a verbal inspiration of the Scriptures. We shall show our readers a three-fold experience in them, which, at all times, has carried profound conviction to other Christians, whose testimony ought at least to appear to them worthy of the most sincere consideration.

Certainly one of the strongest proofs of the divinity of the Scriptures, is this majesty which fills us with astonishment and respect; it is the imposing unity of this book, composed during fifteen hundred years by so many authors, some of whom wrote two centuries before the time of Hercules, of Jason and the Argonauts; others in the heroic times of Priam, of Achilles and Agamemnon; others in the days of Thales and Pythagoras; others in the age of Seneca, of Tacitus, of Plutarch, of Tiberius and Domitian; and who yet pursued one and the same plan, and advanced constantly, as if they themselves understood it, towards that one great end, the history of the world's redemption by the Son of God. It is this vast harmony of all the Scriptures through so many ages; this Old Testament alike with the New, filled with Jesus Christ; this universal history which nothing can stop, which relates the revolutions of Empires even to the end of time, and which, when the pictures of the past are finished, continues them by those of the future, up to the moment when

the empires of the world will have become the possession
of Christ and his saints. On the first page, the earth created to receive the man who sins not; on the following
pages, the earth accursed to receive man who sins always;
on the last page, the new heavens and the new earth to receive man who will sin no more : on the first page, the
tree of life forbidden; paradise lost, sin entering the world
by the first Adam, and death by sin; in the last page,
paradise regained, life restored to the world by the second
Adam, death vanquished, all mourning ended, the image
of God reëstablished in man, and the tree of life in the
midst of the paradise of God. Surely there is in this majestic whole, which begins before the days of man, and
which continues even to the end of time, a powerful and
heavenly unity, an undeviating, universal and immense
convergence, whose grandeur seizes the attention, surpasses
all our human conceptions, and proclaims the divinity of
its author as irresistibly as can in a summer's night, the
aspect of the heaven's brilliant stars, and the thought of all
these worlds of light, which revolve night and day in the
immensity of space. *Μυρία φιλα καὶ σύμφωνα*, says one
of the Fathers of the Church.* But beside the beauties
of this whole, which the Scriptures present, we have still
something to contemplate no less glorious, which reveals
to us also the action of God in their minutest points, and
which attests to us their verbal inspiration.

Three orders of persons, or rather three orders of experiences, furnish us this testimony.

First, if you consult ministers who have devoted their
whole lives to the meditation of the Scriptures, for the daily nourishment of the flock of Christ, they will tell you,
that the more they have given themselves to this blessed

---

* "Myriads of objects in accord and perfect harmony." Theoph-
ilus ad Autolyc. lib. i. c. 36. See also Justin Martyr, ad Græcos
cohort. c. 8.

study, and have applied themselves to look closely into
the oracles of God, the more has their admiration for the
letter of the Scriptures increased. Often surprised by unexpected beauties, they there recognise, even in the slightest expressions, divine foresight, profound relations, spiritual grandeur, which became manifest merely by a more
exact translation or a more profound attention to the details of a single verse. They will tell you that the minister of God, who for a long time holds before the eyes of
his mind, some text of Scripture, feels himself soon compelled to use the language of the naturalist studying with
the microscope, a leaf of the forest, its texture, its nerves,
its thousand pores and innumerable vessels. "He who
made the forest, made also the leaf!" he exclaims. Yes, replies the other, and "he who made the Bible, made also
the verses that compose it." A second order of experiences, the testimony of which we here invoke, is that of the
interpreters of the prophecies. They will unitedly tell
you, with what evidence, when they have given time to
this study, they recognize, that in these miraculous pages,
it must needs be, that each verse, each word, without exception, even the particle apparently the most unimportant, has been given by God. The slightest change in a
verb, in an adverb, or in the simplest conjunction, might
lead the interpreter into the most serious error. And it
has often been remarked, that if the prophecies that are
now fulfilled, were misapprehended before their fulfilment,
it has proceeded in a great degree, from the fact that they
have failed in attention to some of the details of their text.
We might here cite many examples, by way of illustration.

But there is still a third order of persons who testify
more strongly, if possible, the full inspiration of the Scriptures, even of their smallest points. These are the Christians who have felt their power, first in the conversion of

their souls, then in the various conflicts, afflictions and tri-
als that have followed it. Go, seek in the biographies of
these men who were great in the kingdom of God, the
moment when they passed from death to life, by the
knowlege of Jesus Christ; ask also in turn, the Christians
around you who have themselves experienced this virtue
of the word of God; they will give a unanimous testimony. They will tell you that when the sacred Scriptures, taking hold of their conscience, cast them down at
the foot of the cross, there to reveal to them the love of
God, to bathe them in the tears of gratitude and joy;
what affected them thus, was not the whole of the Bible,
nor was it a chapter; it was a verse; almost invariably,
it was a word in this verse; yea, it was a word which
penetrated like the sharp pointed sword wielded by the
hand of God. They felt it to be living and efficacious, a
discerner of the thoughts and affections of the heart, entering the very soul, piercing even to the dividing asunder of soul and spirit and of the joints and marrow. It
was a virtue of God which concentrated itself in one single word, which made it become to them as "a fire and
as a hammer that breaketh the rock in pieces." They
will tell you that the more studious they have become of
the holy word, the more also have they felt growing, by
intimate and deep experience, their respect for its least
important parts; because they have found it, as St. Paul
says, "mighty through God, to the pulling down of strong
holds; casting down imaginations and every high thing
that exalteth itself against the knowledge of God, bringing
into captivity every thought, to the obedience of Christ."
They had read in the moment of their need, a psalm or
some words of the prophets, or some sentence of the epistles, or some narrative of the sacred history; and whilst
they were reading, behold a word came to seize their conscience with a force unknown, drawing, irresistible. It

was but a word; yet this word remained upon their soul, spoke to it, preached to it, sounded there as if all the bells of the city of God were ringing to call them to fasting, to bend the knee, to pray, to meet Jesus Christ, to hope, to rejoice. It was but a word, but this word was of God. It was in appearance, but one of the most delicate chords of this heaven-descended harp; but this chord was tuned in unison with the human heart; harmonies sounded forth, unexpected, delicious, omnipotent, which moved all their being, and was as the voice of many waters. They felt then, that that chord was attached to the very heart of God, and that its harmonies came from heaven. They had there recognised the appeal of Jesus Christ; and his word had been to them powerful as that single word, "MARY!" which astonished Mary Magdalene near the sepulchre.— Like her, they exclaimed, "Rabboni, my Master! It is then thy voice, oh my Savior; thou callest me; I recognise thee! Ah! behold me, Lord; I give myself to thee; speak, thy servant heareth thee."

Such is then the voice of the Church; such has been in all ages the unanimous testimony of the saints; this inspiration which the Bible attributes to itself, we, they say, have recognised. We believe it, not only because it attests it, but also because we have seen it, and because we can ourselves render testimony of it by a happy experience, and an irresistible sentiment.

We might adduce such examples by thousands. Let us content ourselves with naming here two of the noblest spirits that have influenced the destinies of the Church, and served as guides to humanity. Let us remember how the two greatest luminaries of ancient and modern times were kindled; and how it was one single passage of the Scriptures which came, prepared of God, to shed upon their souls the light of the Holy Spirit. Luther, an Augustinian monk, was going to Rome; he was still sick upon his bed, at Bologna, in a strange country, bowed down under the weight of his sins, believing himself about to appear before God. It was then that the 17th verse of the first chapter of the Epistle to the Romans "The, just shall live by faith," came to enlighten all his being, as a ray from heaven. This single sentence had seized him twice with resistless power; first at Bologna, to fill him with strength and an inexpressible peace; then afterwards at Rome itself, to cast him down, and to lift him up, whilst with an idolatrous crowd, he was dragging his body on his knees, up the fabulous staircase of Pilate. This word commenced the western reformation. "Transforming word for the Reformer and the Reformation;" exclaims my precious friend, Merle D'Aubigné. It was by it that God then said: "Let there be light, and there was light." "In truth," says the Reformer himself, "I felt myself as it were, entirely renewed; and this word was for me the very gate of paradise." "*Hic me prorsus renatum esse sensi, et apertis portis in ipsum Paradisum intrasse.*"*

Are we not here reminded again of the greatest of the doctors of Christian antiquity, that admirable Augustine, when in his garden near Milan, unhappy, without peace, feeling too, like Martin Luther, a storm in his soul, lying under a fig tree; "*jactans voces miserabiles, et dimittens habenas lacrymis,*" groaning and pouring out abundant tears, he heard from a young voice, singing and repeating in rapid succession: "*Tolle, lege, Tolle, lege!*" take and read, take and read. He went to Alypius to procure the roll of Paul's Epistles which he had left there; *adripui, aperui, et legi in silentio*; he seized it, he opened it, and he there read in silence the chapter on which his eyes first alighted. And when he came to the 13th verse of the 13th chapter of the Epistle to the Romans, every thing

* L. Opp. lat. in Præf.

was decided by a word. Jesus had conquered; and that grand career of the holiest of the Fathers there commenced. A word, a single word of God had kindled that glorious luminary which was to enlighten the church for ten centuries; and whose beams gladden her even to this present day. After thirty-one years of revolt, of combats, of falls, of misery; faith, life, eternal peace came to this erring soul; a new day, an eternal day arose upon it.

After these words, he desired no more; he closed the book; his doubts had fled. " *Nec ultrá volui legere, nec opus erat* ; for, with the end of this sentence, a stream of light and security was poured into his soul ; and all the night of his doubts had vanished. *Statim quippe cum fine hujusce sententiæ, quasi luce securitatis infusâ cordi meo, omnes dubitationis tenebræ diffugerunt.*"*

Such is then the threefold testimony which we desired to produce, and by which the Church attests to us that there is a wisdom and a power of God diffused through the minutest parts of the Holy Word ; and that all the scriptures are divinely inspired. At the same time, let it be understood, that we have not pretended, in this appeal, to impose the experience of one upon another. Proofs from feeling, we are aware, are proofs only to those who experience it. They have unquestionably, an irresistible force for those who, by experiencing its power, have had a living evidence of the divinity of the word of God ; but nothing would be less logical than to give them as demonstrations to those who are strangers to them. If you had had these experiences, you would have been already more than convinced, and our argument might be spared. We have then presented them to you only as strong historical presumptions, hoping to dispose you by this means, to receive with more favor and with more prompt submis-

* Confessions, Book viii. ch. 12.

sion, the scriptural proofs which we are about to submit to you. An entire generation of educated and pious men, we tell you, attest to you for ages, and by a three-fold experience, that by a closer study of the word of God, they have been led to recognise on evidence, the inspiration of the Scriptures, even in their minutest parts. Let this be to you, at least a powerful recommendation to hear respectively and without prejudice, the testimonies of the Bible to its own nature. We are about to furnish these testimonies ; but, in the mean time, we ask that this voice of the Church may be to you as that cry from a neighboring house : *take and read, take and read.* Go take your Bible, my brother ; *adripe, aperi, lege in silentio ;* take, open, read in silence ; and you yourself shall feel how far its inspiration extends, and you also shall say to yourself with Augustine, after so many combats and so many tears: no more doubt, for the morning star has arisen upon my heart !—and you will have no need to read any farther, in order to banish every doubt.

CHAPTER V.

DIDACTIC SUMMARY OF THE THEOPNEUSTIC DOC-TRINE.

WE have now defined and refuted; it remains for us to prove. But it must be done by the word of God alone. If God, reveals himself, it is for him to tell us, in this very revelation, to what extent he has designed to do it. Far be from us all vain hypotheses on such a subject. They could contain nothing more than our own phantasies, which might dazzle the eye of our faith, but could not enlighten it. The great question is, the entire question; what do the Scriptures say?

It has been asked if the Bible is inspired even in its language. We have affirmed that it is. In other words, (for we have cheerfully consented to reduce our entire thesis to this second expression, equivalent to the first), it is asked if the men of God have given us the Scriptures exempt from all error, great or small, positive or negative. Our answer to this, is affirmative.

The Scriptures are composed of books, of phrases and of words. Without making any hypothesis upon the manner which God has adopted for dictating the one and the other, we maintain, with the Scriptures, that this word is of God, without any exception,—and if any one should still ask us, how God dictated all the words of his book to the sacred writers, we should delay our answer, until some

20

one should show us how God dictated all its thoughts; and we should remind him of that child who said to his father: "My father where did God get his colors to paint all the cherries, such a beautiful red?" "My child, I will tell you, when I shall have learned how he painted all the leaves such a beautiful green." That is all our thesis.

But, what have we done to establish it? We have not yet proved it; the Bible alone can do that. Let us then review what we have accomplished.

Section I.—Retrospect.

To exhibit the doctrine more clearly, we have thought that before coming to its proofs, it would be useful to examine the different objections which it has encountered, and the hypotheses which have often been substituted for it. For that purpose, we have first endeavored to put our finger upon the original error of all those false systems which evade inspiration, by pretending to explain it.—It is the book, we have said, that is inspired; it is of the book we treat, and not of the writers. We may dispense with believing in the inspiration of the thoughts; but we cannot dispense with believing in that of the language. If the words of the book are dictated by God, what are the thoughts of the writer to me? He might have been an idiot, but that which came from his hand, must still be the Bible; whereas, if the thoughts, and not the words were given, it is not the Bible that he gives me, it is little more than a sermon.—Yet we have taken great care to qualify. The Scriptures are entirely the word of man, and the Scriptures are entirely the word of God. This, in our view, is one of their sublimest features. Admire them, O man! for they have spoken for thee and like thee; they have come to meet thee, all clothed with humanity; the eternal Spirit (in this respect at least, and in a certain degree,) has made himself man, to speak to thee, as the eternal Son has made himself man, to redeem thee. To this end he chose, before all time, men "subject to like passions" with thee. For that, he foresaw and he prepared their character, their circumstances, their style, their manner, their time, their path; and it is through this that the gospel is the tenderness and sympathy of God, as it is the "wisdom and power of God."

Yet we have been obliged to consider the objections. The individuality of the writers so constantly impressed on the sacred books, has been particularly alleged as an evidence that their inspiration was intermittent, imperfect, and mixed with the fallible thoughts of human wisdom. Very far from overlooking the fact thus objected, we have both admitted it, and adored in it alike, the wisdom and the goodness of God. But of what importance to the fact of the Theopneusty, is the absence or concurrence of the emotions of the sacred writers? God can employ them or dispense with them. When he speaks to us, must he not do it in the manner and style of men? And if the Almighty makes use of second causes in all his other works, why should he not do it in Theopneusty? Besides, we have said, this individuality, thus objected, shows itself equally in the parts of the Scripture the most incontestably dictated by God. This system of a gradual and intermittent inspiration presents at once the characteristics of complication, temerity and puerility; but that above all, which condemns it, is, that it is directly contrary to the testimony which the Scriptures give of themselves. After all, let no one think that the employment of the personal knowledge and feelings of the writers was accidental. No; all these different writers were chosen before the foundation of the world, for the work to which they were destined; and God prepared them all for it, like St. Paul, from their birth. Oh! how admirable are the sacred books in this very respect; how incomparable they appear;

how quickly we recognise in them the abundance of that divine power, which caused them to be written!

Some have also objected the necessity of translations, and their inevitable imperfection; others, the numerous variations in the ancient manuscripts from which the Bible has been printed. We have answered, that these two facts can in no way affect the question with regard to the primitive text;—were the apostles and the prophets commissioned to give us a Bible entirely inspired and without any mixture of error? That is the question; but at the same time we have been able to triumph with the Church, in view of the condition of these sacred manuscripts and the astonishing insignificance of the variations. The providence of the Lord has watched over the inestimable deposit.

Again, it is objected against verbal inspiration, that the Apostles have, in the New Testament, made use, and such use of the version of the Septuagint: but we have, on the contrary, reminded you that in the sovereign and independent manner in which they have employed it, you have a new proof of the agency of that Spirit who led them to speak.

Finally, it has even been objected, that after all, there are errors in the Scriptures; and these errors have been cited. We have denied the fact. Because some statement in some sentence has not at once been comprehended, the word of God has immediately been blamed for it. We have wished to give some example of the imprudence and error of these reproaches; but at the same time, we have hastened to come directly to this objection, to show its authors that they can attack the inspiration of the language, only by imputing error to the thoughts of the Holy Spirit. What rashness! in saying of the Bible, as Pilate did of Jesus Christ, "what evil hath it done?" they bring it to their judgment-bar! what will you then do to those who buffet it, who spit upon it, and who say to it; " prophesy; who is he that smote thee ?" Ah! come down from your tribunal, come down!

The language of the Scriptures has been accused of erroneous expressions, which betray in the sacred authors, an ignorance, elsewhere very pardonable, it has been said, of the constitution of the heavens and of the phenomena of nature. But here as elsewhere, the objections examined more closely, are changed into subjects of admiration ; for, in making us grind the diamonds of the Holy Scriptures, they have made us bring out unexpected beauties, which but serve to discover to us new reflections of its divinity. Whilst you cannot find in the Bible any of those errors which abound in the sacred books of all the heathen nations, and in all the philosophers of antiquity, it betrays in a thousand ways, in its language, the science of the Ancient of days ; and you will immediately recognise, both by the expressions which it employs, and by those which it avoids, that this language was, for thirty centuries, in an intelligent and profound harmony with the eternal truth of facts. That which you have known since yesterday, it says, I did not mention to you, but I knew it from eternity.

The words of St. Paul too have been objected to ; when the Apostle distinguishes that which the Lord says, from that which he himself says. We believe we have showed that, on the contrary, he could not have given a more convincing proof of his inspiration, than the boldness of such a distinction ; since, with an authority totally divine, he was there revoking the laws of the Old Testament.

That was not all ; we have had to reply to other objections, which present themselves rather under the form of systems, and which would pretend to exclude from inspiration, a part of the book of God.

Some have been willing to admit the inspiration of the

20*

Bible, and to dispute only that of its language; but we have suggested, first, that there exists so necessary a dependence of the thoughts upon the words, that a complete inspiration of the first, without a full inspiration of the latter, cannot be conceived of.   We have desired to show how irrational such a conception would be : and to this end, we have pointed out its illusion, since those who make it, find themselves forced, the moment they would sustain it, to attack the thoughts of the Scripture, as well as its language, and to impute errors to the sacred writers.

We have elsewhere reproached this fatal system with being nothing else than a human hypothesis; fantastically assumed, without being authorized by any thing in the word of God.

It also inevitably leads, we have said, to the most contemptuous suppositions concerning the word of God; whilst at the same time, it does not remove a single difficulty from our mind : since after all, it only substitutes for one inexplicable operation of God, another which is no less so.

But again, we have added : what is the use of this system, since it is incomplete, and since by the admission even of those who sustain it, it is applicable only to one part of the Scriptures ?   Others again have sometimes wished to concede to us the full inspiration of certain books, but to exclude from it the historical writings.   We have showed not only that every distinction of this kind is gratuitous, rash, opposed to the terms of the Scriptures; but also, that these books are perhaps, of all the Bible, those whose inspiration is the most attested, the most necessary, the most evident; those which Jesus Christ has cited with the greatest respect; those which most powerfully search the heart, and which tell the secrets of the conscience.   They foretell the most important future events, in their least details; they constantly announce Jesus Christ; they describe the character of God ; they teach doctrines ; they legislate ; they reveal. They shine with a divine wisdom, both in that which they say, and in that which they suppress ; in their prophetic reserve, in their sublime moderation, in their plenitude, in their variety, in their brevity. To write them, we repeat, required more than men, more than angels.

It has generally been asked, if we could discover any divinity in certain passages of the Scriptures, too vulgar to be inspired. We believe we have showed how much wisdom, on the contrary, shines in these passages, when, instead of judging them hastily, we seek in them the teachings of the Holy Spirit.

Finally, we have entreated the reader to go directly to the Scriptures, and to consecrate to studying them by themselves, with prayer, the time which he may recently have employed in judging them ; and we have warranted him, upon the testimony of all the Church, and from a threefold experience, that the divine inspiration of the least parts of the Holy Scriptures shall quickly reveal itself to him, if he can study them with respect.

We have desired that this Book should not wear so theological an aspect, that christian women and other persons unacquainted with certain theological studies, or with the sacred languages, should fear to undertake the perusal of it. At the same time we should fail to accomplish one part of our design, if the doctrine had not been stated, on some points, with more precision. We shall then ask that, to avoid being led, under another form, to too extended developments, we may be permitted to state it here, more didactically, and to review it in a short catechism. We shall do scarcely more than indicate the place of the points already stated, and we shall give a little expansion to those only of which we have not yet spoken.

Section II.—Short Catechetical essay on the principal points of the doctrine.

I. What do we then understand by Theopneusty?

Theopneusty is the mysterious power exercised by the Spirit of God over the authors of the Holy Scriptures, to make them write them, to guide them in the employment of even the words they were to use, and thus to preserve them from all error.

II. What is said of the spiritual power which was exercised over the men of God, while they were writing their sacred books?

It is said that they were *carried* or *impelled* (φερόμενοι) not by a human will, but by the Holy Spirit; so that they presented at that time the things of God, " not with the words which man's wisdom teacheth, but which the Holy Ghost teacheth."[*] God, saith the apostle,[†] at sundry times, and in divers manners, (πολυμέρῶς καὶ πολυτρό-πῶς) has spoken BY THE PROPHETS;" sometimes in granting them the understanding of that which he was leading them to say; sometimes without giving it to them; sometimes by dreams[‡] and by visions,[§] which he afterward led them to relate; sometimes by words given internally (λόγω ενδιάθετω,) which he led them immediately to utter; sometimes by words sent externally, (λόγῳ προφορικῳ,) which he led them to repeat.

III. But what was passing in their heart and in their understanding, whilst they were writing?

We do not know. This fact, moreover, subjected to

---

[*] 2 Pet. i. 21. 1 Cor. ii. 13. [†] Hebrews i. 1.

[‡] Numb. xii, 6. Job xxxiii, 15. Daniel i, 17; xi, 6; vii, 1. Gen. xx, 6; xxxi, 10. 1 Kings iii, 5. Matt. i, 20; ii, 12–22. Acts ii, 17.

[§] Num. xii, 6; xxiv, 4; Job vii, 14; Gen. i, 15; iii, 3; Psalms lxxxix, 26; Matt. xvii, 9; Acts ii, 17; ix, 10, 12; x, 3, 17, 19; xi, 5; xii, 9; xvi, 9, 10; 2 Cor. xii, 1, 2.

great varieties, could be for us, neither an object of science nor of faith.

IV. Besides; have not the modern authors who have written upon this subject, often distinguished in the Scriptures, three or four degrees of inspiration ?

This is a vain divination; and this supposition, moreover, is in contradiction with the Word of God, which knows but one kind of inspiration. There is nothing true in this question, except the suggestion of what men have done.

Do we not see at the same time, that the men of God were profoundly instructed, and often even profoundly moved by the holy things which they were teaching, the future things which they were predicting, and past events which they were relating ?

They might be, without doubt; they were so most generally; but it was possible that they should not be; and when they were thus instructed, it was in very different degrees, of which we remain ignorant, and the knowledge of which is not required of us.

VI. What must we then think of those definitions of Theopneusty, in which the Scriptures seem to be represented as the merely human expression of a purely divine revelation ; for instance, that of Baumgarten,* who says that inspiration is only the means by which revelation, at first immediate, became mediate, and arranged itself in a book (*medium quo revelatio immediata, mediata facta, inque libros relata est*) ?"

These definitions are not exact, and may give rise to false ideas of Theopneusty.

I say that they are not exact. They contradict facts. Immediate revelation does not necessarily precede inspiration ; and when preceding it, is not its measure. The

* De discrimine revelat. et inspirationis.

vacant air has phrophesied ;* a hand coming out of the wall has written the words of God ;† a dumb animal reproved the folly of a prophet ;‡ Balaam prophesied against his will ; Daniel, without comprehending it ; and the Corinthian Christians, without even knowing the words which the Holy Spirit had put upon their lips.§

Still farther, I say that these definitions engender or conceal false notions concerning Theopneusty. They suppose, in fact, that inspiration is but the natural expression of a supernatural revelation, and that the men of God had only to record humanly, in their books, that which the Holy Spirit had made them see divinely in their understanding. Inspiration is more than that. The Scriptures are not only the thought of God, elaborated by the Spirit of man, to diffuse itself through the words of man ; they are the thought of God, and the word of God.

VII. The Holy Spirit having, in every age, enlightened the elect of God, and having, moreover, imparted to them, in ancient times, miraculous powers ; in which of these two orders of spiritual gifts must we rank Theopneusty?

We must place it in the order of gifts extraordinary and entirely miraculous. The Holy Spirit, in all ages, enlightens the elect by his powerful and internal influence, testifies to them of Jesus,‖ anoints them from the holy One, teaches them all things, and convinces them of all truth.¶ But, besides these *ordinary* gifts of illumination and of faith, the Holy Spirit has bestowed *extraordinary* gifts upon men charged with promulgating and writing the oracles of God. The Theopneusty is one of these gifts.

---

* Gen. iii, 14, &c. iv, 6 ; Exod. iii, 6, &c. xix, 3, &c. ; Deut. iv, 12 ; Matt. iii, 17, xvii, 5, &c.
† Dan. v, 5.   ‡ 2 Peter ii, 16.   § 1 Cor. xiv.
‖ John xv. 26.
¶ 1 John ii. 20, 27. John xiv. 16, 26 ; vii. 38, 39.

VIII. Is then the difference between illumination and inspiration in kind, or only in degree?

The difference is in kind, and not merely in degree.

IX. Yet have not the Apostles received from the Holy Spirit, in addition to *inspiration, illumination* in an extraordinary measure, and in its most eminent degree?

In its most eminent degree, is what no one can affirm; in an extraordinary degree, is what no one can contradict. The Apostle Paul, for example, had not "received the gospel from man, but by revelation of Jesus Christ."*

He wrote "ALL HIS LETTERS," Saint Peter tells us,† not only with words which the Holy Ghost teacheth,‡ as were THE OTHER SCRIPTURES (of the Old Testament,) according to the wisdom given unto him." § He had the knowledge of the mystery of Christ. ‖ Jesus Christ had not promised to his Apostles to give them a mouth only, but also wisdom to testify of him.¶ David, when he seemed but to speak of himself, in the Psalms, *knew* that it was of the Messiah that his words must be understood; "because he was a prophet, and knew that of the fruit of his loins according to the flesh, God would raise up Christ to sit on his throne." **

X. Why then should we not say, that Theopneusty is only illumination in its highest and most abundant degree?

Beware of saying it; for you would then have an idea of inspiration narrow, confused, contingent, and always uncertain. In fact;

1. God, who has often united both these gifts in the same man, has likewise often designed to separate them, to show us that they differ essentially one from the other, and that when united, they are still independent. Every

* Gal. i. 12—16; 1 Cor. xv. 3. † 2 Peter iii. 15, 16.
‡ 1 Cor. ii. 13. § 2 Peter iii. 15, 16. ‖ Eph. iii 3.
¶ Luke xxi. 15. ** Acts ii. 30.

true Christian has the Holy Spirit ;* but every Christian is not inspired ; and a man may speak the words of God, without having received either the affections or the vivifying lights which they impart.

2. It can be showed clearly by a great number of examples, that the one of these gifts was not the measure of the other, and that the theopneusty of the prophets, held no more proportion to their intelligence than to their holiness.

3. So far was the one of these gifts from being the measure of the other, that it can even be affirmed, that the theopneusty appears the more clearly, the more the illumination of the sacred writer is inferior to his inspiration, when you see the prophets, the most enlightened of the Spirit of God, bending over their own pages, after having written them, and seeking to understand the meaning of that which the Spirit who was in them, had just made them express, it must become evident to you, that their theopneusty was independent of their illumination.

4. In supposing even the illumination of the prophet elevated to its highest degree, it was at the same time, never at the height of the divine thought : and there might be, in the word that has been dictated to them, much more meaning than the prophet yet saw. David, without doubt, in singing his psalms,† knew that they pointed to " Him who was to be raised up of the first of his loins to sit on his throne forever." The greater part of the prophets like Abraham their father, saw the day of Christ ; they rejoiced in it ;‡ "they sought what, or what manner of time the Spirit which was in them did signify, when it testified beforehand the sufferings of Christ and the glory that should follow ;"§ . . . and yet, our Savior

* John ii. 20, 27 ; Jer. xxxi. 34 ; John vi. 43.
† Act. ii. 30. ‡ John viii. 56. § 1 Pet. i. 11.

tells us that the simplest christian, the least (in know-ledge) in the kingdom of God, knows more concerning it, than the greatest of the prophets.*

5. These gifts differ from one another by essential characteristics which we shall presently point out.

6. Finally, it is always the inspiration of the book which is presented to us as an object of faith, never the internal state of him who writes it. His knowledge or his ignorance does not affect in the least the confidence which I owe his words; and my soul ought always to look not so much to his knowledge, as to the God of all holiness, who speaks to me by his mouth. The Lord de-signed, it is true, that the greater part of his historians should be also the witnesses of that which they related. This was without doubt, in order that the world might hear them with more confidence, and might not be able to excite reasonable doubts as to the truth of their narra-tives. But the Church, in her faith, looks much higher, the intelligence of the writers is to her imperfectly known and comparatively indifferent: that which she knows, is their inspiration. She never goes to look for the source of it in the bosom of the prophet; it is in that of her God. " Christ speaks in me," says St. Paul to her; "and God hath spoken to our fathers by the prophets."† "Why then look ye upon us," say all the sacred writers to her, " as though it were by our power, or our holiness that we had done this work?"‡ Look up!

XI. If there exist then, a specific difference between the two spiritual graces of inspiration and illumination; in what must we say that it consists?

Although you could not say, yet you would not be the

* Mat. xi. 11; Michaëlis Introd. tom. i. page 116–129. Fr. Translat. (This author thinks that, in this passage, the *least* means *the least prophet*.)

† 2 Cor. xiii. 3; Heb. i 1, (ἐν). ‡ Act. iii. 12.

less obliged, for the preceding reasons, to declare that this difference exists. In order to be able thoroughly to answer this question, you must understand the nature and the mode of both these gifts; whilst the Holy Spirit has never explained to us, neither how he pours the thoughts of God into the understanding of a christian, nor how he places the word of God on the lips of a prophet. At the same time, we can here point out two essential characteristics, by which the e two operations have always showed themselves distinct. One of these characteristics relates to their duration, and the other to their degree.

As to the duration, the illumination is continued; while the inspiration is intermittent; as to the measure, illumination has degrees, whilst inspiration does not admit them.

XII. What do we understand by continued illumination and intermitted inspiration?

The illumination of a saint by the Holy Spirit is a permanent work. When it has commenced for him at the day of his new birth, it then goes on increasing, and accompanies him with its light to the very end of his career. This light, without doubt, is but too much obscured by his unfaithfulness and his negligence; but it never more entirely withdraws from him. "His path," saith the wise man, "is as the shining light, that shineth more and more unto the perfect day."* "When it has pleased God, who separated him from his mother's womb, to reveal his Son in him,† he preserves even to the end, the knowledge of the mystery of Jesus Christ, and can always explain its truths and its glories. As "it is not flesh and blood that have revealed these things to him, but the Father,"‡ this anointing which he has received of the holy one,§ abides in him,

---

* Prov. iv. 18.   † Gal. i. 15.   ‡ Gal. i. 16.
§ 1 John ii. 20–27.

says St. John, and he has no need that any one teach him : but as the same anointing teacheth him of all things, and is truth, and is no lie, and even as it has taught him, they shall abide in him." Illumination then abides with the believer ; but it is not thus with miraculous gifts, nor with Theopneusty, which is one of these gifts.[*]

As to miraculous gifts, they were always intermittent among the men of God, if we except Jesus only. The Apostle Paul, for example, who at one time resuscitated Eutychus, and through whom God performed acts of extraordinary power, so that handkerchiefs and garments that had touched him only, healed the sick on whom they were laid ; at other times could neither comfort his colleague Trophimus, nor his dear Epaphroditus, nor his son Timothy.[†] Such is the case with Theopneusty, which is merely the most excellent of miraculous gifts. It was exercised only at intervals in the prophets of the Lord. The prophets, and even the Apostles, who (as we shall show) were prophets and more than prophets,[‡] did not prophesy so often as they themselves desired. Theopneusty was granted them at intervals ; it descended upon them according to the will of the Holy Spirit (καθὼς τὸ πνεῦμα ἐδίδου αὐτοις ἀπθέγγεσθαι) ; for " prophecy came not by the will of man," says St. Peter, " but they were filled with the Holy Ghost, and spake as the Spirit gave them utterance."[§] God spake by the prophets (ἐν τοῖς προφήταις), says St. Paul, when he willed, at different times, and by different ways (πολυμέρως, πολυτρόπως). " On such a day and at such a time," it is often written, " the word of Jehovah came to such a one (ויהי דבר יהוה אלי)." " The tenth year, at the twelfth day of the tenth month, the word of Jehovah came to me," said the prophet.[‖] " In the fif-

---

[*] 1 Cor. xiv. 1.—Acts xx. 10.
[†] 1 Tim. iv. 20.—Phil. ii. 27.—1 Tim. v. 23.
[‡] Eph. iii. 4, 5 ; iv. 2.—Rom. xvi. 25–27.
[§] Acts ii. 4.   [‖] Jer. i. 1 ; xxix. 1, and elsewhere.

teenth year of the reign of Tiberias, the word of God came
to John, son of Zacharias." (ἐγένετο ῥήμα Θεοῦ ἐπι
Ιωάννην) ;* " and on the eighth day, Zacharias, his father,
was filled with the Holy Spirit, and prophesied, saying . ."†

Thus then, we should not think that the divine infallibility of the language of the prophets (and even of the
Apostles), continued beyond the time of accomplishing
their miraculous task, or that in which the Spirit made
them speak independently of Theopneusty, they were
most frequently illuminated, sanctified, guarded by God
as every holy believer in our day might be ; but then, they
spake no longer as " moved by the Holy Ghost ;" their
words might still be worthy of the most respectful attention ; but it was then a saint who spake ; it was no longer
God : they had again become fallible.

XIII. Can we cite examples of this fallibility of their
language, independently of Theopneusty ?

Such examples are numerous. In the Scriptures we
often see men, who were for a time the mouth of Jehovah, afterward becoming false prophets, and falsely pretending, after the Spirit had ceased to speak by them, that
they still uttered the words of the most High ; " although
the Lord had not sent them, neither commanded them,
nor spoken unto them." " They spake a vision of their
own heart, and were then no more the mouth of the
Lord."‡

Without even speaking here of those wicked men, any
more than of the profane Saul, of Balaam, who were for a long
time numbered among the prophets, can it be thought that
all the words of king David are infallible during the whole
of that long year which he passed in adultery ? Yet these,
say the Scriptures, are " the last words of David, the sweet
singer of Israel : the Spirit of the Lord spake by me, and

* Luke iii. 1, 2.   † Luke 1, 59–67—41, 42.
‡ Jer. xiv. 14 ; xxiii. 11, 16 ; Ezek. xiii. 2, 3.

his word was in my tongue."* Can it be thought that all the words of the prophet Solomon were still infallible, when he fell into idolatry in his old age, and the safety of his soul became a problem to the Church of God? Yet farther, to come down to the *holy apostles and prophets* of Christ (Eph. iii. 5), can it be thought that all the language of Paul himself was infallible, and that he could still say; "Christ spake by him, while there was a sharp contention (παροξυσμός) between him and Barnabas?† Or, when mistaking in the midst of the Council, the person of the high priest, he "insulted the prince of his people," and cried; God shall smite thee thou whited wall! Or yet again, as (some doubt may rest on the character of this reproof,) can it be thought that all the words of the holy apostle Peter were infallible, when at Antioch, he showed himself "so reprehensible" (κατεγνωσμένος); when he feared the messengers of St. James; when he used hypocrisy; and when he compelled the apostle Paul, "to resist him face to face in the presence of all, because he walked not uprightly according to the truth of the Gospel," (οὐκ ἦν ὀρθοποδήσας)?

XIV. What inference should we draw from this first point of difference between illumination and inspiration, as to the duration of these gifts?

We must conclude:

1. That these two operations of the Holy Spirit differ in essence, and not in degree only;

2. That the infallibility of the sacred writers has depended not on their illumination (which, although granted in an extraordinary measure to some among them, was nevertheless common to all the saints,) but, on their Theopneusty only;

---

* 2 Sam. xxiii. 1, 2. † Acts. xv. 39.

3. That the Theopneustic words, having been all miraculous, are all likewise the words of God;

4. That our faith in each portion of the Bible, being no longer founded on the illumination of the writers, but on the inspiration of their writings, need never give itself to the perplexing study of their internal state, of the degree of their light, or of their sanctification; but must lean on God in every thing, on man in nothing.

XV. If the illumination and inspiration of the prophets and apostles has varied so much in the duration of these gifts, how has it been as *to the degree* to which they possessed them?

Illumination has degrees; Theopneusty cannot admit them, a prophet is more or less enlightened of God; but his word is not more or less inspired. It is inspired, or it is not; it is of God, or it is not of God. In it there is neither measure nor degree, neither increase nor decrease. David was illuminated of God; John the Baptist was so far more than David; a simple christian may be so in a higher degree than was John the Baptist; an apostle still exceeded this christian; and Jesus Christ is yet in this, superior to this apostle. But the inspired word of David, what do I say? the inspired word of even Balaam, is of God equally with that of John the Baptist, of Paul, or of Jesus Christ! IT IS THE WORD OF GOD. The most illuminated saint cannot speak by inspiration; while the most wicked, the most ignorant and the most impure of men can prophesy; for " he speaks not of himself ($\dot{\alpha}\varphi$' $\varepsilon\alpha\nu\tau o\tilde{\nu}$, $o\dot{\nu}\varkappa\ \dot{\varepsilon}\ \iota\pi\varepsilon\nu$), but by Theopneusty ($\dot{\alpha}\lambda\lambda\dot{\alpha}\ \pi\varrho o\varphi\dot{\eta}\tau\varepsilon\dot{\nu}\sigma\alpha\iota$.)* In a truly regenerated man are always found the divine and the human spirit, which act at the same time, the one enlightening, the other obscuring; and illumination will increase in proportion as the action of the Divine Spirit sur-

* John xi. 51.

passes that of the human. These two elements have also existed in the prophets, and above all, in the apostles. But thanks to God, our faith in the language of the Scripture depends not on the unknown issue of the conflict between the flesh and the spirit in the soul of the sacred writers. Our faith ascends directly to the heart of God.

XVI. Can great evil result from the doctrine according to which, the language of inspiration would be but the human expression of a superhuman revelation; and if we may so express ourselves, but a natural reflection of a supernatural illumination?

One of these two evils must ever result from it: either the oracles of God will be brought down to a level with the words of the saints; or these will be raised to a level with the Scriptures. This is a fatal consequence, the alternative of which is reproduced in every age. It was inevitable. All truly regenerated men, being enlightened by the Holy Spirit, it follows, according to this doctrine, that they all possess, though in different degrees, perhaps, the element of inspiration; so that, according to the arbitrary idea you shall have formed of their spiritual condition, you will be inevitably led, now to assimilate them to the sacred writers, now to raise them to the rank of men inspired from above.

XVII. Can instances be produced of religious communities, where the first of these evils has been realized? I mean, where men have been led, by this means, to lower the Scriptures to a level with the words of the saints?

All the theories of the learned among the Protestants, which suppose some mixture of error in the Scriptures, are founded upon this doctrine;—from Semler and Ammon, to Eichhorn, Paulus, Gabler, Schruster, and Restig; —from Mr. De Wette, to the more respectful systems of Michaëlis, of Rosenmüler, Scaliger, Capellus, John Le Clerc, or Vossius. According to these systems, the divine light, by which the intellect of the sacred writers was illuminated, might experience a partial eclipse, by the unavoidable influence of their natural infirmities, of a defect of memory, of an innocent ignorance of a popular prejudice; so that their writings bear the mark of it, and we can there discover where the shades have fallen.

XVIII. Can we show that there are also religious societies, in which the second of these evils has been consummated; I mean, where, from having chosen to confound inspiration with illumination, they have raised saints and learned men to the rank of the theopneustic, or inspired men?

For specimens of this, we might adduce, above all others, the Jews and the Latins.

XIX. What have the Jews done?

They have regarded the rabbins of the ages succeeding the period of the dispersion, as gifted with an infallibility, that has placed them on a level with (if not above), Moses and the prophets. They have, without doubt, attributed a species of divine inspiration to the sacred writings; but they have forbidden any explanations of the oracles, except those furnished by their traditions. They have called the immense body of those commandments of men, *the oral law*, (תורה שבעל פה) the *doctrine*, or the *Talmud*, (תלמוד) distinguishing it as *Mishna*, or *Second Law*, (משנה) and as Gemanah; complement, or perfection, (גמרא). They have proclaimed it as transmitted by God to Moses, by Moses to Joshua, by Joshua to the prophets, by the prophets to Esdras, by Esdras to the Doctors of the great Synagogue, and by these to the Rabbis *Antigonus, Soccho, Shemaia, Hillel Schammai;* until, at last, *Judas the holy* committed it to the *Traditions*, or *Repetitions* of the law, (משנה, δευτέρωσεις,) which, in later times, with their Commentary, or Complement, (the *Gemarah*,) formed the *Talmud of Jerusalem*, and then that of *Babylon*.

"One of the greatest obstacles we find among the

Jews," says the missionary M'Caul, "is their invincible prejudice in favor of their traditions and commentaries; so that we cannot persuade them to purchase our Bibles without notes or comments."*

"The law, they say, is salt; the Mishna, pepper; the Talmuds, spices." "The Scriptures are water; the Mishna, wine; the Gemarah, spiced wine." "My son," says Rabbi Isaac, "learn to pay more attention to the word of the Scribes, than to the word of the law." "Turn your children, (said Rabbi Eleazar, upon his death-bed, to his scholars, who were asking him the way of life,) turn your children from the study of the Bible, and put them at the feet of the Sages." "Learn, my son, (says Rabbi Jacob,) that the words of the Scribes are more excellent than those of the Prophets." †

XX. And what has resulted from these enormities?

By them, millions and millions of immortal souls, however far they have wandered on the earth, however wearied and heavy laden, however despised and persecuted in every place, have been able to carry, among all the nations of the world, the book of the Old Testament untouched and complete, and not to cease reading it in Hebrew, every Sabbath, in thousands of synagogues, for eighteen hundred years; . . . . yet without being able to recognise in it, that Jewish Messiah whom we all adore, and the knowledge of whom would be their instant deliverance, as it is one day to be their happiness and their glory!

"And Jesus said unto them, full well ye reject the commandment of God, that ye may keep your own traditions."‡

XXI. And what have the Latins done?

---

* Letters from Warsaw, March 22, 1827.
† In the Jerusalem Talmud.—Engel. method., at the word Juifs.
‡ Mark vii. 9, 13, and Matt. xv, 3, 9.

They have considered the fathers, the popes, and the
Councils of the successive ages of the Church of Rome, as
endowed with an infallibility which puts them upon the
level, if not above, Jesus, prophets and apostles. They
have, it is true, greatly differed from each other upon the
doctrine of the inspiration of the Scriptures; and the
faculties of Douay and Louvain, for example, have set
themselves strongly* against the opinion of the Jesuits,
who were unwilling to see in the operation of the Holy
Spirit, any thing more than a direction, which preserved
the sacred writers from error; but they have all forbidden
any other explanation of the Holy Scriptures, than that
which is according to the traditions.† They believed
they had a right to say, in all their Councils, with the
apostles and prophets of Jerusalem; "*It hath seemed good
to the Holy Spirit and to us.*" They have declared that
it belonged to them to judge the true sense of the Holy
Scriptures. They have called the immense body of these
human commandments, *the oral Law, unwritten traditions,
the unwritten Law.* They have styled them, transmitted
from God, and dictated by the mouth of Jesus Christ, or
of the Holy Spirit, by a continual succession.

"Seeing," says the Council of Trent,‡ "that the saving
truth, and the discipline of manners is contained in the
written books and the unwritten traditions, which having
been received by the Apostles, from the mouth of Jesus
Christ, or the inspiration of the Holy Spirit, in the succession of time, have been handed down even to us; following the example of the Apostolic Fathers, the Council
receives with the same affection and reverence (pari pietatis

* Censure of 1588. † Council of Trent, Sess. 4, 2d. decree of 28th
April, 1546. Bellarmin, *De Eccl.* lib. iii. cap. 14; lib. iv. cap.
3, 5, 6, 7, 8. Coton, lib. ii. Cap. 24, 34, 35. Du Perron contre
Tilenus.
‡ Council of Trent. 1st decree. Session 4.

et reverentiæ affectu,) and honors all the books of the Old and New Testament, (seeing God is their author,) and *likewise the traditions* concerning faith and practice, as having been dictated by the mouth of Jesus Christ or of the Holy Spirit, and preserved in the Catholic Church by a perpetual succession ?"   "If any one does not receive the said books entirely, and with all their parts, as holy and canonical, as they have been accustomed to be read in the Catholic Church, and in the ancient vulgar trans. lation," (that of Jerome,* which abounds, especially in Job and the Psalms, in very serious and very glaring faults, and has even been abundantly corrected in after times by other Popes), " or, in good earnest, despises the said traditions, let him be accursed !"

They have also put the bulls of the Bishop of Rome and the decrees of their synods above the Scriptures. " The Holy Scriptures," they say, " do not contain all that is necessary to salvation, and are not sufficient."† " They are obscure."‡   " It is not for the people to read the Holy Scriptures.§   We must receive with obedience of faith, many things that are not in the Scriptures."‖   We must serve God according to the traditions of the elders."¶

The Bull *Exsurge* of Leo. X.** puts in the number of Luther's heresies, his saying : " that it is not in the power of the church or Pope to establish articles of faith."

The Bull *unigenitus*†† condemns forever, as being " re.

* It was in vain that at the Council, the Abbey Isidor Clarius represented that there was rashness in attributing inspiration to a writer who himself declared that he had none. Fra Paolo, Tom. 1, liv. ii. Sec. 51.   † Bellarmin *de verbo Dei*, lib. iv.

‡ *Id.* lib. iii.   Charon, Veritè 3.   Coton lib. 2. Cap. 19. Bayle Traitè.   § Bellarmin, *de verbo Dei*, lib. ii. cap. 19.

‖ Bellarmin, lib. iv.   Cap. 3.   Coton, lib. ii. Cap. 24.   Du Perron contre Tilenus.   ¶ Bellarmin, lib. iv, Cap 5.   Coton, lib. ii. cap. 34, 35.   Council of Trent, Sess. 4.

** 1520 Counc. Harduini, T. ix. p. 1893.

†† Of Clement XI. of September 8, 1713.

spectively false, captious, scandalous, rash, pernicious, suspected of heresies, savoring of heresies, heretical, impious,
blasphemous, etc." the following propositions: "It is
useful, at all times, in all places and for all sorts of persons to study the Scriptures, and to know their spirit, their
piety and their mysteries," (upon 1 Cor. xvi. 5.)* "The
reading of the Holy Scriptures by a man of business,
shows that it is for all the world," (upon Acts, viii. 28.)†
"The holy obscurity of the word of God is not a reason
why the laity should not read it," (on Acts, viii. 31.")
"The Sabbath ought to be sanctified by the reading of
books of piety, and especially of the Holy Scriptures. It
is the milk which God himself, who knows our hearts, has
given them. It is dangerous to attempt to wean him from
it," (on Acts, xv. 21.) "It is an illusion to imagine that the
knowledge of the mysteries of religion ought not to be com-
municated to that sex, (the female sex) by the reading
of the holy books, after that example of the confidence
with which Jesus shows himself to this woman, (the Sama-
ritan woman)." "It is not from the simplicity of woman,
but from the proud science of man, that the abuse of the
Scriptures has arisen, and that have arisen the heresies,
(on John iv. 26). "It is, to shut the mouth of Jesus Christ
to christians, to snatch from their hands the holy book,
or to keep it closed to them, in depriving them of the
means of understanding it, (1 Thes. v. 2.)" "To forbid
the reading of the Bible to christians, is to refuse the
light to the children of light, and to inflict on them a kind
of excommunication, (Luke, xi. 33.)‡

More recently, in 1824, the Encyclical letters of Pope
Leo XII., complain grievously of the Bible Societies,
" which violate say they, the traditions of the Fathers, and
the Council of Trent, in scattering the Scriptures in the

* Propos. 79.   † Prop. 80.
‡ Prop. 82, 83, 84, 85.

vulgar languages of all the nations." (" *Non vos latet,
venerandi fratres, Societatem quamdam, dictam vùlgo*
Biblicam, *per totum orbem audacter vagari, quæ, spre-
tis S. S. Patrum traditionibus* (! ! !) *et contra notissi-
mum Tridentini concilii decretum, in id collatis viribus
ac modis omnibus intendit, ut in vulgares linguas natio-
num omnium sacra vertantur vel potius pervertantur
Biblia.*") " In order to turn away this pest," adds he, " our
predecessors have published many constitutions, . . . tending to show how pernicious to faith and practice is this
perfidious invention! (*ut ostendatur quantoperé fidei
et moribus vaferrimum hocce inventum noxium sit !*")

XXII. And what is the result of these enormities?

It is that, by them, millions and millions of immortal
souls in France, in Spain, in Italy, in Germany, in Amer-
ica, even in the Indies, although they possess every where,
the books of the Old and New Testaments uninjured and
complete, although they have not ceased to read them in
Latin every Sabbath, in thousands of temples, during
twelve hundred years, . . . have been turned away from
the fountain of life; have given, like the Jews, " more attention to the words of the scribes than to those of the
law," have turned away their children, according to the
counsel of Eleazar, " from the reading of the Bible, to
place them at the feet of the wise men ;" have found, with
Rabbi Jacob, " the words of the scribes more excellent
than those of the prophets." It is thus that they have
been able to maintain for twelve centuries, doctrines the
most contrary to the word of God,* upon the worship of
images ;† upon the exaltation of the priesthood ; upon their

* Exodus, xx. 4, 5.

† Quisquis elanguerit erga venerabilium imaginum adorationem
(προσκύνησιν) hunc anatematizat sancta nostra et universalis
synodus ! (was it written to the Emperor, in the name of all the
Second Council of Nice.) (Conc. tom. vii. p. 583.)

forced celibacy; upon their auricular confessions; upon the absolution which they dare to give; upon the magical power which they attribute, even to the impurest of them, of creating their God by three Latin words, *opere operato;* upon an ecclesiastical priesthood of which the Scriptures have never spoken; upon the invocation of the dead; upon the spiritual preëminence of the city which the Bible has called Babylon; upon the unknown *tongues* in worship; upon the celestial empire of the blessed but humble woman, to whom Jesus himself said; " Woman, what have I to do with thee ?"—upon the mass; upon the forbidding the cup to the laity; upon the forbidding the Scriptures to the people; upon the indulgences; upon purgatory; upon the universal episcopacy of an Italian priest; upon the forbidding of meats; so that just as they annul the only priesthood of the Son of Man, in establishing other priesthoods by thousands; just as they annihilate his divinity in recognising thousands of demi-gods or dead men, present in every place, hearing every where the most secret prayers of men, protecting cities and kingdoms, accomplishing miracles in favor of their adorers; . . . they in the same manner annihilate the inspiration of the Scriptures, in recognising by thousands, other writings which share its divine authority, and which surpass and engulf its eternal infallibility !

It is against just such pretensions made by the heretics of his day, that St. Ireneus said; " when we would· convince them by the Scriptures, they treat the Scriptures as if they were imperfect, or wanting authority, or uncertain, and as if the truth could not be found there without the aid of tradition, because the latter was given, not by writing, but by the living voice."[*]

" Well do ye make void the commandment of God by your tradition !" said the Savior. Benè irritum facitis præceptum Dei, ut traditionem vestram servetis !" (Mark vii. 9).

* Adv. Hæres. lib. iii. cap. 2.

XXIII. Without pretending in any way to explain how the Holy Spirit may have dictated the thoughts and the words of the Scriptures (since the knowledge of this mystery is neither given, nor required), what may we recognise in this divine action ?

Two things; first, an *impulse*, that is an action upon the *will* of the men of God, to lead them to speak and to write; and secondly, a *suggestion*, that is to say, an action upon their *understanding* and upon their *organs*; to produce, first, within them, more or less exalted notions of the truth which they were about to utter; and again *without* them, human expressions the most divinely adapted to express the eternal thought of the Holy Spirit.

XXIV. Must we yet admit that the sacred writers were but the pens, the hands, the secretaries of the Holy Spirit ?

They have been, without doubt, the pens, the hands, the secretaries; but they have been almost always, and in different degrees, living pens, intelligent hands, docile secretaries, moved and sanctified by the truths they uttered. In order that even in these cases, our faith might rest on God, and not lean upon man, the Holy Spirit has chosen on many other occasions, to employ ignorant hands, inert pens, and secretaries without light and without holiness.

XXV. At the same time, has not the word of God often been written in reference to particular occasions ?

Yes, without doubt; and the occasion was as much prepared by God, as the writer. "The Holy Spirit," says Claude,* "used the pen of the evangelists, . . . and of the prophets. He furnished them the occasions of writing; he gave them the desire and the strength for it; the matter, the form, the order, the arrangement, the expression, are of his immediate inspiration and of his direction."

* Claude, posthumous works, vol. iv. p. 228.

XXVI. But may we not clearly recognise, in the greater part of the sacred books, the individual character of the writer?

We are careful not to overlook it; and on the contrary, we admire this feature. The individual character so far as it comes from God, and not from sin and the fall, was prepared and sanctified of God, for the work to which God had destined it.

XXVII. Ought we then to think that every part of each one of the sacred books of the holy Scripture was equally inspired of God?

The Scripture, in describing itself, admits no distinction. All the sacred books, without any exception, are the word of the Lord. THE ENTIRE SCRIPTURE, says Saint Paul ($\pi\acute{\alpha}\sigma\alpha\ \gamma\varrho\acute{\alpha}\varphi\eta$), IS INSPIRED OF GOD.

This declaration, we have already said, is susceptible of two constructions, according as we prefer to place the verb understood before or after the Greek word which we here translate by *inspired of God*. Both these constructions irrefutably establish that, in the thought of the apostle, all, without exception, in each book of the Scriptures, is indited by the Spirit of God. In fact, in both, the apostle equally attests that these SACRED LETTERS ($\tau\alpha$ $\mathcal{\iota}\varepsilon\varrho\acute{\alpha}\ \gamma\varrho\acute{\alpha}\mu\mu\alpha\tau\alpha$), of which he had just spoken to Timothy, are all, *theopneustic Scriptures*.

Now, we know that in the days of Jesus Christ, the whole church designated ONLY ONE AND THE SAME COLLECTION OF BOOKS, as *the Scripture*, or *the Scriptures*, or *the holy letters*, or *the law and the prophets*, ($\gamma\varrho\acute{\alpha}\varphi\eta$,[*] or $\acute{\eta}\ \gamma\varrho\acute{\alpha}\varphi\eta$,[†] or $\alpha\iota\ \gamma\varrho\alpha\varphi\alpha\iota$,[‡] or $\acute{o}\ \nu\acute{o}\mu o\varsigma\ \varkappa\alpha\acute{\iota}\ o\iota\ \pi\varrho o\varphi\acute{\eta}\tau\alpha\iota$,[§] or $\tau\acute{\alpha}\ \mathcal{\iota}\varepsilon\varrho\alpha\ \gamma\varrho\acute{\alpha}\mu\mu\alpha\tau\alpha$).[||] They were the 22 Sacred Books

---

[*] 2 Peter, 1–20; John, xix. 37.   [†] John x. 35; xvii. 12.

[‡] John v. 39.—Matt. xxi. 42; xxvi. 54—Rom. xv. 4—1 Cor. xv. 3.

[§] Acts xxiv. 14; Luke xvi. 29, 31, 17; Matt. v. 17, 18; John x. 34.   [||] 2 Tim. iii. 14, 15.

which the Jews received from their prophets, and about which they were perfectly agreed.*

This entire and perfect theopneusty of the Jewish Scriptures was so entirely, in the days of Jesus Christ, the doctrine of all this ancient people of God (as it was that of Jesus Christ, of Timothy, and of St. Paul), that we read this testimony of it in the Jewish general, Josephus (who had already attained to his thirtieth year,† at the epoch when the apostle Paul was writing his second epistle to Timothy). Never, says he, in speaking of "the 22 books"‡ of the Old Testament, which he calls τα ιδία τράμματα, as St. Paul here calls them τα ιερα γράμματα, "Never, although so many ages have already passed away, has any one dared either TO TAKE AWAY from it, or TO ADD to it, or TO TRANSPOSE any part of it ;§ for it is for ALL THE JEWS, as a thought born with them (ΠΑΣΙ δε συμφύτον ἐστιν), from their earliest infancy,‖ to call them THE INSTRUCTIONS OF GOD, to abide in them, and, if necessary, to die with joy to maintain them."

"They are given us (he says again) by the inspiration which comes from God (κατά τήν ἐπίπνοιαν τήν ἀπό τοῦ θεοῦ). But as to the other books composed after the time of Artaxerxes, they are not regarded as worthy of the same faith."¶

We do not cite these passages of Josephus here as an authority for our faith, but as a historical testimony, which shews us in what sense the Apostle Paul spoke, and which

* See Krebs & Lœsner or 2 Tim. iii. 15.

† He was born in the year 37. See his life. Edit. Aureliæ Allobr, p. 999.

‡ Against Appion, lib. 1, p. 1037. Δύο μόνα πρὸς τοῖς εἴκοσι βυβλία,

§ Οὔτε ΠΡΟΣΘΕΙΝΑΙ τις οὐδὲν, οὔτε ΑΦΕΛΕΙΝ αὐτῶν, οὔτε ΜΕΤΑΘΕΙΝΑΙ τετολμήκεν.

‖ Εὐθὺς ἐκ της πρώτῆς γενέσεως ὀνομάζειν αὐτα ΘΕΟΥ ΔΟΓΜΑΤΑ. According to others ; *from the first generation.*

¶ Πίστεως δε οὐχι ὁμοίας ἠξιωται.

22*

attests to us that in mentioning the Sacred letters (τά ἱερά γράμματα), and in saying that they are all *Theopneustic writings*, he would attest to us, that in his eyes, there was nothing in the Sacred books, which was not dictated by God.

Now, since the books of the New Testament are ἱερα γράμματα, *holy Scriptures, the Scripture, the holy letters*, as well as those of the Old ; since the Apostles have placed their writings, and St. Peter, for example, has placed ALL THE EPISTLES OF PAUL (πάσας τας ἐπιστολας), in the same rank as THE OTHER SCRIPTURES (ὡς καί τας λοιπας ΓΡΑΦΑΣ); we must infer thence that all is inspired of God, in all the sacred books of both the Old and the New Testament.

XXVIII. But if all the sacred books τά ἱερα γραμματα) are theopneustic, how can we recognise such or such a book as sacred, and another as not sacred ?

It is in a great measure a question altogether historical.

XXIX. Yet have not the Reformed Churches maintained that it was by the Holy Spirit that they recognised the divinity of the sacred books ; for example, the confession of faith of the Churches of France, does it not say in its fourth article, that, " we know these books are canonical, and a very sure rule for our faith, not so much by the common accord and consent of the Church, as by the testimony and persuasion of the Holy Spirit, which enables us to distinguish them from the other ecclesiastical books" ?

This maxim is perfectly true, if you apply it to the whole collection of the sacred books. In this sense the Bible is evidently a book αὐτόπιστος, which has need *only of itself* to produce belief in its divinity ; for to him who studies it " with sincerity and as before God",[*] it presents itself with evidence and by itself, as a miraculous

---

[*] 2 Cor. ii. 17.

book ; it reveals the secrets of the conscience ; it discerns the thoughts and intentions of the heart. It has foretold the future ; it has changed the face of the world ; it has converted souls ; it has created the church. It produces thus in the hearts of men, " a testimony and an interior persuasion of the Holy Spirit," which attests its inimitable divinity, independently of any human testimony. But we do not think that any one can confine himself to this mark, to discern such or such a book, such or such a chapter, such or such a verse of the word of God, and to establish its celestial origin. We ought to admit as divine the entire code of the Scriptures, before each of its parts can have proved to us by itself, that it is of God. It is not for us to judge this book ; it is this book that shall judge us.

XXX. Yet has not Luther said* in starting from a principle laid down by St. Paul† and by St. John,‡ that " the touchstone by which we may recognise certain Scriptures as divine, is this ; do they preach Christ, or do they not preach him ?" And, among the moderns, has not Dr. Twesten said " that the different parts of the Scriptures are more or less inspired, just in proportion as they partake of the character of *preaching ;* and that inspiration extends to words and historical statements only in that which relates to the christian conscience, in that which comes from Christ, or that which serves to show us Christ" ?‖

Christ is, without doubt, the way, the truth, and the life ; the spirit of prophecy without doubt, is the witness of Jesus :¶ but this touchstone in our hands, may indicate falsely : 1st, because many writings speak admirably of

* In his preface to James and Jude.
† 1 Cor. iii. 9, 10. 1 John, iv. 2.
‡ Ob sie Christum treiben, oder nicht.
‖ Vorlesungen über die Dogmatik, 1829, I. B. p. 421–429.
¶ John xiv. 6. Rev. xix. 10.

Christ, without being inspired; 2dly, because although every thing, in the inspired Scriptures, relates to Jesus Christ, we cannot at first, detect this divine character; and, 3dly, in fine; because we ought to BELIEVE, before SEEING it, that " all Scripture is profitable for doctrine, for reproof, for correction, for instruction in righteousness; that the man of God may be perfect, thoroughly furnished unto every good work."[*]

XXXI. What reasons have we then for recognising as sacred, the books which now form the collection of the Scriptures?

For the Old Testament, we have the testimony of the Jewish Church; and for the New Testament, the testimony of the Universal Church.

XXXII. What are we here to understand by the testimony of the Jewish Church?

We must understand the consent of all the Jews, Egyptians and Syrians, Asiatics and Europeans, Sadducees and Pharisees,[†] ancient and modern, good and bad.

XXXIII. What reason have we for holding as divine, the books of the Old Testament, which the Jewish Church has given us as such?

It is written that "the oracles of God were committed to them :"[‡] which signifies that God, in his wisdom, chose them to be, under the almighty control of his providence, sure depositories of his written word.

XXXIV. Should our faith then depend on the Jews?

---

[*] 2 Tim. iii 16.

[†] See Josephus, against Appion, book 1. p. 1037.—Philo in Eichhorn.—Joseph in Nov. Repert., p. 239.—De Ægypticis Judæis. cf. Eichhorn. Einleit ins. A. T. P. I. § xxi. p. 73, 89, 91, 113, 114, 116.—De Sadducæis, § xxxv. p. 95.—Et Semler (App. ad liberal. V. T. interpret, p. 11.—Eichhorn., Allg. Bibl. der. bibl. Literal T. iv. p. 275, 276.

[‡] Romans iii. 2.

The Jews have often fallen into idolatry; they have denied the faith; they have killed their prophets; they have crucified the King of kings; they have hardened their hearts for nearly two thousand years; they have filled up the measure of their sins, and "wrath is come upon them to the uttermost."* Yet, "the oracles of God were committed to them;" and, although these oracles condemn them; although a veil remains upon their hearts when they read the Old Testament; † although they have, for ages, despised the word of God, and adored their Talmud; they HAVE NOT BEEN ABLE not to give us unharmed and complete the *book of the Scriptures ;* and the historian Josephus might yet say of them, that which he wrote of them eighteen hundred years ago: "after that so many ages have already passed away (τοσούτου γαρ αἰῶνος ἤδη παρωχηκότος,) no one, among the Jews, has dared to ADD, RETRENCH or TRANSPOSE any thing in the Holy Scriptures."‡

XXXV. What have then been the security, the cause and the means of this fidelity of the Jews?

We shall answer to this question very briefly. Its security has been the promise of God; its cause has been the providence of God; and its means has been the concurrence of the five following circumstances:

1st. The religion of the Jews, which has carried even to superstition, their respect for the letter of the Scriptures;

2d. The indefatigable labors of the Masorites, who have watched over it with so much care, even in its least accents;

3d. The rivalship of the Jewish sects, none of which would ever have authorized the unfaithfulness of the others;

---

* Thess. xi. 16. † 2 Cor. iii. 15. ‡ See this quotation at the xxvii. question.

4th. The extraordinary dispersion of this people into all the countries of the world, long before the destruction of Jerusalem; for "Moses of old time hath in every city, (pagan) them that preach him, being read in the synagogues every Sabbath day;"*

5th. Finally, the innumerable multitudes of the copies of the sacred book, scattered among all nations.

XXXVI. And as to the New Testament, what must we now understand by the testimony of the Catholic Church?

We must understand by it, the universal consent of the ancient and modern churches, Asiatic and European, good and bad, which call on the name of Jesus Christ; that is to say, not only the faithful sects of the blessed Reformation, but the Greek sect, the Arminian sect, the Syriac sect, the Roman sect, and the Unitarian sects.†

XXXVII. Should our faith then be founded upon the Catholic church?

All the churches have erred or have been liable to error. Many have denied the faith, persecuted Jesus Christ in his members, denied his divinity, annihilated his cross, reëstablished the worship of statues and of graven images, exalted the priests, shed the blood of the saints, prohibited the Scriptures to the people, destroyed by fire the people of God who desired to read them in their native tongue, established in the temple of God, him who sits there as God, overruled the Scriptures, worshiped traditions, made war on God, and cast the truth to the ground. Notwithstanding all this, the new oracles of God have been entrusted to them, as those of the Old

---

* Acts xv. 21. Josephus often attests the same fact.

† We believe that we may employ the name *Church* after the example of the Scriptures, as designating sometimes every thing gathered in the Gospel nets, sometimes only that which is pure and living. And as to the name *sect* (ἁιρεσις Acts xxiv. 14; xxvi. 5; xxviii. 21), after the example of the apostle, we employ it here neither in a good nor a bad sense.

Testament were to the Jews. And although these oracles condemn them, although they have for ages despised the Scriptures, and almost adored their traditions, they HAVE NOT BEEN ABLE not to give us unharmed and complete the book of the Scriptures of the New Testament; and we may say of them, that which Josephus has said of the Jews: "after that so many ages have passed away, never has any one in *the churches* dared to add any thing to or take anything from the holy Scriptures; they have been compelled, *in spite of themselves*, to transmit them to us in their integrity."

XXXVIII. Yet, has there not been, in Christianity, a powerful sect, which for three hundred years, has introduced into the canon of the Scriptures, apochryphal books, disavowed of the Jews,* (as even the pope Saint Gregory attests,)† and rejected by the fathers of the ancient church,‡ (as attests Saint Jerome ?§)

That, it is true, was done for the Latin sect, by the fifty-three persons who composed on the 8th April, 1546, the famous council of Trent, and who pretended to represent THE UNIVERSAL CHURCH OF JESUS CHRIST.‖ But they have done it only for the Old Testament, which was entrusted to the Jews, and not to the Christians. Neither this council, nor any of the churches, even the most cor-

---

* Josephus against App. liv. i. 8. Eusebius E. H. book iii. ch. 9, 10.

† Exposition of Job, Hist. of Counc. of Trent by Fra Paolo, tom. i. liv. 2, Sect. 47.

‡ Origen (Eusebius E. H. liv. iv. c. 26). Athanasius (Paschal letter). St. Hilary (prologue in Psalmos. p. 9, Paris, 1693). St. Epiphan., Lardner, vol. iv. p. 312. St. Gregory Nazianzen (Carm. 33, Op. tom. ii. p. 98).

§ Preface to book of Kings; or Prologo. Galeato. See Lardner, vol. 5, p. 16–22.

‖ Forty-eight bishops and five cardinals, all or almost all Italians. Fra Paolo, t. i. liv. 2, § 57.

rupted and the most idolatrous, HAVE EVER been able to add one single apochryphal book to the New Testament. It is thus the Jews HAVE NEVER BEEN ABLE to introduce a single human book into the Old Testament, and have ever excluded from it those which the fifty-three ecclesiastics of Trent have pretended to add to it in the name of the Universal church.

XXXIX. And what has been the security, the cause and the means of this fidelity of the Universal church in transmitting to us the oracles of God in the New Testament?

We shall answer this question briefly.

Its guarantee has been the promise of God; its cause has been the Providence of God, and its means has been especially the concurrence of the following circumstances:

1. The religion of the ancient christians, and their extraordinary respect for the sacred text; a respect which showed itself on every occasion, in their churches,* in their councils,† in their oaths,‡ and even in their domestic customs;§

2. The labors of learned men, in different ages, for the preservation of the sacred text;

3. The abundant quotations of the Scriptures made by the fathers of the church;

4. The mutual jealousy of the sects into which the Christian church has been subdivided;

* Photius contr. Manich., i. t. 1; apud Wolf. anecd., p. 32. sq.—J. Ciampini rom. vetera monum., i. p. 126, sq.

† Cyrill., Alex. in Apol. ad Theodos., imp. Act. Concil. ed. Mansi. t. vi. col. 579; vii. col. 6; ix. col. 187; xii. col. 1009, 1052, al.

‡ Corb. byz., i. p. 422, al.

§ See St. Jerome, pref. on Job. St. Chrysost. Hom. 19, *De Statuis.* The women, says he, were accustomed to suspend copies of the gospels on the necks of their children. See the 68th canon of the vi. Counc. in Trullo.

5. The versions made from the earliest ages in many ancient languages ;

6. The number and the abundant dissemination of the manuscripts of the New Testament ;

7. The dispersion of the new people of God, to the very extremities of Asia, and to the farthest limits of the west.

XL. Does it then result from these facts, that the authority of the Scriptures for us, is, as Bellarmin* has declared, founded upon that of the church ?

The doctors of Rome, it is true, have gone so far as to say that, without the testimony of the Church, the Scriptures would have no more authority than Titus Livy, than the Koran, or than the fables of Esop ;† and Bellarmin, having doubtless a horror of these impious sentences, has wished to distinguish the authority of the Scriptures *in itself* and *in reference to us* (quoad se et quoad nos). In this last sense, he says, the Scriptures have no authority but by the testimony of the Church. Our answer shall be very simple.

Every manifestation having three causes, an objective, a subjective, and an instrumental cause ; we may say also, that the knowledge which we receive of the authority of the Scriptures has first, for its *objective cause*, the Holy Bible itself, which proves its divinity by its own beauty and by its own works ; in the second place, for its *subjective* or efficient *cause*, the Holy Spirit,‡ which confirms and seals to our souls the testimony of God ; and thirdly, in fine, for its instrumental cause, the Church, not the Roman, nor the Greek, more ancient than the Roman,

* Lib. ii. de Conciliis, c. 12.

† Hosius contra Brentium, lib. iii. Eckius, de auth. Ecclesiæ. Bayle Tractat. i. catech. 9, 12. Andradius, lib. iii. Defens Conc. Trident. Stapleton adv. Whitaker, lib. i. c. 17.

‡ Isa. liv. 13, lix. 21.

23

nor even the Syrian, more ancient than both, but the universal Church.

The pious Saint Augustine expresses this threefold cause in his book against the epistle of Manicheus called *fundamenti.** Speaking of the time when he was yet a Manichean, he says,† "I should not have believed the Gospel, if I had not been led to it by the authority of the Church;" but he is careful to add: "Let us follow those who invite us to believe, at once, while we may not yet be in a condition to see; so that being rendered more capable by the very exercise of faith, we may deserve to comprehend what we now simply believe. Then it will no longer be man, it will be God himself within us, who will strengthen and illuminate our soul."

Here then the church is a servant, not a mistress; a depositary, not a judge. She exercises an office, not an authority; *ministerium, non magisterium.*† She gives her testimony, not her sentence. She discerns the canon of the Scriptures, she has not made it. She has recognised their authenticity, she has not constituted it. And as the men of Shechem believed in Jesus Christ, not from the report of the sinful, but penitent woman, who called them to him; so we say to the Church; now, we believe not because of thy saying; we have heard him ourselves, and know that this is indeed the Christ, the Savior of the world. We have believed then *per eam*, and not

---

* Edition of Mabillon, vol. viii.

† Evangelio non crederem (according to the African custom, for credidissem, as confess, lib. ii. c. 8: Si tunc amarem, for amavivissem) nisi me ecclesiæ commoveret (commovisset) authoritas (ch. 5.) Eos sequamur qui nos invitant priùs credere, quùm nondum valemus intueri, ut ipsâ fide valentiores facti, quod credimus intelligere mereamur, non jam hominibus, sed ipso Deo intrinsecùs mentem nostram firmante et illuminante (c. 14).— Opera August:, Paris, Mabillon, t. VIII.

‡ Turretin. Theol. elenct. vol. 1. loc. 2 ques. 6.

propter eam ; by means of her, and not because of her. We found her on her knees ; she showed us her master ; we have recognised him, and we have ourselves knelt with her. If I mingle in the last ranks of an imperial army, if I request them to point out to me their prince, to conduct me to him, they will do in respect to him, for me, what the Church does for the Scriptures. They will not call their regiment *the ecumenical army ;* and above all, they will not say that their emperor has authority by their testimony alone, whether as it regards themselves or us; whether it be *quoad se* or *quoad nos* (as says Bellarmin.) The authority of the Scriptures is in no way founded on the authority of the Church ; it is the Church which is founded on the authority of the Scriptures.

XLI. If the authenticity of the Scriptures is proved in a great measure by history, how is their Theopneusty then established ?

By the Scriptures alone.

XLII. But is such an argument rational ? Is it not begging the question, and is it not proving inspiration by inspiration ?

There would be a begging of the question, if, to prove that the Scriptures are inspired, we should invoke their own testimony, as if they were inspired. But we must beware of proceeding thus. We consider the Bible, first, simply as a historical document, worthy of our respect by its authenticity, and by means of which we may know the doctrine of Jesus Christ, as one would learn that of Socrates by the books of Plato, or that of Leibnitz, by the writings of Wolff. Now, this document declares to us in every page, that the whole system of the religion which it teaches, is founded on the great fact of a miraculous intervention of God in the revelation of its history, and of its doctrines.

The learned Michaëlis himself, whose views of inspiration are so lax, declares that the authenticity of the apostolic writings necessarily results from their inspiration.

There is no middle ground, says he; if their narrative is true, they are inspired; if they were not inspired they could not be sincere; but they are sincere; therefore they are inspired. There is then, nothing in such a train of reasoning that can wear the appearance of 'begging the question.'

XLIII. If it is by the Bible itself that the doctrine of a certain inspiration in the sacred books is established, how can it be proved that this inspiration is universal, and that it has extended even to the minutest details of their instructions?

If it is the Scriptures that teach us their own Theopneusty, it is they alone also that can teach us in what this Theopneusty consisted. To admit their inspiration, on their own testimony alone, we must be well assured that they are authentic; but to admit their full inspiration, something more is needful; for we can invoke their testimony as a witness already recognised as divine; they are no more merely authentic books, which shall say to us: I am inspired; they are authentic and inspired books, which shall say to us: I am altogether inspired. The Scriptures are *inspired*, we affirm, because, being authentic and true, they declare themselves inspired; but the Scriptures are also *plenarily inspired*, we add, because, being inspired, they say that they are so totally and without any exception.

It is then simply a doctrine that the Bible here teaches us, just as it teaches us all other doctrines. And just as we believe that Jesus Christ is God, and that he became man, because the Bible tells us so; thus also we believe that the Holy Spirit is God, and that he has dictated all the Scriptures.

XLIV. Who are the writers who have opposed the doctrine of inspiration?

Before enumerating them here, we ought to make a general observation ; it is that, with the alone exception of Theodore of Mopsuesta, that philosophical theologian, whose numerous writings, so deeply stained with Pelagianism, were condemned for their Nestorianism, in the fifth universal Council, (Constantinople, 553,) and whose principles on the subject of Theopneusty were very loose ; with the exception, we say, of Theodore of Mopsuesta, there cannot be cited, in the long course of the first EIGHT CENTURIES OF CHRISTIANITY, one single writer, who was ignorant of the plenary inspiration of the Scriptures ; if he is not in the bosom of the most violent heresies which have tormented the Christian Church ; I mean, among the Gnostics, the Manicheans, the Anomians, and the Mohammedans.   St. Jerome himself, who has sometimes indulged himself, when speaking of the style of certain parts of the sacred books, in a language, the temerity of which must be reproved by all pious men,* yet maintains, even for such passages, the entire inspiration of all the parts of the Holy Scriptures ;† and he sees even there, under what he ventures to call the grossness of the language, and the apparent folly of the reasonings, intentions of the Holy Spirit, full of skill and of depth.   And if, transporting ourselves from the days of St. Jerome to four hundred years later, we come to the celebrated Agobard, whom Dr. Du Pin pretends to make the first of the Fathers of the Church that have abandoned the doctrine of a verbal inspiration, ‡ it is quite unjustly, says Dr. Ruddelbach, that such an accusation is brought against that bishop.   It

---

* Qui solœcismos in verbis facit, qui non potest hyperbaton reddere sententiamque concludere.—(Comment. on Titus, lib. 1. ad cap. i. 1.)—and on Eph. lib. ii. (ad cap. iii. 1.)   See also his Comment. on Galatians.

† Proem. on Philemon ; Comment. on Galat. lib. ii.

‡ Du Pin of the Sorbonne, Proleg on Bible, lib. 1. v. 256.

23*

is true that, in disputing against the Abbey Fredegise,[*] concerning the latitude permitted to the Latin translators, in regard to the words of the sacred text, he maintained that the dignity of the word of God consists in the power of the meaning, and not in the pomp of the words; but he took care to add, that "the authority of the Apostles and Prophets remains unimpaired, and that it is not permitted to any one to believe that they could have placed a letter otherwise than they have done; because their authority is stronger than heaven and earth."[†]

If then we would arrange, in the order of time, the men who have set themselves against the entire theopneusty of our sacred books, we must place :

In the second century; the Gnostics, (Valentinius, Cerdon, Marcion his pupil, &c.,) they believed in two equal, independent principles, contrary and co-eternal, the one good and the other bad; the one, Father of Jesus Christ; the other, author of the law; and by maintaining this theory, they rejected the Pentateuch, while admitting, in the New Testament, the Gospel of Luke and one portion of the epistles of Paul.

In the third century; Maneus or Manicheus, who styling himself the paraclete, promised by Jesus Christ, corrected the books of the Christians, and added to them his own.

In the fourth century; the Anomians or ultra-arians (for Arius himself spoke more reservedly,) who maintained, with Aetius, their head, that the Son, a created intelligence, *unlike the Father*,[‡] inhabited 'a human body without a human soul. They spoke of the Scriptures with a degree of irreverence equivalent to the denial of their entire inspiration. "When they are pushed by Scripture reasons, says St. Epiphanus, they escape by this language:

[*] Agobard, adv. Fredeg., lib. c. 9—12.

[†] Rudelbach, Zeitschrift, 1st number, 1840, page 48.

[‡] Ανομοις; thence their names.

It is as man that the Apostle has said these things or those :" " why do you oppose to me the Old Testament ?" What adds the holy bishop ? " It was a necessary consequence," says he, " that those who deny the glory of Christ, deny still more that of the Apostles."*

In the fifth century ; Theodore of Mopsuesta, head of the school of Antioch, 'an able philosopher and a learned theologian, but rash. Of his numerous works, there remain to us only fragments preserved by different authors. His books, we have said, were condemned (two hundred years after his death,) at the council of Constantinople. They cited, there, for example, his writings against Appoloniarius, when he said, that the Book of Job is but a poem proceeding from a pagan heart :—that Solomon had without doubt received λόγον γνώσεως but not λογον σοφίας ; that the Canticles are but a long and insignificant epithlamium, without prophetic, historical, or scientific character, and in the style of the Sympasion of Plato, etc. etc. †

In the seventh century; Mohammed (whose false religion is rather a heresy of Christianity, and who speaks of Christ at least as honorably as do the greater part of the Socinians), Mohammed recognised and quoted often as inspired, the books of the Old and New Testament, but he pronounced them corrupt, and, like Maneus he added his own.

In the twelfth and thirteenth centuries; as it appears, there arose and was formally stated first among the Jewish talmudists, the theory of modern divines, who have chosen to classify different passages of the Holy Scriptures under different degrees of inspiration, and to reduce theopneusty to proportions more or less natural. It was under the

* Ephiphan., advers. hær. lxx, vi.—Aetii salutat. confut., vi.
† Acta concilii Constantinop. ii. collat. iv, 65, 71, apud Harduin. Acta concilii, tom. iii, p. 87—89.

double influence of the Aristotelian philosophy and of the theology of the Talmud, that the Jews of the middle ages, in this respect very different from the ancient Jews,* imagined this theory. It was in the time of Solomon Jarchi, David Kimchi, of the Averroes, of Aben-Ezra, Joseph Albo, and above all, of *Moses Maimonides*, that Spanish Jew who was called *the eagle among the learned.* Maimonides borrowing the vague terms of peripateticism, taught that prophecy is not the exclusive product of the action of the Holy Spirit; but that in the same manner when the *intellectus agens* (the intellectual influence in man) associates itself more intimately with the reason, it gives birth to the *secta sapientum speculatorum ;* and that when this agent operates on the imagination, there arises from it the *secta politicorum, legislatorum, divinatorum*, and *præstigiatorum ;* so likewise when this superior principle exerts its influence in a more perfect manner, and at once on these two faculties of the soul, it produces the *secta prophetarum.* Almost all the modern learned Jews have adopted the ideas of Maimonides; and this appears likewise to have been the modern theory of M. Schleiermacher on inspiration. It is by starting from these principles that the learned have admitted several degrees of inspiration in the prophets. Maimonides sometimes numbered eight, sometimes eleven. Joseph Albo reduced them to four, and Abarbanel to three. They applied these distinctions of the different degrees of inspiration to the division of the Old Testament into Law, Prophets and Hagiographies (תורה נביאים כתובים.) The *Kethubim*, according to him, had not received the spirit of prophecy (רוח נבואה) but only the Holy Spirit, (רוח הקדש),

---

* See Josephus against Appion, lib. i. c. 7, 8; and Philo, ed. Hæschel, p. 515 et p. 918.

which in his estimation was but a faculty of man, by which he uttered words of wisdom and holiness.*

The modern German School of the adversaries of inspiration appears then to be but a reproduction of the theory of the rabbins of the thirteenth century, or is merely borrowed from the Talmudist doctors of our day.

In the sixteenth century, Socinus,† and Castellio‡ maintained that the sacred writers failed sometimes in memory, and were liable to error on subjects of small importance.

In the seventeenth century, three ranks of adversaries according to the celebrated Turretin,§ fought against inspiration. There were beside the unbelievers properly called (*atheos et gentiles*); 1. the fanatics (enthusiastæ), who accused the Scriptures of imperfection, to exalt their own revelation; 2. the followers of the Pope, (*pontificii*) who feared not, said he, to betray the cause of Christianity, by alleging the corruption of the original text, (*fontium*) in order to raise their Vulgate translation; 3. rationalists of different classes, (*libertini*) who while remaining in the church, ceased not to shake the authority of the Scriptures, by objecting to difficult passages and apparent contradictions, ἄπορα καὶ ἐναντιωφανῆ.

In the last half of the eighteenth century, this third class of opponents increased greatly in Germany. Semler gave the first impulse to what he termed the liberal interpretation of the Scriptures; he put aside all inspiration, denied all prophecy, and regarded every miracle as allegory or exaggeration.‖ At a later period, Ammon established positive rules for this impious manner of explaining mi-

* Moses Maïmonides, more nebuchim, part ii, ch. 37 and 45. Rudelbach (ut supra), p. 53.

† De Author, Script.   ‡ In Dialogis.

§ Theol. elenctic., loc. 2, quæst. 5.

‖ Preface of the *Compendium de Schultens*, on the Proverbs, by Vogel. Halle, 1769, p. 5.

raculous facts.* A legion of writers equally rash, Paulus, Gabler, Schuster, Restig, and many others made an abundant practical application of these principles in their writings. Eichhorn, more recently, has reduced the rationalist doctrine of prophesy to a system.† Mr. de Wette, in his *preliminary manual* appears to have seen no real prediction in the prophets, and to discover no other difference between those of Israel and those of the pagan nations, than the spirit of morality and sincerity which characterises the monotheism, and which purified (he says) the Hebrew prophecies, while it was wanting in the *seers* among the Pagans.‡ Mr. Hug, in his introduction to the writings of the New Testament,§ says nothing about inspiration. Michaëlis admits it for one part of the Scriptures, and rejects it for the other. So did Le Clerc, in the last century. ‖ Rosenmüller is still more unequal.

In these latter years, however, among the Germans, the more respectful theologians have admitted different degrees of inspiration in the different parts of the Scriptures, distinguishing at the same time, the passages which, they say, do not relate to salvation; and pretending to see in them, as formerly did Socinus and Castellio, faults of memory and errors, on subjects, say they, of trivial importance.

Among the English, we have also recently seen men, otherwise respectable, permit themselves to rank under different classes of inspiration, the different sentences of the word of God.

XLV. Can we cite many illustrious writers in the

* De interpret, narrationum mirab, N.T.(preface to his Ernesti.)

† Einleitung in das Alte Testament; 4th edit. Gœting. 1824. tome. iv. p. 45.

‡ Zweyte verbessete Auflage. Berlin, 1822, p. 279, Lehrbuch. Ammerkungen.

§ Einleitung, etc·, 2d edit. 1821.

‖ Sentiments of some Dutch Theologians, Letter xi, xii. La Chambr. Traité de la Religion, tome iv. p. 159 and following.

church, who have maintained the plenary inspiration of the Scriptures ?

It is the uniform doctrine of THE ENTIRE CHURCH up to the days of the reformation. "Scarcely," says Rudelbach, "is there a single point in respect to which there has prevailed, in the first eight centuries of the Church, a greater and more cordial unanimity."*

We recommend to the reader desirous of seeing these historical testimonies, the dissertation recently published, upon this subject by the learned writer of Glauchau that we have just named. The author, first passing in review the first eight hundred years of the Christian era, establishes, by very numerous citations from the Greek and Latin fathers, the following principles:

1. The ancient Church teaches with a unanimous voice, that all the canonical writings of the Old and the New Testament ARE GIVEN BY THE HOLY SPIRIT of God; and that it is upon this foundation alone, and independently of the fragmentary understanding of them which human imperfection can acquire, that the Church based her faith in the perfection of the Scriptures.

2. The ancient Church, in consequence of this first principle, maintains as firmly the INFALLIBILITY of the Scriptures, as their *sufficiency* ($\alpha\dot{\upsilon}\tau\alpha\varrho\varkappa\epsilon\tilde{\iota}\alpha\nu$) and as their *plenitude.* She does not only attribute to their sacred authors the *axiopisty,* a credibility fully merited, but also the *autopisty,* that is to say, a right to be believed independently of their circumstances, or of their personal qualities, and on account of the infallibility and heavenly authority which has caused them to speak.

* Kaum istirgend ein Punct, worüber im Alterthume eine groessere und freudigere Einstimmigkeit herrschte. (Zeitschrift von Rudelbach und Guerike, 1840. 1st vol. p. 1 to 47: Die Lehre von der Inspiration der heiligen Schrift, mit Berücksichtigung der neüsten Untersuchungen darüber, von Schleiermacher, Twetsen und Steudel.)

3. The ancient Church considering all Scripture as the word of God addressed to man and dictated by the Holy Spirit, has always maintained, that in it is found NOTHING ERRONEOUS, nothing useless, nothing superfluous; and that in this divine work as in that of creation, we may always recognise in the midst of the richest abundance, the greatest and wisest economy. Each word then has its end, its design, its sphere of action. "*Nihil otiosum, nec sine signo, neque sine argumento, apud eum*" (Irenæus; πᾶν ῥῆμα . . . ἐργαζόμενον τό ἑαυτοῦ ἔργου" (Origen). It is in establishing and defending with power, both these features of the Scriptures, that the ancient Church has made known the high and the deep idea that she had of their theopneusty.

4. The ancient Church has always maintained that the doctrine of the Holy Scripture is EVERY WHERE THE SAME, and that the Spirit of the Lord proclaims one and the same testimony throughout. She has powerfully opposed this science falsely so called, (1 Tim. vi. 20), which alreadyin the first ages, presented itself in the doctrine of the Gnostics, and which, pretending to attribute imperfection to the Old Testament, imagined contradictions between one apostle and another.

5. The ancient Church believed that inspiration should, above all, be considered a passive state; and still, as a state in which the human faculties, FAR FROM BEING STIFLED or laid aside by the action of the Holy Spirit, were raised by its power, and filled with its light. She has often compared the souls of the apostles and prophets " to a stringed instrument, that the Holy Spirit should touch, and draw thence the divine harmony of life." (Athenagorus.)* " Their task was simply to present themselves to the powerful action of the Holy Spirit, so that his di-

* Legatio pro Christianis, c. 9.

vine plectrum descending from heaven upon the human viol, caused it to reveal to us the knowledge of the mysteries of heaven (Justin Martyr.")* But in their sight, this viol, passive as it was in respect to the action of God, was still a heart of man, a soul of man, an intellect of man, renewed by the Holy Spirit, and filled with divine life.

6. The ancient Church, while maintaining this continuous action of the Holy Spirit, in the composition of the Scriptures, powerfully repulsed the false notions that certain among the learned, chiefly among the Montanists, sought to propagate, concerning the active influence of the Spirit of God and the passive state of the spirit of man in the theopneusty; as if the prophet ceasing to be master of his senses, had been in the condition the pagans attribute to their sybils (μανία or ἔκστασει). While the Cataphrygians maintained that an inspired man loses his senses under the overwhelming influence of divine powers (*excidit sensu, obumbratus scilicet virtute divina*)† the ancient Church believed, on the contrary, that the prophet *does not speak in a state of ecstacy* (non loquitur in ἔκστασει), and that by this test we may distinguish true from false prophets. This was the doctrine of Origen against Celsus (lib. vii. c. 4); also of Miltiades, Tertullian, Epiphanus, Chrysostom, Basil and Jerome against the Montanists.

7. The ancient Church, seeking, by OTHER DEFINITIONS which we shall not point out here, to render the idea of theopneusty clearer, and relieve it of the difficulties by which it was sometimes obscured, showed again by this means how dear this doctrine was to her.

8. The ancient Church believed that, in order to

---

* Ad Græcos cohortatio, c. 8.

† Tertullian, adv. Marcion, lib. iv, ch. 22.

‡ Hieronym. Proem. in Nahum. Præfat. in Habacuc, in Esaiam. Epiphan, adv. hæreses, lib. 2. Hæres, 48. c. 3.

merit the name of the action of God, inspiration ought to extend TO THE WORDS, as well as the things.

9. The ancient Church,—by its constant mode of QUOTING the Scriptures, to establish and defend its doctrines;—by its manner also of expounding them and of COMMENTING on them;—and finally, by the USE of them which she recommends to all Christians without exception, as a privilege and a duty; the ancient Church by these three habits of her life, shows (still more strongly, if possible, than by direct declarations,) how profoundly she was attached to a verbal inspiration.

And it is not only by her exposition of the word, that the ancient church shows us to what point the entire inspiration of the Scriptures was for her an indisputable axiom; she shall show it to you still more strongly, if you will follow her in her attempts to RECONCILE THE APPARENT CONTRADICTIONS in the gospel narratives. Whenever she attempts an explanation, she does not insist on it; but she hastens to conclude that, whatever the value of her explanation, a reconciliation of these passages exists necessarily, and that the difficulty is only apparent; because its origin is in our ignorance, and not in the Scriptures. " Whether it be so, or not (says she with Julius Africanus), is of no moment, the gospel remains entirely true (τό μέντοι Ἐυαγγέλιον πάντως ἀληθεύει) !"* That is always her conclusion upon the perfect solubility of all the difficulties which may be found in the word of God.

10. The ancient Church was so strongly attached to the doctrine of the personality of the Holy Spirit, and of his sovereign action in the composition of all the Scriptures, that she never found any difficulty in admitting at the same time the greatest variety and the *greatest liberty*

* In his letter to Aristides; upon the harmony of the gospels relating the two genealogies of Christ. (Euseb. E. H. lib. i. c. 7).

in the phenomena, in the occasions, in the persons, in the
characters, and in all the exterior circumstances, under
the concurrence of which, this work of God was accomplished. At the same time that she recognised with St.
Paul that, in all the operations of this Spirit, "it is one
and the self same Spirit who divideth to every man
severally as he will;" (1 Cor. xi. 11), she equally
admits that, in the work of theopneusty, the divine effi-
ciency is exercised in the midst of great liberty in respect
to the human manifestations. And let it be well observed
that, in the ancient Church, you never see one class of
writers adopting one of these views (that of the divine
causality and sovereignty), and another class attaching
themselves exclusively to the other (that of human personality and of the diversity of the occasions, of the affections, of the lights, of the style and other circumstances
of the writer). "If it were thus," says Rudelbach, "one
might justly accuse us of having ourselves forced the
solution of the problem, instead of exposing with fidelity
the views of the ancient Church." But no; on the contrary, you will often see one and the same author exhibit
both these points of view at once and without scruple:
the action of God and the personality of man. This we
see, for example, in Jerome; who, in speaking of the
peculiarities of the sacred writers, is always fixed in the
notion of a word poured by God into their minds. This
we see again in Ireneus, who, while insisting more than
any other upon the action of God in the inspiration of the
Scriptures, is the first of the fathers of the Church who
relates to us in their details, the different personal circumstances of the evangelists. You will find the same in
Augustine; you will find it even in that father of ecclesiastical history, Eusebius of Cæsarea, who gives so many
details upon the few authors of the gospels; and who at
the same time avows, on the plenary inspiration of the
canonical Scriptures, the most rigorous principles.

11. The ancient church shows us still more completely by two other signs, her idea of inspiration ; on the one side, by the care she has taken to ESTABLISH THE RELATIONS of the doctrine of the theopneusty with the doctrine of the gifts of grace ; on the other, by the care she has taken to PRESENT THE PROOFS of inspiration.

12. Finally, if the ancient church presents this spontaneous (ungesuchte) and universal harmony in the doctrine of inspiration, it cannot be believed, as some imagine, that this great phenomenon belongs to some particular system of theology, or can be explained by such a system. Nor must this admirable harmony be regarded as the germ of a more complete theory which was afterwards to` establish itself in the church. No, the very oppositions which from time to time, were made by the heretics of the first centuries, and by THE NATURE OF THE ANSWERS which were made by the ancient Church, on the contrary, show us clearly that this doctrine was profoundly rooted in the conscience of the church. All the time that the fathers, in defending any truth by passages of the Bible, were forcing their adversaries to defend themselves only by denying the plenary inspiration of these divine testimonies, the Church has regarded the question as settled. The adversary assumed the place of a judge ; there was nothing more to say to him, he denied the Scriptures to be the word of God! what could be done, but show him the deformity of his own argument, and to say to him : see where you are ! as one shows to a man who has disfigured himself, his image in a glass. This is what the fathers have done.

Such are the facts ; such is the voice of the Church.

We had at first collected, with the intention of giving it here, a long series of passages, taken first from Ireneus,*

---

* Advers. hæreses, lib. ii, c. 47.—Lib. iii, c. 2.—Lib. iv, c. 34.

from Tertullian,* from Cyprian,† from Origen,‡ from Chrysostom,§ from Justin Martyr,‖ from Epiphanius,¶ from Augustine,** from Athanasius,†† from Hilary,‡‡ from Basil the great,§§ from Gregory the great,‖‖ from Gregory of Myssa,¶¶ from Theodoret,*** from Cyril of Alexandria,††† from the most esteemed Fathers of the succeeding ages; and finally from the holiest writers of the reformation.‡‡‡ But we have at once perceived that all these names, if we gave merely names, would present themselves

---

* De animâ, c. 28.—Advers. Marcion., lib. iv, c. 22. De Præscrip. adv. hæret., c. 25.—Advers. Hermog., c. 22.

† De opere et eleemos., p. 197-201.—Adv. Quirin., Adv. Judæos, præfat.

‡ Homil. xxxix in Jerem. (already quoted above, ch. iv, sect. 1.)—Homil. ii, in eumd. (cap. xix and L.)—Homil. xxv, in Math. —Ejusd. Philocalia, lib. iv.—Commentar. in Matthæum., p. 227-428. (edit. Huet.)—Homil. xxvii, on Numb.—In Levit., hom. v.

§ Homil. xlix on John.—Homil., xl, on John., v.—Homil., ix, on 2 Tim. iv.—Serm. 53, de util. lect. script.— 3. de Lazarod.

‖ Apol., I, c. 33 and 35, 50, 51.—Dialog. contr. Tryph., c. 7. —Ad Græcos cohort., c. 8.

¶ Σύντομος λόγος περὶ πιστεως—De Doct. Christi, lib. ii, c.9.—De Pastor., cap. 2.—Epist. xlii.

** Epist. xcvii, (ad Hieron.)—De unitate Ecclesiæ, c. iii, t. ix, p. 341 (Paris, 1694.)

†† Contra Gentes, t. I, p. 1.—De Incarnat. Christi (Paris, 1627.)

‡‡ Ad Constant. Aug., p. 244.—De Trinit., lib. viii, (Paris 1652).

§§ Comment. on Isa. t. I, p. 379 (ed. Bened.)—Hom. xxix advers. calumniantes S. Trinit.—In Ethicis regul. xvi, lxxx, cap. 22.

‖‖ Moralia in Job, præfat., c. i.

¶¶ Dialog. de animâ et resurr., tom. I, edit. græcolat., p. 639.— De cognit. Dei cit. ab Euthymio in Panoplia. Tit. viii.

*** Dial. I, Ατριπτ—Dial. II, Ασυγχυι—In Exod. Qu. xxvi. –In Gen., Qu. xlv.

††† Lib. vii, cont. Jul. Glaphyrorum in Gen., lib. ii.

‡‡‡ See Lardner, vol. II, p. 172, 488, 495.—Haldane, Insp. of H. Scrip., p. 167 to 176.

merely as a vain appeal to human authority ; and that if we gave them with their quotations, they would too much extend this chapter.

Eagerly then, we hasten to quote the greatest of teachers, our master Jesus Christ, and to make him heard when he speaks of the Scriptures, and above all, heard when he quotes them. Among the most ardent defenders of their verbal inspiration, we know no man who has ever expressed himself with more respect for the totally divine authority and permanence of their least expressions, than the man Jesus. And we do not fear to say that, if any modern writer should quote the Bible for the statement of some doctrine in the manner of Jesus Christ, he must immediately be ranked among the highest partisans of the doctrine we defend.

CHAPTER VI.

SCRIPTURAL PROOF OF THE THEOPNEUSTY.

LET us then open the Bible. What does it say of its own inspiration ?

SECTION I.—ALL SCRIPTURE IS THEOPNEUSTIC.

We shall begin by quoting again this passage so often repeated (2 Tim. iii. 16:) *all holy Scripture is Theopneustic*, that is to say, all is given by the Spirit or by the breath of God.

We have showed that this sentence admits neither of exception nor of restriction.

It admits not of exception ; it is the whole Scripture, all that *is written*, (πᾶσα γραφή) that is to say, the thoughts that have already put on the clothing of language. It admits of no restriction ; all Scripture is so far a work of God, that it is represented to us as given by the breath of God, in the same manner as the word of a man is given by the breath of his mouth. The prophet is the mouth of the Most High. The import of this declaration of St. Paul remains the same in both constructions of his language ; whether we place, as our version does, the affirmation of the phrase upon the word θεόπνευστος (*divinely inspired*), the verb understood (*all Scripture is given by inspiration of God, and is profitable, &c. ;*) or make θεόπνευστος only a determinative adjective, and confine the verb of affirmation to the following words, (all Scripture given by inspiration of God, is profitable, &c.) This last construction would give even more force than the former, to the Apostle's declaration. For then, his proposition, necessarily referring to the Holy letters, (τὰ ἱερα γράμματα) of which he had just spoken, would suppose as an admitted and incontestible principle, that to call them Holy letters, is to indicate thereby, that they are writings inspired by God.

It will be well however to draw this same truth from some other declaration of our sacred books.

SECTION II.—ALL THE WORDS OF THE PROPHETS ARE GIVEN BY GOD.

St. Peter, in his Second Epistle, at the close of the first chapter, speaks thus; "knowing this first, that no prophecy of the Scriptures is of any private interpretation. For the prophecy came not in old time by the will of man: but holy men of God spake as they were moved by the Holy Ghost."

Remark, on this passage :

1. That it here refers to *written* revelations, προφητεία γραφῆς, ;

2. That those who have given them to us, are called *holy men of God ;*

3. That *never* (οὐ πότε) did any one of these writings come by the impulse or the government of the *will of man ;*

4. That those holy men were impelled and borne by the Holy Spirit, when they wrote and spoke;

5. Finally, that these writings are called, *prophecy.*

Before advancing farther, it will be well to determine with precision, the Scripture meaning of these words; *prophecy, to prophesy, prophet,* (נבּיא) because this knowledge is indispensable to our investigation, and also throws great light over the whole question.

Varied and inaccurate meanings have been generally attached to the Bible term *prophet,* but an attentive examination of the passages in which it is used, will soon convince us that, in the Scriptures, it always designates— a man whose lips utter the word of God.

Among the Greeks, those who were first called by this name, were the interpreters and organs of the *prophecies* spoken in the temples (ἐξηγητὴς ἐνθέων μαντείων). This use of the term is eloquently expressed by a passage from Plato, in his Timæus.* The most celebrated prophets of pagan antiquity were those of Delphos. They conducted the pythoness, to the tripod, and were themselves commissioned to interpret and digest the oracles of their God. And it was afterward only by an extension of this first meaning, that the name of *prophet* was given by the Greeks to the poets, who, beginning their songs by the invocation of Apollo and the muses, were supposed to utter the language of the gods, and to speak under their inspiration.

A prophet, in the Bible, is then, a man in whose mouth God puts the word he would cause to be spoken to man ; and it was also in allusion to the plenitude of this sense, that God said to Moses ; " I have made thee a god to Pharaoh, and Aaron thy brother shall be thy prophet ;" (Exod. ii. 1,) as he had before said, (chap. iv. verse 16,) "He shall be to thee instead of a mouth, and thou shalt be to him instead of God."

Listen to the prophets in the Scriptures, as they testify of the Spirit which caused them to speak, and of the divine authority of their language. You will ever hear from them the same definition of their office and of their inspiration. They speak ; it is true, their voice is heard ; their frame is agitated, their very soul is often moved ; but their words proceed not from themselves alone ; they are at the same time, the words of the Most High. "The mouth of the Lord of hosts hath spoken ; the Most High hath spoken," say they unceasingly.† " I will open my mouth in the midst of them," says the Lord to his servant Eze-

---

* T. ix. Chap. Bipont., p. 392.

† Mic. iv. 4.—Jer. ix. 12 ; xiii. 13 ; xxx. 4 ; l. i ; li. 12.—Isa. viii. 11.—Amos, iii: 1.—Deut. xviii. 21, 22.

kiel. "The spirit of the Lord spake by me, and his word was in my tongue," said the royal psalmist,* "Hear the word of the Lord." It is thus that the prophets announce their messages†. "The word of the Lord was then upon me," say they often. "The word of God came unto Shemaiah;" "The word of God came to Matthew. The word came unto John in the wilderness.‡ The word that came to Jeremiah from the Lord; the word that was given to Jeremiah; the burden of the word of the Lord to Israel by Malachi;§ the word of the Lord that came unto Hosea;‖ in the second year of Darius the king, came the word of the Lord by Haggai the prophet;" this word descended on the men of God when it would, and often in the most unlooked for manner. Thus God, when he sent Moses, said to him; "I will be thy mouth;"¶ and when he made Balaam speak, he "put his word," it is written, "in the mouth of Balaam."** Thus the apostles, making, in their prayer, a quotation from David, express themselves in these words; it is THOU Lord, who HAST SPOKEN by the MOUTH of David thy servant.†† And St. Peter addressing the multitude of disciples: "men and brethren, it must needs be that this Scripture should be fulfilled, which the HOLY SPIRIT hath before spoken, BY THE MOUTH of David, concerning Judas."‡‡ Thus, the same apostle, declared to the people of Jerusalem, in Solomon's porch; "But those things which God BEFORE HAD SHOWED BY THE MOUTH OF ALL HIS PROPHETS, &c.§§

* 2 Sam. xxxiii. 1. 2.   † Isa. xxviii. 14.

‡ 1 King, xxi 22; 1 Chr. xvii. 3; Luke, iii. 2.

§ Jer. xi. 1; xiii. 1; xxi. 1; xxv. 1; xxvi. 1; xxvii. 1; xxx. 1; and frequently elsewhere.—See Isa. i. 2; Jer. i. 1, 2, 9, 14; Ezek. iii. 4, 10, 11; Hos. i. 1, 2; Malachi, i. 9; &c.

‖ Hos. i. 1, 2.   ¶ Exod. iv. 12, 15.

** ἐνέβαλεν (οἱ lxx.) Num. xxiii. 5.

†† Acts, iv. 25.

‡‡ Acts, i. 16.   §§ Acts, iii. 18.

To the Apostles, then, David in all his songs, and all
the prophets in their writings, whatever may have been
the pious emotions of their souls, were but the mouth of
the Holy Spirit. It was David, WHO SPOKE; they were
the prophets WHO ANNOUNCED, but it was God also WHO
SPOKE BY THE MOUTH of David, his servant; it was God
WHO HAD ANNOUNCED BY THE MOUTH of all his prophets.
And let this expression so often repeated in the Gospels,
and so conclusive, be carefully examined in the Greek:
" in order that that might be fulfilled which was spoken
OF THE LORD, BY THE PROPHET (ὑπό τοῦ κυρίου ΔΙΑ τοῦ
προφήτου,) saying,"* . . . It is in a sense altogether analogous, that the Holy Scriptures give the name of prophets to the lying imposters among the Gentiles, in the
temples of the false gods; whether they were vulgar
cheats, falsely pretending to divine visions; or were really
the mouth of an occult power, of a wicked angel, and of a
spirit of Python.†

And it is still in the same sense, that St. Paul in quoting
a verse from Epimenides, poet, priest, and divine, among
the Cretans, called him one of their prophets; because
all the Greeks consulted him as an oracle; and Nicias
went, on the part of the Athenians, to take him from
Crete, to purify their city; and Aristotle, Strabo,‡ Suidas §
and Diogenes Laertius,‖ tell us that he pretended to announce the future, and to discover unknown things.

From all these quotations, it remains thus established,
that in the language of the Scriptures, the prophecies are
" words of God, put into the mouth of men." It is thus
then, by an evident abuse, that, in the vulgar language,
some pretend to understand by this word, only a miracu-

---

*Mat. i. 22; ii. 5, 15, 23; xiii. 35; xxi. 4; xxviii. 35.

†Acts, xv. 6. See 1 Sam. xxviii. 7. 1 Chron. x. 13. Levit.
xix. 26, 31; xx. 26, 27. Isa. viii. 19.   ‡ Geogr. lib. x.

§ In voce, (Επίμεν.)   ‖ Vita Epimen.

lous *prediction.* The prophets could reveal the past as well as the future: they denounced the judgments of God, they interpreted his word; they sang his praises; they consoled his people; they exhorted souls to holiness; they rendered testimony to Jesus Christ. And as *no prophecy came by the will of man;** a prophet as we have already given to understand, was a prophet only by intervals, *and as the spirit made him speak.* (Acts, ii. 4.)

A man prophesied sometimes without anticipating it, sometimes again, without knowing it, and sometimes even without willing it.

I have said, without anticipating it; and often even at the very moment when he might be least expecting it. Such was the old prophet of Bethel. (1 Kings, xiii. 20.) I have said; without knowing it; such was Caiaphas. (John, xi. 51). I have finally said; without willing it. Such was Balaam, when wishing three times to curse Israel, he was thrice unable to utter any thing but blessings. (Numbers, xxiii. xxiv.)

We will give other examples of it, to complete the demonstration of what a prophecy is in general, and thus to arrive at a more full comprehension of the extent of the action of God in that which St. Peter calls *written prophecy.* (προφητείαν γραφῆς.)

We read in Numbers, xi. 25 to 29; that as soon as the Lord had caused the Spirit to rest on the seventy elders, "they prophesied;" but (it is added) "they did not continue." The Spirit came upon them in an unexpected moment; and after he had thus "spoken by them," and his word had been upon their tongue," (2 Sam. xxiii. 1, 2), they preserved no longer any thing of this miraculous gift, and were prophets only a day.

We read, in the 1st book of Samuel, (chap. x.) with what unexpected power, the spirit of the Lord seized the

---

* 2 Peter, i. 21.

young King Saul, at the moment when, seeking his father's asses, he met a company of prophets, who were coming down from the holy place: " What has happened to the son of Kish? they asked one another. Is Saul also among the prophets?"

We read in the eleventh chapter, something still more striking—Saul sends men to Rama to seize David; but immediately when they have met Samuel and the assembly of the prophets over whom he presided, the Spirit of the Lord comes upon these men of war; and " they also become prophets." Saul sends others; and " they also prophesy." Finally, Saul himself goes, " and he also prophesies, all that day and night, before Samuel." The Spirit of God, it is said, CAME UPON HIM." But it is particularly, by an attentive study of the twelfth and fourteenth chapters of the first Epistle to the Corinthians, that we arrive at the exact knowledge of what was the divine, and what the human action in the prophecy.

The apostle there lays down rules to the Corinthian Church, for the right employment of this miraculous gift. His counsel will shed great light on this important subject. The following facts will at once be recognised in this passage.

1. The Holy Spirit, at that time, conferred a great variety of gifts upon believers, for the general good (xii. 7, 10); to one, that of miracles; to another, that of healing; to another, the discerning of spirits; to another, the use of foreign languages, which the speaker himself did not understand, while uttering them; to another, the power of interpreting them; and to another, that of *prophesying*, that is, of speaking in his own language, words dictated by God.

2. One and the same Spirit distributed the divers miraculous powers at his own pleasure.*

* Verse 2. See also Eph. iv. 7; Act xix 1–6.

25

3. These gifts were a just subject of zeal and christian ambition (ζηλοῦτε, 1 Cor. xiv. 1, 39). But the gift which they were to regard as most desirable, was *that of prophesying;* for they might speak an unknown tongue, without edifying any one; and this miracle was rather useful to unbelievers than to believers; whilst the gift of prophesying edified, exhorted and consoled (1 Cor. xiv. 1–3).

4. This prophecy, that is to say, these words that descended miraculously upon the lips which the Holy Spirit had chosen for such an office, this prophecy put on very different forms. Sometimes an instruction; sometimes a revelation; sometimes too it was a miraculous interpretation of that which others had miraculously spoken in foreign tongues.*

5. There was evidently in these prophecies, a work of man and a work of God. They were the words of the Holy Spirit; but they were also the words of the prophet. It was God who spake; but in men, but by men, but for men; and you would there have found the sound of their voice; perhaps too the habitual turn of their style; perhaps too, allusions to their personal experience, to their present position, to their individuality.

6. These miraculous facts were continued in the primitive church during the long career of the apostles. Saint Paul, who wrote the letter to the Corinthians, twenty years after the death of Jesus Christ, speaks to them of these gifts as of a common and habitual order of things, which had existed then for sometime among them, and was still to continue.

7. The prophets, although they were the mouth of God, to announce his words, were yet not absolutely passive, while they were prophesying.

" The spirits of the prophets, says St. Paul, are subject

---

* Verses 26, 31, and Sam. x. 6; xviii. 10.

to the prophets," (1 Cor. xiv. 32) : that is to say ; that the men of God, while the prophetical word was upon their lips, could yet prevent the utterance of it, by the repressive action of their own will ; almost as a man suspends, when he chooses, the otherwise almost involuntary course of his respiration. Thus, for example, if *some revelation* came down upon one who was sitting in the assembly, " the first who was speaking, must cease, and be re-seated to give place to him."

Let us now apply these principles and these facts to the prophecy of Scripture (τῇ προφητείᾳ γραφῆς), and to the passage of St. Peter, for the exposition of which, we have brought them forward.

" No prophecy of the Scripture, he says, is of any private interpretation ; for the prophecy came not in old time, by the will of man ; (2 Peter i. 21), but holy men of God spake as they were moved by the Holy Ghost."

See then the full and entire inspiration of the Scriptures clearly established by the apostle ; see the Scriptures compared to those prophecies which we have just been defining. They " came not by the will of man," they were entirely dictated by the Holy Spirit ; they give the very words of God ; they are entirely (ἔνθεος and θεόπνευστος) given by the breath of God. Who would then dare, after such declarations, to maintain, that the expressions in the Scriptures are not inspired ? They are WRITTEN PROPHECIES (πᾶσα προφητεία γραφῆς). One only difficulty can then be presented to our conclusion. The testimony and the reasoning upon which it rests, are so conclusive, that there is no escape but by this objection : we agree it may be said, *that the written prophecy* (προφητεία γραφῆς) has without contradiction, been composed by that power of the Holy Spirit, which operated in the prophets ; but the rest of the book, as also the Epistles, the Gospels and Acts, the Proverbs, the book of

Kings, and so many others purely historical, have no claim to be placed in the same rank.

Let us then stop here ; and before replying, let us see first, how far our argument has been carried.

It should already be admitted, that at least *all that part of the Bible* called PROPHECY, whatever it may be, was *completely* dictated *by God;* so that the very words, as well as the thoughts, were given by him.

But then, who will allow us to establish a distinction between any one book whatever, and the other books of the Bible ? Is not every thing in it given by prophecy ? Yes, without doubt, every thing there is equally dictated by God ; this we are now to prove.

SECTION III.—ALL THE SCRIPTURES OF THE OLD TESTAMENT ARE PROPHETIC.

And first ; all the Scriptures are indiscriminately called, THE WORD OF GOD. This title at once by itself, would be sufficient to show us that, if Isaiah commenced his prophecies by inviting the heavens and the earth to hear, because the Lord hath spoken ; (Isa. i. 2,) the same summons should address us from all the books of the Bible ; because they are all called, "the Word of God." "Hear, O heavens, and thou earth, attend ; for the Lord hath spoken !"

We can no where find a single passage which permits us to detach one of its parts from the others, as less divine than they. To say, that the entire book "is the word of God ;" is it not to attest that the very phrases of which it is composed, were dictated by him ?

Now the entire Bible is not only named the " word of God" (ὁ λόγος τοῦ θεοῦ); it is called without distinction, THE ORACLES OF GOD (τά λόγια τοῦ θεοῦ). (Romans iii. 2.) Who does not know what the oracles were, in the opinions of the ancients ? Was there then a single word which could express more absolutely a complete and verbal inspiration ? And as if this term employed by St. Paul, did not suffice, we again hear Stephen, "filled with the Holy Ghost," call them LIVING ORACLES (λόγια ζῶντα) ; "Moses, says he, received the living oracles, to give them to us." (Acts vii. 38.) All the Scriptures, without exception, are then a continued word of God ; they are his miraculous voice ; they are written prophecies, and his living oracles. Which of their different parts would you then dare to retrench ? The apostles often divide them *into two parts*, when they call them "Moses and the Prophets." Jesus Christ divided them *into three parts* * when he said to his apostles, "All things which are written concerning me in Moses, the Prophets, and the Psalms, must be fulfilled." From this division, in which our Lord conformed to the language of his time, the Old Testament was composed of these three parts ; Moses, the Prophets and the Psalms ; as the New Testament consists of the Gospels, the Acts, the Epistles and the Apocalypse. Which then of these parts of the Old Testament, or which of these four parts of the New, would you dare to separate *from the prophetic Scriptures* (προφητείας γραφῆς) or from the inspired word (ἔνθεου λόγου—γραφῆς θεόπνευστοῦ) ?

Would it be Moses ? But what is there more holy or more divine in all the Old Testament, than the writings of that man of God ? He was so great a prophet, that his holy books are placed above all the rest, and are called by way of distinction, THE LAW. He was so fully a prophet, that another prophet, in speaking of his books alone, said: "The law of the Lord is perfect ; (Ps. xix. 7,) the words of the Lord are pure words ; they are silver refined in a furnace, seven times purified." (Ps. xii. 6). He was so much a prophet, that he compares himself to nothing less than the Son of God. It is this Moses, who said to the

* Luke xxiv. 44.

25*

children of Israel: "The Lord our God will raise you up
a PROPHET LIKE UNTO ME, from among your brethren;
hear him." (Acts vii. 37)! He was so much a prophet,
that he was accustomed to preface his orders with these
words: "Thus saith the Lord." He was so much a
prophet, that God had said to him: "Who hath made
man's mouth, or who maketh the dumb, . . . have not I,
the Lord? Now therefore go, and I will be with thy
mouth, and teach thee what thou shalt say." (Exod. iv.
11, 12). He was finally, so much a prophet, that it is
written: "And there arose not a prophet since in Israel,
whom the Lord knew face to face." (Deut. xxxiv. 10.)

What other part of the Old Testament would you exclude from the prophetic Scriptures? Would it be the
second; that which Jesus Christ calls the Prophets, and
which comprehends all the Old Testament except Moses and the Psalms, and sometimes includes even the
Psalms? It is worthy of remark that Jesus Christ,
and the apostles, and all the people, habitually applied
the title of *Prophets, to all the authors* of the Old Testament. Their habitual designation of the entire Scriptures
was: "Moses and the Prophets." (Luke xxiv. 25, 27,
44. Matt. v. 17; vii. 12; xi. 13; xii. 40. Luke xvi.
16, 29, 37; xx. 42. Acts i. 20; iii. 20; x. 5; &c. &c.)
Jesus Christ called all their books, *the Prophets.* They
were prophets. Joshua then was as fully a prophet of
the Lord as Isaiah, Jeremiah, Ezekiel, Hosea, Daniel and
all the others, even to Malachi. All of them wrote then
the *prophetic writings* ($\pi\varrho o\varphi\eta\tau\epsilon\iota\alpha\nu\ \gamma\varrho\alpha\varphi\tilde{\eta}\varsigma$); all of them
wrote the words of which St. Peter tells us: "that none
of them spoke by the will of man;" all those ($\iota\epsilon\varrho\alpha$
$\gamma\varrho\dot\alpha\mu\mu\alpha\tau\alpha$), those "Holy letters," which the apostle declares, "divinely inspired."* The Lord said of them all,
as of Jeremiah: "Lo, I have put my words in thy

* 2 Tim. iii. 15.

mouth ;"* and of Ezekiel : "Son of man, go, and speak MY words to them, speak to them, and say to them, that the Lord, the Eternal HATH THUS SPOKEN !"†

And that all the phrases, all the words were given them by God, is shown clearly by a fact stated more than once, and which the study of their writings places before our eyes ; to wit, that they were charged with transmitting to the Church, oracles whose meaning remained still veiled to them. Daniel, for example, declares more than once, that he was unable to seize the prophetical sense of the words that he uttered or wrote.‡ The types, imprinted by God on all the events of the primitive history, could not be recognised, until many ages after the existence of the men charged with relating to us their features ; and the Holy Spirit declares to us, that the prophets, after having written their holy pages, applied themselves to study them with the most respectful attention, as they had done the other Scriptures, searching WHAT THE SPIRIT OF CHRIST, which was in them, DID SIGNIFY, when he foretold the sufferings of Christ." § Do you see them, those men of God, bowed over their own writings ? They are there meditating the words of God and the thoughts of God. Are you astonished at it, since they have just been writing for the elect of the earth, and for the principalities and powers of heaven, ‖ the doctrines and the glories of the Son of God ; and since they are " things into which the angels desire to look " ?

. So much for Moses and the Prophets ; but can you say it of the Psalms ? Were they less given by the spirit of prophecy, than all the rest ? Are not the authors of the Psalms always called prophets ? ¶ And if they are some-

* Jer. i. 1, 2, 9.   † Ezek. iv. 10, 11.
‡ Dan. xii. 4, 8, 9; viii. 27; x. 8, 21.
§ 1 Peter i. 10, 11, 12.   ‖ Eph. iii. 10, 11.
¶ Matt. xiii. 35; for Asaph, Ps. lxxviii.

times, like Moses, distinguished from the other prophets, is it not evidently in order to assign them a more eminent place ? David was a prophet. (Acts ii. 3.) Hear him himself tell what he is: "The Spirit of the Lord has SPOKEN BY ME," says he, "and HIS WORD WAS UPON MY TONGUE." (2 Sam. xxiii. 1, 2.) Whatever David wrote, even his least words, were written by him, "SPEAKING BY THE HOLY SPIRIT," says our Lord, (Mark xii. 36.) The Apostles also, in quoting him, in their prayer, have taken pains to say: "That must be fulfilled which was spoken by the Holy Ghost through the mouth of David." (Acts i. 16.) "Who, by the mouth of thy servant David, hast said," (Acts iv. 25.) What do I say ? The Psalms were, to such a degree, dictated by the Holy Spirit, that the Jews, and that Jesus Christ himself, called them by the name of the LAW:* all their words made *law:* their least words were of God. "Is it not written in YOUR LAW ?" said Jesus Christ, in quoting them; and in quoting them even *for one single word,* as we shall presently be called to show.

All the Old Testament is then, in the scriptural sense of that expression, a PROPHETIC WRITING. ($\pi\varrho o\varphi\eta\tau\varepsilon\iota\alpha\ \gamma\varrho\alpha\varphi\tilde\eta\varsigma$.) It is then plenarily inspired of God; since, according to the testimony of Zacharias, "it is God who hath spoken by the mouth of his holy prophets, which have been since the world began;"† "and since," according to Peter, "the prophecy came not, in old time, by the will of man, but holy men of God spake as they were moved by the Holy Ghost."‡

It is true that, as yet, the preceding arguments, and the testimonies on which they are founded, directly regard only the Old Testament; and it may, perhaps, be object-

* John x. 35; xii. 34.
† Luke i. 7.
‡ 2 Peter i. 21. See also Matt. i. 21; xxii. 43; Mark xii. 36.

ed, that we have thus far proved nothing for the New. We shall commence, before replying, by asking if it is probable that the Lord would have given successive revelations to his people, and that, at the same time, the most recent and the most important of these revelations should be inferior to the first?

We will ask, if it would be rational to imagine that the first Testament, which contained only "the shadow of things to come," could have been dictated by God, in all its contents, while the second Testament, which presents to us the great object, the substance of the shadows, and which describe to us the works, the character, the person, and the very words of the Son of God, should be less inspired than the other. We will ask if it can be believed that the Epistles and the Gospels, destined to revoke many of the ordinances of Moses and the prophets, should be less divine than Moses and the prophets; and that the Old Testament should be entirely a word of God, whilst it was to be displaced, or, at least, modified and consummated, by a book, partly the word of man, and partly the word of God!

But there is no necessity for resorting to these powerful inductions, to establish the prophetical inspiration of the Gospel, and even its superiority to Moses and the prophets.

SECTION IV.—ALL THE SCRIPTURES OF THE NEW TESTAMENT ARE PROPHETICAL.

The Scripture, in its constant language, places the writers of the New Testament in the same rank with the prophets of the Old; and even, when it establishes any difference between them, it is always to place those that came last, above the first, as far as one word of God is superior (not in divinity, certainly, not in dignity, but in authority,) to the word which has preceded it.

Let the following passage of the Apostle Peter be particularly noticed. It is very important, as it shows us that, in the life-time of the Apostles, the book of the New Testament was already almost entirely formed, to make one alone with that of the Old. It was twenty or thirty years after the Pentecost, that St. Peter was pleased to quote " ALL *the Epistles of Paul,* his well beloved brother ; " and that he spoke of them as " sacred writings," which, already in his day, made part of the Holy Letters ($\ell\epsilon\rho\omega\nu$ $\gamma\rho\acute{\alpha}\mu\mu\alpha\tau\omega\nu$,) and were to be classed " with *the rest of the Scriptures,* ($\dot{\omega}\varsigma$ $\varkappa\alpha\iota$ $\tau\alpha\varsigma$ $\lambda o\iota\pi\grave{\alpha}\varsigma$ $\gamma\rho\acute{\alpha}\varphi\alpha\varsigma$.) He assigns them the same rank ; and he declares to them, that " ignorant men could not pervert them, but to their own destruction."

We quote this important passage, " Even as our beloved brother Paul also, according to the wisdom given unto him, hath written unto you ; as also in ALL HIS EPISTLES, speaking in them of these things ; in which are some things hard to be understood, which they that are unlearned and unstable, wrest, as they do also the other Scriptures, unto their own destruction."*

The Apostle in the second verse of the same chapter, had already represented himself and his fellow-apostles as occupying the same rank and invested with the same authority as the sacred writers of the old Testament, when he had said, " Remember the words which were *before* spoken by the Holy PROPHETS, and the commandments which you have received from US APOSTLES of the Lord and Savior." The writings of the Apostles were then, whatever those of the Old Testament were ; and since the latter are a WRITTEN PROPHECY, that is to say, a word entirely God's, the former are nothing less.

But we have said, the Scripture goes farther, in the rank which it assigns to the writers of the New Covenant.

* 2 Peter iii, 15, 16.

It teaches us to consider them as even superior to those of the ancient, by the importance of their *mission*, by the glory of the *promises*, which were made to them, by the greatness of the *gifts* conferred upon them, and finally by the eminence of the *rank* which is assigned them.

I. Let us first compare their *mission* with that of the ancient prophets; and we shall quickly see, by that alone, that their inspiration could not be inferior to that of their predecessors.

When Jesus sent forth the Apostles whom he had chosen, he said to them: "Go ye therefore, and teach all nations to observe all things whatsoever I have commanded you: and, lo, *I am with you* alway, even unto the end of the world. Amen."* "Ye shall receive power, after the Holy Ghost is come upon you: and ye shall be witnesses unto me, both in Jerusalem, and in all Judea, and in Samaria and unto the uttermost part of the earth."† Peace be unto you; *as* my Father *hath sent me,* even so *send I you.*‡

Such was their mission. They were the immediate *envoys* (ἀποστόλοι) of the Son of God; they went to all the nations; they had the assurance that their Master would be always present with the testimony which they were to render of him in the Holy Scriptures. Did they then need less inspiration when going to the very extremities of the earth, than the prophets needed in going to Israel; —when making disciples of all the nations, than the prophets in instructing only the Jews? Had they not to promulgate all the doctrines, all the ordinances and all the mysteries of the kingdom of God? Had they not to carry the keys of the kingdom of heaven, so that whatever they

---

* Matt. xxviii, 19, 20. † Acts i, 8.
‡ John xx, 21.

should bind or unbind on earth,* should be bound or unbound in heaven? Had not Jesus Christ conferred the Holy Spirit on them, expressly in order that whosesoever sins they should remit or retain, should be remitted or retained? Had he not breathed upon them, saying; " Receive ye the Holy Ghost?" Had they not revealed the unheard of character of the Word made flesh, and of the Creator stooping to assume the form of a creature, and even to die upon a cross? Had they not to repeat his inimitable words? Had they not to fulfil upon the earth, the miraculous, intransmissible functions of his representatives and of his ambassadors, as though it were Christ who spoke by them?† Were they not called to such a glory, that in the last and great regeneration, "when the Son of Man shall sit in the throne of his glory, they also shall sit upon twelve thrones, judging the twelve tribes of Israel"?‡ If then the prophetical spirit was necessary to the first men of God, in order to present the Messiah under shadows; was it not much more so to them, to produce him in the light of his actual life, and to set him forth as crucified in the midst of us ;§ so that whosoever rejects them, rejects him, and whosoever receives them receives him?"‖ Judge then from all these features of their mission, what must have been the inspiration of the New Testament, compared with that of the Old; and say if, whilst this was entirely and totally prophetic, that of the New could have been inferior to it.

II. But this is not all: let us again hear the promises which have been made to them, for the accomplishment of such a work. Words cannot declare it more forcibly. These promises were especially addressed to them on three great occasions: first, when they were sent for the first time to preach the kingdom of God ;¶ in the second place, when Jesus himself delivered public

---

* Matt. xviii. 18, xvi, 19.　† 2 Cor. v, 20.　‡ Matt. xix. 28.
§ Gal. iii. 1.　‖ Luke x. 16 ; Matt. x. 40.　¶ Matt, x. 19, 02.

discourses upon the gospel, before an immense crowd, assembled by myriads around him;* in the third place, when he uttered his last denunciation against Jerusalem and the Jews.†

"But when they deliver you up, take no thought HOW or WHAT (πῶς ἤ τί) ye shall speak; for it shall be given you in that same hour what ye shall speak. For it is NOT YE that speak, but the SPIRIT of your father which speaketh in you." "And when they bring you unto the synagogues, and unto magistrates and powers, take ye no thought, HOW or WHAT ye shall answer, or WHAT ye shall say. For the HOLY GHOST shall teach you IN THE SAME HOUR, what ye ought to say." "Take no thought beforehand, what ye shall speak, NEITHER DO YE PREMEDITATE; but WHATSOEVER shall be GIVEN you in that hour, that speak ye; for it is NOT YE THAT SPEAK, but the Holy Ghost."

On these different occasions, the Lord gives his disciples the assurance, that *the most entire inspiration* should control their language, in the most difficult and important moments of their ministry. When they should have to speak to princes, they were to exercise no solicitude; they were *not even to think upon it ;* because there should be then *immediately given* them of God, not only *the things,* which they should have to say, but also *the words* with which they should express them; not only τί but πῶς λαλήσονται. (Matt. x. 19, 20.) They were to rely entirely upon him; this should be given them by *Jesus ;* it should be given them *in the same* hour; it should be given them in such a way, and in such a plenitude, that then they might be able to say, it is NO MORE THEY, but the Holy Spirit, the SPIRIT OF THEIR FATHER speaking IN THEM; and that then also, it was not only wisdom

---

* Luke xii. 12. † Mark xiii. 11. Luke xxi. 14, 15.

that could not be gainsaid, which was given them; it was A
MOUTH !*

" Settle it therefore in your hearts, not to meditate before, what ye shall answer; for I will give you a mouth
and wisdom, which all your adversaries shall not be able
to gainsay nor resist."

Then, (as with the ancient prophets, Isaiah, Jeremiah,
Ezekiel,) it should be the Holy Spirit, who should speak
by them, as " God hath spoken by the mouth of all his
holy prophets, since the world began."†   In one sense, it
would indeed be *they* who would speak; but it would be
the Holy Spirit, (Luke xii. 12,) who should teach them,
in that same instant, what to say; so that, in another
sense, it would be the *Spirit* himself, speaking by their
lips.

We ask if it was possible, in any language, to express
more absolutely the most entire inspiration, and to declare with more precision, that the words themselves were
then guaranteed of God, and given to the Apostles.

It is very true that, in these promises, reference is not
directly made to the aid which the apostles were to receive
as writers, but rather to that which they were to expect,
when they should have to appear before priests, before
governors, and before kings. But is it not sufficiently
evident that, if the most entire inspiration was insured
them, for temporary occasions,‡ to stop the mouths of
some wicked men, to avert the dangers of the day, and to
secure interests of the smallest importance; yet if it was
promised them, that then the very words of their reply
should be given them, by a calm, powerful, but inexplicable operation of the Holy Spirit; is it not abundantly
evident, that the same aid could not be refused to these
same men, when they should have, like the ancient pro-

---

* Matt. x. 20. Mark xiii. 11. Luke xxi. 14, 15.
† Acts iii. 21. Luke i. 17.   ‡ 2 Pet. i. 21. 1 Cor. ii. 13.

phets, to continue the book of the oracles of God, to transmit to all ages the laws of the kingdom of heaven; to describe the glories of Jesus Christ, and the scenes of eternity? Could any one imagine that the very men who, before Ananias, or Festus, or Nero, were so much "the mouth of the Holy Spirit," that then "it was no more they that spake, but the Spirit;" should become, when writing "the eternal gospel," ordinary beings, merely enlightened, stripped of their former inspiration, speaking no more by the Holy Spirit, and employing thenceforward, only the words dictated by human wisdom? (θελήματι ἀνθρώπου, καὶ ἔν διδακτοῖς ἀνθρωπίνης σοφίας λόγοις.)* It is inadmissible.

III. See them commencing their apostolic ministry on the day of Pentecost; see what *gifts* they receive. Tongues of fire descend on their heads; they are filled with the Holy Spirit; they come down from their upper chamber, and all the people hear them proclaim, in fifteen different languages, the wonderful works of God; AS THE SPIRIT GIVES THEM UTTERANCE† they speak THE WORD OF GOD (ἐλάλουν τὸν λόγον τοῦ θεοῦ.)‡ Surely, then, *the words* of these unknown tongues must have been given them, as well as *the things*, the expression as well as the thought, the τί as well as the πῶς. (Matt. x. 19; Luke xii. 11.) Can we then suppose that the Spirit would have taken the pains to dictate thus to them all they should say, for preaching at the corners of the streets, for words which passed with their breath, and which reached, at most, only some thousands of men, whilst these very men, when they afterwards came to write, for all the ages of the Church, the "living oracles of God," should see themselves deprived of their former aid? Can we suppose, that after having been greater than the ancient pro-

---

* 2 Pet. i. 21; 1 Cor. ii. 13. † Acts ii. 2. ‡ Acts iv. 31.

phets, in order to preach in the public place; they were less than these prophets, and became ordinary men, when they took up the pen to complete the book of the prophecies, to write their Gospels, their Epistles, and the book of their Revelations? The inconsistency and inadmissibility of such a supposition is manifest.

4. But we have something to say here, still more simple and more peremptory: we mean to speak of the *rank* assigned them; and we shall be able to confine ourselves to this single fact, after having spoken of the prophets of the Old Testament. It is, that the Apostles were all PROPHETS, and more than PROPHETS. Their writings are then, WRITTEN PROPHECIES (προφητειϰαί γραφαι), as much as, and more than those of the Old Testament; and we are thus led to conclude yet once more; that all Scripture, in the New Testament, as in the Old, is inspired of God, even in its least parts.

I have said that the Apostles were all prophets. They declare so frequently. But, not to multiply quotations needlessly, we content ourselves here with an apeal to the two following passages of St. Paul.

The first is addressed to the Ephesians (iii, 4, 5,): "In the few words WHICH I WROTE afore, ye may understand my knowledge in the mystery of Christ, which in other ages was not made known unto the sons of men, as it is NOW revealed unto his holy APOSTLES and Prophets by his Spirit."

It is then clearly manifest here: the *apostle* and *prophet* Paul, the *apostles and prophets* Matthew, John, Jude, Peter, James, have received, by the Spirit, the revelation of the mystery of Christ, and they have written of it AS PROPHETS.

It is still of the same mystery and of the writings of the same prophets, that the same Apostle is speaking, in the second of the passages I have referred to; I mean, in the last chapter of his Epistle to the Romans.*

"Now to Him that is of power to stablish you according to my gospel, and the preaching of Jesus Christ (according to the revelation of the mystery, which was kept secret since the world began, but is now made manifest, and by the SCRIPTURES OF THE PROPHETS or prophetic writings;) (διά τε γραφῶν προφητικῶν), according to the commandment of the everlasting God, made known to all nations for the obedience of faith; to God the only wise, be glory through Jesus Christ, for ever, Amen."

Behold then again, the authors of the New Testament named PROPHETS; behold their writings called PROPHETIC WRITINGS (γραφαί προφητικαί), which is the synoneme of Peter's προφητεια γραφῆς. And since we have already recognised that no prophecy ever came from the personal and private will of him that attested it; but that it was, as moved by the Holy Ghost, that holy men of God spoke; the prophets of the New Testament have then spoken, as those of the Old, and according to the commandment of the Eternal God. They were all prophets.†

But even that is not enough; for, we have said they were MORE THAN PROPHETS. This is a remark of the learned Michaëlis.‡ In spite of his loose principles on the inspiration of a part of the New Testament, this observation has not escaped him. It is clear, according to him, from the context, that, in the sentence of Jesus Christ upon John the Baptist (Matt. xi. 9–11), the words *great* and *least* of the 11th verse, apply only to the name of *prophet*, which precedes them in the 9th verse; so that Jesus Christ there declares that if John the Baptist is *the*

* Rom. xvi. 25–27.

† See again Luke xi. 49.—Eph. ii. 20; iii. 5; iv. 11.—Gal. i 12.—1 Pet. i. 12.—1 Cor. xi. 23.—1 Thess. ii. 15.

‡ Introd., t. I. p. 118, French edit.

greatest of the prophets—if he is even *more than a prophet* —*the least of the prophets of the New Testament* is still greater than John the Baptist, that is to say, greater than the greatest of the prophets of the Old Testament.*

Moreover, this superiority of the *Apostles and Prophets* of the New Testament, is more than once attested to us in the apostolical writings. Wherever the various offices established in the churches are spoken of, the Apostles are placed before the Prophets. Thus, for example, in a very remarkable passage of his 1st Epistle to the Corinthians, where he aims to shew the gradation of excellence and dignity of the various miraculous powers bestowed by God on the primitive Church, the Apostle Paul thus expresses himself: " God hath set some in the church, *first*, APOSTLES ; *secondarily*, PROPHETS ; *thirdly*, TEACHERS ; after that, miracles ; then gifts of healing, helps, government, diversities of tongues."†

In the 4th chapter of his Epistle to the Ephesians, at the 11th verse, he again places the apostles ABOVE the prophets.

In the 2d chapter, 20th verse, he calls them APOSTLES AND PROPHETS. And in the 14th chapter of 1st Corinthians, he places himself ABOVE the prophets whom God had just raised up in that church. He desires that each of them, if he has truly obtained the Holy Spirit, should employ the gifts he has received, to recognise in Paul's words, God's commandments ; and he is so impressed with the assurance that what he writes is dictated by the inspiration of God, that after having given ORDERS to the churches, and having closed them with words which nothing but the highest inspiration can authorize, *Thus I ordain in all the Churches ;* he does more ; he goes on to rank himself ABOVE THE PROPHETS ; or rather, he him-

---

* Ibid, and Luke vii. 28—30.   † 1 Cor. xii. 28.

self as as a prophet, summons the spirit of prophecy in them, to recognise the words of Paul as the words of the Lord; and he closes with these remarkable words: "What! CAME the word of God out FROM YOU? or came it unto you only? If any man THINK himself to be A PROPHET, or SPIRITUAL,* let him acknowledge that the things that I WRITE UNTO YOU, are the COMMANDMENTS of the LORD."

The Apostles' writings are then, (as those of the ancient prophets), "commandments of the Eternal God;" they are "written prophecies, (προφητεία γραφῆς)" as much as the *Psalms, Moses, and the Prophets,* (Luke xxiv. 44); and all their authors might then say with Paul: CHRIST SPEAKETH BY ME, (2 Cor. xiii. 3; 1 Thess. 11, 13); my word is the word of God, and my discourses are taught me by the Holy Spirit, (1 Cor. ii. 13); just as David, before them, had said: "The Spirit of the Lord hath spoken by me, and his word was upon my tongue."†

Hear them too, when they themselves tell us what they are. Would it be possible to declare more clearly than they have done, that the words as well as the subject were given them by God? "As to us," they say, "*we have the mind of Christ,* (1 Cor. ii. 16); "for this cause also thank we God without ceasing, because, when ye received THE WORD OF GOD which ye heard of us, ye received it not as the word of men, but (as it is in truth) THE WORD OF GOD." (1 Thess. ii, 13.) "He, therefore, that despiseth, despiseth NOT MAN, but God, who also hath given unto us his Holy Spirit." (1 Thess. iv. 8.)

Such finally, then, is the word of the New Testament. It is like that of the Old, a word of prophets, and of greater prophets even than those who preceded them; so that,

* Πνευματικος. 1 Cor. xiv. 37.—See too xv. 45, and Jude 19.
† 2 Sam. xxiii. 2.

for example, as Michaëlis has very well remarked,* an
Epistle, which commences with the words: "Paul, an
APOSTLE of Jesus Christ,"† thereby attests to us more
strongly, its Divine authority and prophetic inspiration,
than did even the writings of the most illustrious prophets
of the Old Testament, when they opened their messages
with these words: "Thus saith the Lord ;‡ the vision of
Isaiah ; the word that Isaiah saw ;§ the word of Jeremiah,
to whom came the word of the Lord ;‖ hear the word of
the Lord ;"—or other analogous expressions. And if there
is, in the New Testament, a book in which similar in-
scriptions are not found, its theopneusty is no more thereby compromised than that of such or such a book of the
Old Testament (the second or ninety-fifth Psalm, for example), which, although the name of the prophet who
wrote them is not inscribed, are none the less quoted as
divine, by Jesus Christ and his apostles.¶

It may have been sometimes objected, that Luke and
Mark were not, properly speaking, apostles, and that consequently, they had not received the same inspiration as
the other sacred writers of the New Testament. They
were not apostles, it is true ; but they certainly were
prophets ; and they were even greater than the greatest
under the Old Testament. (Luke, vii, 28, 30.)

Without here insisting on the ancient traditions** which
say of both, that they were of the number of the seventy

* Introd. tom. 1, p. 118, 119, &c. French Edit.
† Rom. i. 1; Gal. i. 1; 1 Cor. i. 1, &c.; 1 Pet. i. 1; 2 Pet. i. 1;
‡ Isai. lvi. 1. ; xliii. 1, *et passim.*
§ Isai. i. 1; ii. 1, *et alibi.*
‖ Jer. i. 1, 2.
¶ Acts iv. 25 ; xiii. 33; Heb. i. 5; iii. 7, 17 ; v. 5; iv. 3, 7.
** Epiphan., Hæres., 51 and others.—Orig., De rectà in Deum
fide.—Doroth. in synopsi.—Procop. Diacon., apud Bolland., 25
april.

disciples whom Jesus first sent out to preach through
Judea, or at least of the hundred and twenty on whom
descended flames of the Holy Spirit, on the day of Pentecost, do we not know that the apostles had received the
power of conferring, by the laying on of hands, miraculous gifts on all who had believed, and that they used
this power in all the countries and in all the cities whither
they went ?   And since Luke and Mark were the companions in labor, that Paul and Peter chose from among so
many other prophets, is it not sufficiently manifest that these
two apostles must have called down upon such associates,
the gifts which they elsewhere bestowed upon so many
other believers ?   Do we not see Peter and John first
going down to Samaria, in order to confer these gifts on
the believers of that city ; then afterwards Peter coming
to pour them out at Cæsarea, upon all the pagans who had
heard the word, in the house of Cornelius the captain.*
Do we not see St. Paul bestowing them abundantly upon
the faithful of Corinth, upon those of Ephesus, and upon
those of Rome ?†   Do we not see him, before employing
his dear son Timothy as a fellow laborer, bringing down
upon him spiritual powers.‡   And is it not sufficiently
evident that Peter must have done as much for his dear
son Mark,§ as Paul for his companion Luke ?‖ Silas,
whom Paul had taken to accompany him, (as he took
Luke also, and John, surnamed Mark,) was a prophet in Jerusalem.¶   The prophets abounded in all these
primitive churches.   Many, we see, went down from
Jerusalem to Antioch ; there were a great number of them
at Corinth ; Judas and Silas were such in Jerusalem ;

* Acts viii. 15, 17; x, 45.
† Acts xix. 6, 7.—1 Cor. xii. 28; xiv.—Rom. i. 11; xv. 19, 29.
‡ 1 Tim. iv. 14.—2 Tim. i. 6.   § 1 Pet. v. 13.
‖ Acts xiii. 1; xvi. 10; xxvii. 1.—Rom. xvi. 21.—Col. iv. 14.
—2 Tim. iv. 11.—Phil. 24.—2 Cor. viii. 18.   ¶ Act. xv. 32.

Agabus was such in Judea; four virgins, still young, daughters of Philip the evangelist, were such in Cæsarea;[*] and we see in the Church of Antioch, many believers who were prophets and teachers;[†] among others, Barnabas (the first companion of Paul,) Simeon, Manahem, Saul of Tarsus himself, and finally that Lucius of Cyrene, who is supposed to be the Lucius whom Paul (in his epistle to the Romans) calls his kinsman,[‡] and whom (in his epistle to the Colossians) he names *Luke the physician*:[§] in a word, that St. Luke, whom the ancient Fathers have indifferently named Lucas, Lucius, and Lucanus.

It becomes then sufficiently evident, from the facts, that St. Luke and St. Mark were at least in the rank of those prophets whom the Lord had raised up in such great numbers in all the churches of the Jews and Gentiles; and that from among all the others, they were chosen by the Holy Spirit, to write, with the apostles, three of the sacred books of the New Testament.

But still further (and let it be well remarked), this prophetic authority of St. Mark and of St. Luke is very far from resting on mere suppositions. It is founded upon the very testimony of the apostles of Jesus Christ. It must not be forgotten, that it was under the protracted government of those men of God, that the divine canon of the Scriptures of the New Testament was collected and transmitted to all the Churches. By a remarkable effect of the Providence of God, the life of the greater part of the apostles was extended to a great number of years. St. Peter and St. Paul edified the Church of God for more than thirty-four years after the resurrection of their Master. St. John continued his ministry, in the pro-

---

[*] Act. xi. 38.—1 Cor. xii. 19, 20; xiv. 31, 39.—Act. xi. 28; xvi. 9, 10.

[†] Act. xiii. 1, 2.   [‡] Rom. xvi. 21.   [§] Col. iv. 14.

vince of Asia, in the heart of the Roman Empire, for even
more than thirty years yet after their death. The book
of Acts, which was written by St. Luke after his Gospel,*
had been already long circulated among the churches, (I
mean at least ten years) before the martyrdom of St.
Paul.

Now St. Paul, long even before going to Rome, had already made the gospel to abound from Jerusalem to Illyrium;† the apostles were in continual correspondence
with the christians of every country; they were every
day overwhelmed by the care of all the churches.‡ St.
Peter, in his second letter, written to the universal
Church of God, spoke to them already of ALL THE EPIS-
TLES of St. Paul, as incorporated with the Old Testament.
And for more than half a century, all 'the christian
churches were formed and guided under the superintendence of those men of God.

It is then, with the assent and under the prophetic government of those apostles commissioned to bind and to
unbind, and to be, after Christ, the twelve foundations of
the universal Church, that the *canon of the Scriptures*
was formed; and that the new people of God received its
" living oracles," to transmit them to us.§ And it is thus
that the gospel of Luke, that of Mark, and the book of
the Acts, have been received by common consent, under
the same titles, and with the same submission as the apostolic books of Matthew, of Paul, of Peter and of John.
These books have then for us the same authority as all the
others; and we are called to receive them equally, " not
as the word of men, but, as they are in truth, the word of
God, which effectually works in all those that believe."‖

We trust that these reflections will suffice to show how
unfounded is the distinction, which Michaëlis ¶ and other

---

* Acts i. 1.   † Rom. xv. 19.
‡ 2 Cor. xi. 28.   § Acts vii. 38.—Rom. iii. 2.
‖ 1 Thes. ii. 13.   ¶ Introd. tome i. p. 112 to 129 ed. Eng.

German writers have pretended to establish, in regard to inspiration, between these two Evangelists and the other writers of the New Testament. It even appears to us, that it is for the very purpose of preventing any such supposition, that Luke has taken pains to place at the head of his Gospel, the four verses which constitute its preface. In fact, you there see him placing the certainty and divinity of his history in strong contrast with the uncertainty and human character of the narrations *which a great number of persons* (πολλοί) *had undertaken to compose* (ἐπεχείρησαν ἀναταξασθαι), upon the evangelical facts, facts (adds he) RENDERED *perfectly certain among us*, that is to say, among the Apostles and Prophets of the New Testament (τῶν πεπληροφορημένων ἐν ἡμῖνπραγμάτων): the original word signifying the greatest degree of certainty; as may be seen, (Rom. iv. 21—xiv. 5, 2. 1 Tim. iv. 5, 17). *It seemed good also*, adds St. Luke, *having had perfect understanding of all things, from the very first*, (from on high) *to write unto thee in order.*[*]

St. Luke had obtained this knowledge from ABOVE; that is, by " the wisdom which cometh from on high and which had been given to him." It is very true that this last expression in this passage, is ordinarily understood to mean *from the beginning*, and as if, instead of the word ἄνωθεν (*from on high*), we had the same word απ' αρχῆς (*from the beginning*), which is in the second verse. But it has appeared to us that the opinion of Erasmus, of Gomar, of Henry, or Lightfoot, and of other commentators, should be preferred as more natural, and that we must here take

---

[*] Παρακολουθηκότι.—Thus Demosthenes, de Coronâ, t. 53 : Παρακολουθηκὼς τοῖς πράγμασιν dπ' ἄρχῆς.—Theophrast., Char. Proem., 4 : Σὸν δὶ παρακολουθῆσαὶ καὶ ειδῆσαι, ει ὀρθῶς λέγω.—Josephus, in the first lines of his book against Appion, opposes this same word, τὸν παρακολουθηκότα (*diligenter assecutum*), to τῷ πυνθανομένῳ (*sciscitanti ab aliis*).

the word ἄνωθεν in the same sense in which St. John and St. James have employed it, where they have said : "Every good gift cometh *from above* (James i. 7) ; thou shouldst have no power over me, except it were given thee *from on high* (John xix. 11) ; except a man be born again (*from on high*), he cannot see the kingdom of God (John iii. 3) ; the wisdom which cometh *from above* is first pure." (James iii. 15–17).

The prophet Luke had then obtained from on high, an exact knowledge of all things which Jesus began both to do and to teach, until the day he was taken up.

At the same time, whatever rendering of these words is preferred, it is by other arguments that we have shewed how Luke and Mark were prophets ; and how their writings, transmitted to the church by the authority of the Apostles, are themselves incorporated with those of the Apostles, as well as with all the other prophetic books of the eternal word of God.

Observe then precisely how far our argument has conducted us, and what the very authority of the Holy Scriptures has led us to recognise. It is first ; that the Theopneusty of the words of the prophets was entire ; that the Holy Spirit spake by them, and that the word of the Lord was upon their tongue. It is again—that all that has been written in the Bible, having been written by prophecy, all the sacred books are *Holy Letters* (ἱερα γράμματα) *written prophecies* (προφητεια γραφῆς), and *Scriptures divinely inspired* (γραφαι θεόπνευσται). Every thing then is of God.

In the meantime, let it be remembered (we wish to repeat it once more here, although we have already had more than one occasion to say it), that it is not necessary to suppose, among the prophets of the Old or of the New Testament, a state of excitement and of enthusiasm which carried them out of themselves : we must, on the contrary,

27

guard against such a thought.   The ancient church attached so great importance to this principle, that, under
the reign of the Emperor Commodus, according to Eusebius, Miltiades, the illustrious author of a christian Apology, "composed a book expressly to establish" against
Montanus and the false prophets of Phrygia, "*that the true
prophets ought to be masters of themselves, and ought not
to speak in ecstacy.*"*   The power of God was exercised
upon them, without taking them entirely out of their ordinary state.   " The spirits of the prophets," says St. Paul,
" are subject to the prophets. '†   Their intellectual faculties were then directed, and not suspended.   They knew,
they felt, they willed, they remembered, they comprehended, they approved.   They could say, " it hath seemed to me good to write;" and as the apostles, "it hath
seemed good to us and to the Holy Spirit to write."‡   And
then the words were given to them as well as the thoughts;
for, after all, words are but second thoughts, which relate
to the language, and which make from it select expressions.§   It is no easier and no more difficult to explain the
gift of the one than that of the others.

---

* Hist. Eccl., lib. iv. chap. 17.—'Εν ᾧ ἀποδείκνυσι περὶ τοῦ μηδεῖν
Προφήτην ἐν ἐκστάσει λαλεῖν.—See too Niceph., lib. iv. c. 24.—See
the same principles in Tertullian (against Marcion, lib. iv. chap.
·22); in Epiphanius (Adv. hæreses, lib, ii. hæres., 48, c. 3); in
Jerome (Proemium in Nahum.); in Basil the Great (Commentary
on Isa. proem., 5).

† 1 Cor. xiv. 32.   ‡ Act. i. 3 ; xv. 28.

§ We have translated our author here literally, because he has
not expressed himself clearly; and it is the only sentence of his
book which has appeared to us obscure.   If we may intrude our
own explanation, we would state that we think his views might be
thus expressed :   " The words were given as well as the thoughts;
for, after all, the words, that is the enunciation of the thoughts, is
also the product of a second effort of the mind after it has conceived
the thought; an effort which relates to the language, and which
consists in choosing from it appropriate expressions."   A friend
has furnished us this illustration of the author's idea.   Imagine

Yet there is something in reference to the Theopneusty, in the Holy Scriptures, which to us is still more impressive, if it be possible, than all the declarations of the apostles and of Jesus Christ himself; it is their examples.

SECTION V.—THE EXAMPLES OF THE APOSTLES AND OF THEIR MASTERS ATTEST THAT, FOR THEM, ALL THE WORDS OF THE HOLY BOOKS ARE GIVEN BY GOD.

Let it first be remembered what use the apostles themselves make of the word of God, and in what terms they quote it. See how then, they not only content themselves with saying, " *God says ;* * *the Holy Spirit has said ;* † *God says by such a prophet ;* " ‡ but see also when they quote it, how they esteem its least parts; with what respect they speak of it; with what attention they consider each of its words; with what religious assurance they often insist on one single word, to deduce from it the most serious consequences and the most fundamental doctrines.

For ourselves, we must avow, nothing impresses us so strongly as this consideration; nothing has produced in our soul so intimate and so powerful a confidence in the entire theopneusty of the Scriptures.

The preceding reasonings and the testimonies appear to us sufficient to carry conviction to all attentive minds;

these holy men commanded to contemplate a building, and to make an exact representation of it to men; and at the same time, plates engraved with a perfect image of it were given them; their sole duty being to paint them. That is plenary inspiration. The *building* of the house was the first effort of the architect, and the *representation* of it was the second effort of the same mind. None but God could construct the building; none but he could copy it infallibly. And he has done it.

* Eph. iv. 8; Heb. i. 8.

† Act. xiii. 16; xxviii. 25; Heb. iii. 1; x. 15, and elsewhere.

‡ Rom. ix. 25.

but we feel that, if we had a personal necessity of confirming our faith upon this truth, we should not go so far to seek our reasons ; it would be sufficient for us to inquire, how the apostles of God esteemed the Holy Scriptures. Was it, in their opinion, inspired ; was its language inspired ? What, for example, did Saint Paul think of it ? For we have no pretensions to be more enlightened theologians than those twelve men. We abide by the dogmatics of St. Peter, and the exegesis of St. Paul ; and of all the systems on the inspiration of the Scriptures, it is theirs which we are determined to prefer.

Hear the apostle Paul, when he quotes them, and when he comments on them. He then discusses their smallest expressions. Often, in order to draw from them the most important conclusions, he makes use of arguments which would be treated as puerile or absurd, if we had employed them before the doctors of the Socinian school. Such a respect for the words of the text, if we should be guilty of it, would send us back to the XVIth century, to its rude orthodoxy, to its superannuated theology. Remark with what reverence the apostle pauses at the·least expression ; with what confident expectation of the Church's submission, he there points out the employment of such a word in preference to any other; with what investigation and cordiality he presses out each word of it between his hands, even to the last drop.

Out of the multitude of examples which we might produce, let us for brevity's sake, confine ourselves to the Epistle to the Hebrews.

See in chapter xi. v. 8, how, after having quoted these words, " Thou hast put all things under his feet," the sacred author reasons from the authority of the word *all.*

See, in the 11th verse, how, in quoting the xxii. Psalm, he reasons from this word, *my brethren,* to derive from it the human nature which the Son of God was to assume.

See, in chapter xii. v. 27, how, in quoting the prophet Haggai, he reasons from the employment of this word; *once.* " Yet once."

See, in verses 5, 6, 7, 8 and 9, with what expansion he reasons from these words, " *my son,*" from the 3d chap. of Proverbs: " My son, despise not the chastening of the Lord."

See, in chap. x. how, in citing the xl. Psalm, he reasons from the words, " Lo! I come," opposed to the words, " Thou wouldest not."

See, in chap. viii. v. 8 to 13, how, in quoting Jeremiah xxxi. 31, he argues from the word *new.*

See, in chapter iii. v. 7 to 19, and iv. 1 to 11, with what earnestness, in quoting the xcvth Psalm, he argues from the word " *to-day,*" from the words " *I have sworn,*" and especially from the words " *my rest,*" illustrated by this other word of Genesis, " And God *rested* the seventh day."

See, in v. 2, 3, 4, 5, and 6, how he reasons from these words " *servant*" and " *house,*" borrowed from Numbers: " My servant Moses, who is faithful in all my house."

See, above all, in chapter x. the use which he makes successively of all the words of the cxth Psalm; observe how he takes up each expression, one after the other, to deduce from it the highest doctrines: " The Lord hath sworn;" " he hath sworn by himself;" " thou art a priest;" " thou art a priest forever;" " thou art a priest after the order of Melchizedec; " of Melchizedec king of Zedec; " and of Melchizedec king of Salem." The exposition of the doctrines contained in each one of these words, fills three chapters, the 5th, 6th, and 7th.

But I stop here. Is it possible not to conclude from such examples, that, for the holy apostle Paul, the Scriptures were inspired of God, even to the least important expressions? Let each of us then rank himself in the school of this man, "to whom was given the understanding of the mystery of Christ by the Spirit of God, as to a holy apostle and prophet.* We must, of necessity, either hold him for an enthusiast, and reject in his person the testimony of the holy Bible; or receive, with him, the precious and fruitful doctrine of the plenary inspiration of the Scriptures.

O! ye, who shall read these lines, in what school will ye then sit down? in that of the apostles, or in that of the doctors of our age? "If any man shall take away from the words of this book (I testify, says St. John,) God shall take away his part out of the book of life, and out of the holy city, and from the things which are written in this book." "And, if (says St. Paul) any man preach any other Gospel, let him be accursed."†

But again, let us leave the apostles, (prophets as they were, sent of God to establish his kingdom, pillars of the Church, mouths of the Holy Spirit, ambassadors of Jesus Christ;) let us leave them, for the moment, as if they were still too much enveloped in their Jewish traditions, and in their rustic prejudices; let us go to the Master. Let us ask him how he esteemed the Scriptures. This is the great question. The testimonies which we have just cited, are peremptory, without doubt; and the doctrine of a full and entire Theopneusty is as clearly taught in the Scriptures, as perhaps the resurrection of the dead; that alone is enough for us; but, notwithstanding, we will still avow it, here is an argument which renders all others superfluous to us:—How did Jesus Christ quote the Bible? what did he think of the letter of the Scriptures? what use did he make of it, he who is its object and inspirer, its beginning and its end, its first and its last—he, whose Holy Spirit, says St. Peter, animated all the prophets of the Old Tes-

* Eph. iii. 4, 5.   † Rev. xxii. 18. Gal. i. 8, 10.

tament—(1 Pet. ii. 11,) he, who was in heaven in the bosom of the Father, at the same time that he was seen here below, conversing among us, and preaching the Gospel to the poor ?   I am asked, what do you think of the Holy Letters ?   I reply, what did my Master think of them ? how did he quote them ? what use did he make of them ? what were their least parts to him ?

Oh ! tell them thyself, Eternal Wisdom, uncreated Word, Judge of judges ! and whilst we are going to repeat to them here the declarations of thy mouth, show them that majesty in which the Scriptures appeared to thee, that perfection which thou didst recognise in them, that permanence, above all, which thou hast assigned to their least iota, and which shall make them survive even the universe, after the heavens and the earth shall have passed !

We shall not hesitate to say it : when we hear the Son of God quote the Scriptures, everything is said for us upon their theopneusty ; we have no need of any other testimony.   All the declarations of the Bible are equally divine, without doubt ; but this example of the Savior of the world has told us all in a moment.   This proof requires no protracted nor profound research : the hand of a little child seizes it as powerfully as that of a man of learning.   If any doubt should then assail your soul, let it turn to the Lord of lords ; let it see him kneeling before the Scriptures !

Follow Jesus, in the days of his flesh.   With what grave and tender respect he constantly holds in his hands the " volume of the book," to quote all its parts, and to point out its least verses.

See how a word, a single word, whether of a song, or of a historical book, has for him the authority of a law. Observe with what confident submission he receives *all the Scriptures*, without even disputing their sacred canon ;

because he knows that "salvation is of the Jews," and
that, under the infallible providence of God, "the oracles
of God were committed to them." What do I say; that he
receives them? from his cradle to his tomb, and from his
resurrection from the tomb to his disappearance in the
clouds, what does he carry everywhere with him; in the
desert, in the temple, in the synagogue? What does he
still quote, in his resurrection-body, at the moment when
already the heavens are about to exclaim, "Lift up your
heads, ye everlasting gates, and let the King of glory enter"? It is the Bible; it is ever the Bible; it is Moses,
the Psalms, and the Prophets: he quotes them, he explains them; but how? it is verse by verse; it is word
after word!

In what a frightful and painful contrast, after such a
spectacle, do those misguided men present themselves to
us, who, in our day, dare to judge, to contradict, and to
try to mutilate the Scriptures!

We tremble, when we have followed with our eyes the
Son of Man, commanding the elements, stilling the tempest, and bursting the sepulchre, whilst, filled with so profound a respect for the sacred volume, he declared that
he was to return one day, to judge, from this book, the
living and the dead; we tremble, and our heart bleeds,
when afterwards, crossing the threshold of a rationalist
academy, we there see, seated in his professoral chair, a
poor mortal, a learned, miserable sinner, responsible, hand-
ling, without reverence, the word of his God; when we
follow him accomplishing this wretched task before young
men eager for instruction, as future guides of an entire
people, capable of so much good, if you lead them to the
high places of faith, and of so much evil, if you train
them to the contempt of those Scriptures which they are
one day to preach! With what peremptory decision they
exhibit the phantasmagoria of their hypotheses; they re-

trench, they add, they commend, they condemn; they pity the simplicity, which, reading the Bible as Jesus Christ read it, attaches itself, like him, to all the words, and can find no error in the word of God; they decide what interpolations or what retrenchments, (which Jesus Christ never suspected,) the holy Scriptures must have undergone; they purify the chapters which they have not understood; they point out mistakes in them, reasonings badly conducted or badly concluded, prejudices, imprudences, vulgar errors!

God forgive me for being obliged to write the words of this frightful dilemma; (but the alternative is inevitable!) Either Jesus Christ exaggerated and reasoned badly, when he thus quoted the Scriptures, or these imprudent and unhappy men, ignorantly blaspheme their divine majesty. It pains us to write these lines. God is our witness that we would willingly have withheld them, and then have blotted them out; but, we hesitate not to say with a profound feeling, it is in obedience, it is in charity, that they have been written. Alas! in a few years, these professors and their pupils will be sleeping in the same tomb; they must wither like the grass; but then not a tittle of this divine book shall have passed away; and as surely as the Bible is truth, and as it has changed the face of the world, so surely shall we see the Son of Man returning upon the clouds of Heaven, and "judging by this eternal word, the secret thoughts of men."[*]

" All flesh is grass, and all the glory of man is as the flower of grass: the grass withereth, and the flower thereof fadeth away; but the word of God abideth forever; and this is the word which is preached unto us;" it is this word which shall judge us. Now then, we are about to finish our proof, in reviewing, under this aspect, the ministry of Jesus Christ. Let us follow him from the

---

[*] Rom. ii. 16.   John xii. 48.   Matt., xxv. 31.

age of twelve years to his descent into the tomb, or rather to his disappearance in the clouds; and, in all the course of this incomparable career, let us see what the Scriptures were for Him, who "upholdeth all things by the word of his power."

See him first, at the age of twelve years. He has grown, as a human child, in wisdom and in stature; he is in the midst of the doctors, in the temple of Jerusalem; he ravishes, by his answers those who hear him; for "he knew, said one, the Scriptures without having studied them."*

See him, when he has commenced his ministry; behold him filled with the Holy Ghost; he is led to the desert, there to sustain, like the first Adam in Eden, a mysterious combat with the powers of darkness. The impure spirit dares to approach him, to overthrow him; but how shall the Son of God repel him; he who has come to destroy the works of Satan! only by the Bible. His sole weapon, in those encounters, the sword of the Spirit, in his divine hands, shall be the Bible. He shall quote, three times, the book of Deuteronomy.† At each new temptation, he, the Word made flesh, shall defend himself by a sentence of the oracles of God, and even by a sentence whose entire force lies in the employment of a single word, or of two words; first, of these words, (ἄρτῳ μόνῳ) *bread alone ;*—then of these words; *Thou shalt not tempt the Lord* (ὀυκ εχπεειράσεις Κύριον)—then finally, of these two words; (θεόν προςχυνήσεις) *thou shalt worship God.*

What an example for us! All his answer, all his defence, is this: "It is written;" "get thee behind me, Satan, for it is written;"—and as soon as the terrible and mysterious combat is closed, angels draw nigh to serve him.

* John vii. 13, 15.
† Deut. viii. 3; vii. 16; vi. 13; x. 20.—Matt. iv. 1-11.

But, observe, again, that such is for the Son of Man, the
authority of each word of the Scriptures, that the foul
spirit himself, that being so mighty in wickedness, who
knows what all the words of the Bible are in his
eyes, does not imagine a surer means of conquering his
will, than citing to him (but at the same time distort-
ing it) a verse of the xci. Psalm ; and immediately Jesus
Christ, to confound him, is content to reply again, "It is
written."

See how his sacerdotal ministry commenced ; by the
employment of the Scriptures. And see how his prophetic ministry is opened, immediately afterwards ; by
the employment of the Scriptures.

Let us again follow him, as engaged in his work, he
goes from place to place, to do good ; always enlisting in
his poverty his creating power, for imparting comfort to
others, never to himself. He speaks, and it is done ; he
casts out devils ; he calms the tempests ; he awakens the
dead. But, in the midst of all these grandeurs, see how
he estimates the Scriptures. The word is ever with him.
He bears it with respect, not in his hands, (he knows it
thoroughly), but in his memory and in his incomparable
heart. Behold him, when he speaks of it. When he un-
rols the sacred volume, it is as if he were opening the
window of heaven, to make us hear the voice of Jehovah.
With what reverence, with what submission he expounds
them, he comments on them, he quotes them word after
word ! Behold his entire employment ; to heal and to
preach the Scriptures ; as afterward, to die, and to accomplish the Scriptures !

Behold him who comes, "as he was wont," into a synagogue, on a Sabbath day ; "for he taught in their con-
gregations," it is said.* He enters that of Nazareth. What
will he do there ; he, "the Eternal Wisdom, possessed by

* Luke iv. 15, 16.

Jehovah in the beginning of his way, before his works of old, brought forth before the mountains were settled, before the hills ?* He shall rise to take the Bible; he shall open at Isaiah; he shall there read a few sentences; then, having closed the book, he shall sit down; and, as all eyes are fixed on him, he shall say, "This day, is this Scripture fulfilled in your hearing."†

See him, journeying through Galilee. What does he there? He is still holding in his hands, the volume of the book; and he is explaining it line after line, word after word; he holds up its most important expressions for our respect, as he would the law of "the Ten Commandments, pronounced on Sinai."

See him again in Jerusalem, before the pool of Bethsaida; what is he urging on the people? "Search the Scriptures!" (John v.)

See him in the holy place, in the midst of which he had dared to exclaim, "There is one here greater than the holy place," (Matt. xii. 26). Follow him before the Sadducees and Pharisees, whilst he alternately reproves them in these words, "It is written," as he had done to Satan.

Hear him replying to the Sadducees who denied the resurrection of the body. How does he refute them? By A SINGLE WORD from a HISTORICAL passage of the Bible; by a single verb in the present tense, instead of the same verb in the past tense. "Ye err," said he to them, "NOT KNOWING THE SCRIPTURES. Have ye not read what God has declared to you, saying: I am the God of Abraham?" Thus he proved to them the doctrine of the resurrection. God, upon Mount Sinai, four hundred years after the death of Abraham, said to Moses; not, "I was," but "I am the God of Abraham; I am so now, אנכי אלהי אברהם which the Holy Spirit renders: Ἐγώ εἰμι ὁ Θεὸς Ἀβραάμ

* Prov. viii. 22, 25.   † Luke, iv. 21.

There is then a resurrection; for God is not the God of some handful of dust, the God of the dead, the God of non-entity; he is the God of the living. " These men are then living with God."*

See him afterwards before the Pharisees. It is still by the letter of the word that he confounds them.

Some of them had already followed him to the borders of Judea, beyond Jordan, and had come to question him on the subject of marriage and divorce. What might Jesus Christ have done? He could surely have replied from his own authority, and have given his own laws. Is he not the King of kings and Lord of lords? But no; it is to the Bible he again appeals, to found here a doctrine; it is to the simple words, taken from an entirely historical passage of Genesis: HAVE YE NOT READ, that He who made them from the beginning, made them male and female; so that they are no more twain, but one flesh? What then God hath joined together, let not man put asunder.†

ᐧ But hear, above all, when in the temple, he would prove to other Pharisees, by the Scriptures, the divinity of the expected Messiah. He again insisted here, to demonstrate it, upon the use of A SINGLE WORD, which he was about to take from the book of the Psalms. " If the Messiah," said he to them, " is the Son of David, how did David, BY THE SPIRIT, call him LORD? when he says, (in Ps. cx.); the Lord said unto my Lord, Sit thou at my right hand? If then David calls him Lord, how is he his Son?" ‡

Why was there not some one of the Pharisees suggesting the ready reply which modern times have furnished: What! do you pretend to insist on a single word, and

* Matt. xxii. 31, 32.
† Gen. i. 27; ii. 24; Matt. xix. 4, 5, 6.
‡ Matt. xxii. 43.

28

more, upon a term borrowed from a poetry eminently lyrical, in which the royal Psalmist may, without injury, have employed a too vivid construction, exaggerated expressions, and words which he doubtless had not then logically weighed in his mind, before casting them into his verse? Would you follow the at once fanatical and servile method of a minute interpretation of each expression? Would you adore even to the letter of the Scriptures? Would you construct an entire doctrine upon a word?

Yes, I will, replies Jesus Christ; yes, I will support myself upon a word; because this word is of God, and because with one word he created the light. To cut all your objections short, I declare to you, that IT IS BY THE SPIRIT, that David wrote all the words of his Songs; and I ask you how, if the Messiah is his Son, David, BY THE SPIRIT, can call him his Lord, when he says: "the Lord said to my Lord"?

Students of the word of God, and you especially who are to be its ministers, and who, in order to prepare yourselves for preaching it, wish first to have received it into a good and honest heart, see what each saying, each word of the book of God was for our Master. Go, then, and do likewise!

But still farther. Hear him again, even on his cross. He was there pouring out his soul an offering for sin; all his bones were out of joint; he poured himself out like water; his heart was melted like wax within him; his tongue cleaved to the roof of his mouth;* he was about rendering up his spirit to his Father. But what did he first? He would gather all his remaining strength, to repeat a psalm which the Church of Israel had sung for a thousand years in her religious festivals, and which spoke successively all her griefs and all her prayers:

* Psalm xxii. 16—18.

" *Eli, Eli, lamma Sabachthani !* " (My God, my God, why hast thou forsaken me?) He did yet more: hear him. There remained yet in the Scriptures one unfulfilled word; they must yet give him vinegar upon that cross; the Holy Spirit had declared it a thousand years before, in the lxixth Psalm. "After this, knowing that all things were now accomplished, that the Scripture might be fulfilled, Jesus said, I thirst. And when Jesus had received the vinegar, he said, It is finished! and he bowed his head and gave up the ghost." *

Had David known whilst he was saying this 69th Psalm upon Shoshannim, and the 22d upon Ajeleth, the prophetical sense of each one of these words; of these hands and feet pierced, of this gaul poured out, of this vinegar, of these garments divided, of this robe taken by lot, of this mocking multitude, wagging the head and shooting out the lip? To us it matters little whether he understood it or not; the Holy Spirit at least understood it; and David was speaking by *the Spirit*, Jesus tells us. The heavens and the earth must pass; but there is not in this book a jot or tittle that can remain unaccomplished (John x, 35 ; xii. 34.)

Yet there is something still more striking, if it be possible. Jesus Christ rises from the tomb; he has vanquished death; he is about to return to the Father, to resume that glory which he had with the Father, before the world was. Follow him then in these rapid moments which he yet bestows on the earth. What words are to fall from his reänimated lips? They are words from the Holy Scriptures. Still he quotes them; he explains them; he preaches them still. See him first upon the road to Emmaus, journeying with Cleopas and his friend; afterwards, in the upper chamber; and still later upon the borders of the lake. What does he? he expounds the sacred books

* John xix. 28—30.

he begins at Moses, and continues through all the Prophets and the Psalms; he shows them what has been said concerning himself, in all the Scriptures; he opens their understandings, that they may comprehend; he makes their hearts burn while he opens up the Scriptures.*

But we have not finished. All these quotations show us what the Holy Bible was to Him in whom are hidden all the treasures of wisdom and knowledge, (Col. ii. 3,) and by whom all things consist. (Col. i. 1.) But let us hear again, upon the letter of the Scriptures, two declarations and one final example of our Lord.

"It is easier, says he, for heaven and earth to pass away, than for one tittle (κεραία) of the law to fail;"† and, by the law, Jesus Christ understood the body of the Scriptures, and, even more particularly the book of the Psalms.‡

What word could we imagine, which should express with more precision and more force, the principle that we defend, I mean, the authority, the entire theopneusty, and the permanence, of all the parts and of the very letter of the Scriptures? Students of the word of God, behold the theology of your Master. Be then theologians after his pattern; have the same Bible with the Son of God!

But let us hear yet another declaration. Our Lord made it in his Sermon on the Mount.

"Until heaven and earth pass away, not one jot or tittle shall pass *from the Law*. (Matt. v. 18.) All the words of the *Scriptures*, even to the smallest letter and the smallest part of a letter, are then, equivalent to the words of JESUS CHRIST; for he has also said; The heavens and the earth shall one day pass away, but MY words shall not pass. (Luke xxi- 33.)

Men who combat these doctrines, demand of us if we

---

* Luke xxiv. 27—44.
† Luke xvi. 17.   ‡ John x. 34; xii. 34.

dare pretend that the Holy Scriptures are a law of God, even in its words, as a hysop or an oak is a work of God, even to its leaves. We reply, with all the Fathers of the Church, Yes; or rather, Jesus Christ, our Savior and our Master, lifts his hands towards heaven, and replies: Yes, even in its "words; even to (ἰῶτα ἓν, ἢ μία κεραία) a single iota, or a single fragment of a letter!"

But, after these two declarations, let us finally consider a last example of our Lord, which we have not yet adduced.

It is still Jesus Christ who is going to quote the Scriptures, but in claiming, for their least word, such an authority, that we are obliged to rank him in the number of the most ardent partisans of the verbal inspiration, and that we think, that in searching through the writings of our most rigidly orthodox divines, there cannot be found the example of respect for the letter of the Scriptures and for the plentitude of their theopneusty carried farther.

It was on a day in winter, as Jesus was walking in the temple under the colonnade of the Eastern portico; the Jews surrounded him; and he then said to them (John x. 27); "I give eternal life to my sheep; they shall never perish; no one shall pluck them out of my hand; I and the Father are one." They were astonished at such language; but he became still more startling, until finally the Jews, crying out against the blasphemy, brought stones to kill him, and said to him: "We stone thee, because being man, thou makest thyself God."[*]

We would now call particular attention to the different features of the answer of Jesus Christ. He is about to quote one word taken from a hymn, and he is about to found all his doctrine on this single word; for "he made himself equal with God," says John in another place (v.

[*] John x. 27, et. seq.

28*

18). In order to sustain the sublimest and most mysterious of his doctrines, to legitimate his most unheard-of pretension, he supports himself on a word of the Psalm lxxxii. But, remark it well; before pronouncing this word, he is careful to interrupt himself; he pauses in a solemn parenthesis, and exclaims with authority : " *and the Scriptures cannot be broken*" (και ού δύναται λυθῆναι ή γράφη)!

Has this been sufficiently regarded ?   Not only is the Lord's argument here entirely founded upon the use made of a single word by the Psalmist; and not only is he going to erect on this single term, the most astounding of his doctrines; but also, in quoting thus the book of Psalms, to make us better comprehend, that in his view, the book is entirely a writing of the 'Holy Spirit, in which each word must serve to us as a law, Jesus calls it by the name of LAW, and he says to the Jews : " Is it not written in your law, I have said ye are gods?"   These words are placed in the middle of a song ; they might seem to have escaped from the unreflecting fervor of the prophet Asaph, or from the ardent strain of his poetry.   And if the plenary inspiration of *all that is written* were not admitted, we should be tempted to tax them with indiscretion, since the imprudent use which the Psalmist might have made of them, might have led the people to practices, condemned in other parts of the word of God, and to idolatrous thoughts.   Why then, yet once more, was there not found there, in Solomon's porch, some rationalist scribe of the Jewish universities, to say to him : " Lord, you cannot justify yourself by this expression?"   The use which Asaph made of it, could have been neither deliberate nor proper.   Although inspired in the thoughts of his piety, he certainly did not weigh his smallest word, with a minute forethought of the use which might be made of them a thousand years afterwards.   It would then be imprudent to pretend to insist on them.   But now, observe how our

Lord prevents the profane temerity of such an evasion. Behold him: he recollects himself with solemnity; he had just pronounced concerning himself words which would be blasphemous in the mouth of an archangel: " I and the Father are one ;" but he interrupts himself, and as soon as he has said : " Is it not written in your law, I have said, ye are gods"; he pauses, and fixing his eyes authoritatively upon the doctors who surround him, he exclaims : " AND THE SCRIPTURES CANNOT BE BROKEN." As if he had said : " Beware! there is not in the sacred books, a single word which can be reproved, nor one single word which can be neglected. That which I quote to you from the lxxxii Psalm, is traced by the hand which made the heavens. If then he would give the name of gods to men, inasmuch as they are christs, (anointed) and types of the true Christ, of the anointed, and in taking care at the same time immediately to suggest, " that they died as men ;" how much more appropriate is this name to me "the Father of eternity,* the Immanuel, the man-God, the Messiah, who do the works of my Father, and whom the Father hath marked with his seal ?"

We will then ask here of every serious reader, (and our argument, it should be well observed, is entirely independent of the orthodox meaning or of the Socinian meaning which may be given to these words of Jesus Christ); we will ask; is it possible to admit that the being who makes such a use of the Scriptures, DOES NOT BELIEVE IN THEIR PLENARY VERBAL INSPIRATION? And if he had believed that the words of the Bible had been left to the free choice and to the pious fantasies of the sacred writers, would he ever have broached the idea of founding such arguments upon the employment of such a word? The Lord Jesus, our Savior and our Judge, believed then in the most complete inspiration of the

* Isa. ix. 5; vii. 14.   John vi. 27.

Scriptures; and, for him, the first rule of all hermeneutics, and the beginning of all exegesis, was this simple maxim, applied to the least expressions of the written word: "AND THE SCRIPTURES CANNOT BE BROKEN."

Let the Prince of life, the light of the world, then rank us all in his school! What he has believed, let us receive. What he has respected, let us respect. This book, to all the words of which he has submitted his heart as a Savior, and all the thoughts of his holy humanity, let us press it to our diseased hearts, and submit to it all the thoughts of our fallen humanity. Let us seek God there in the least passages; let us plunge into it every day all the roots of our being, as the tree planted near the running waters, which gives its fruit in its season, and whose leaf never fades. Let us be, in a word, as the righteous man of the Psalms, "who takes his delight in the law of the Lord, so that he meditates therein day and night." Then the Holy Spirit, who wrote it, word after word, in his eternal book, will write it also, with his almighty fingers, upon the table of our hearts; and will there make us comprehend with efficacy these words of God our Savior: "Be thou healed, and be thou saved; go, son, thy sins are forgiven thee; thy faith hath saved thee; go in peace! All things are possible to him that believeth."

CHAPTER VII.

CONCLUSION.

But we must conclude.

From all that we have read, it results that there are in the world only two schools, or but two religions: that which places the Bible above every thing; and that which places something above the Bible. The first was evidently that of Jesus Christ; the second was that of the rationalists of all denominations and of all ages.

The motto of the first is this; all the written word is inspired of God, even to a single iota or title; the Scriptures cannot be broken.

The device of the second is this: there are human judges of the word of God.

Instead of placing the Bible above every thing, it is on the contrary, either science or reason, or human tradition, or some new inspiration, that it places above the Bible. Thence, all the rationalists; and thence all their false religions.

They correct the word of God, or they complete it; they contradict it, or they interdict it; they teach their pupils to read it with irreverence, or they prohibit the reading of it.

The rationalists, for instance, who now profess Judaism, place above the Bible, if not their own reason, at least that of the IId. IIId. IVth. Vth. and VIth. centuries; that is the human traditions of their Targums, the Mishna and the Gemara of their two enormous Talmuds. That is their Alcoran: they have stifled the law and the prophets beneath its enormous weight.

The rationalists who profess the religion of Rome will in their turn, place above the Bible, not their own reason, but, first, the reason of the VIIth, VIIIth, IXth, Xth, XIth, XIIth and XIIIth centuries, which they call *tradition* (that is, the reason of Dyonisius the Less, of Hincmar, of Radbert, of Lanfranck, of Damascenus, of Anastasius the Librarian, of Burkardt, of Ives of Chartres, of Gratian, of Isidorus the Merchant); and then, that of a priest ordinarily Italian, whom they call *Pope*, and whom they declare *infallible in the definition of matters of faith.** Did the Bible require us to worship the virgin, to serve the angels, to pray for pardons, to worship images, to confess to priests, to refrain from marriage, to refuse meats, to pray in unknown tongues, to forbid the Scriptures to the people;† to have a sovereign Pontiff? And when they speak of a future Rome,‡ is it otherwise (all the first Fathers of the Church are agreed on this point),§ than in de-

---

* It is the doctrine of the ultramontanes, maintained both by popes, (Pascal, Pius, Leo, Pelagius, Boniface, Gregory), and by councils. Bellarmin, Duval and Arsdekin assure us that it is the sentiment of all the theologians of any distinction. Hæc doctrina communis est inter omnes notæ theologos. (Arsdekin, Theol., vol. I, p. 118. Antwerp, 1682.)

† Prohibemus etiam, ne libros Veteris Testamenti aut Novi laïci permittantur habere; nisi forte psalterium, vel breviarium pro divinis officis, aut horas beatæ Mariæ, aliquis ex devotione habere velit. Sed ne præmissos libros habeant in vulgari translatos, arctissimè inhibemus. (The XIVth canon of the Council of Toulouse, under pope Gregory IX. in 1229. Concilia Labbæi. t. ii., part 1, Paris, 1671.)

‡ 2 Thess. ii. 1 to 12.—Rev. xiii. 1 to 8; xviii. 1 to 24.

§ St. Jérôme, *Exhortation to Marcella, to induce her to emigrate*

signating it as the seat of the Man of Sin, as the centre of
an immense apostacy; as a Babylon, drunk with the
blood of the saints and of the witnesses of Jesus Christ, who
has made all the nations drink of the wine of the fury of
her fornication; as the mother of the fornicators and of
the abominations of the earth?

The rationalists who profess an impure protestantism,
and who reject the doctrines of the Reformation, will
place above the Bible, if not the reason of Socinus and of
Priestly, of Eichhorn and of Paulus, of Strauss and of
Hegel, at least their own. There is a mixture, they will
say, in the word of God. They try it, they correct it;
and with the Bible in their hands, they will tell you;
No divinity in Christ, no resurrection of the body, no Holy Spirit, no devil, no demons, no hell, no expiation in
the death of Jesus Christ, no native corruption in man, no
eternity of punishment, no miraculous facts (what do I
say?) no reality in Jesus Christ!

The rationalists finally, who profess mysticism (the
Illuminati, the Tremblers, the Paracelcists, the Bourig-
nonists, the Labadists, the Bœhmists,) will put above the
sacred text of the Scriptures, their hallucinations, their
internal word, their revelations, and the Christ within.
They will speak with disdain of the letter, of the literal
sense of the evangelical facts, of the man Jesus, or of
the external Christ (as they style him), of the cross of
Golgotha, of preaching, of worship, of the sacraments.
They are above these carnal aids! Hence their aversion

from Rome to Bethlehem: "Read John's Revelation, and observe
what is said of the woman in scarlet, &c. : . . . the seven hills,
and of coming out from Babylon, &c." Tertullian; "Sic et Babylon apud Johannem nostrum romanæ urbis figura est, &c." (*Adv.
Judæos. Parisiis*, 1675).—St. Chrysostom (*Hom.* 4; *in 2 epis. ad.
Thessal.*, c. 2); "That which hindered (in his time, he says) the
manifestation of the Man of Sin, was the Roman Empire" Τουτ'
ἐστιν ἡ ἀρχὴ Ρώμαϊκῆ. Ὁκιν ἄρθη ἐκ μέσου, τότε ἐκεῖνος ἥξει.

to the doctrines of the judicial justice of God, of the reality of sin, of the divine wrath against wickedness, of grace, of election, of satisfaction, of the imputed righteousness of Christ, of future punishment.

Disciples of the Savior, hear him in his word, there he will speak to you; there is our reason, there our wisdom, there our inspiration; there our sure tradition; there is the lamp to our feet, the light of our paths, "sanctify me by thy truth, O Lord; thy word is truth!"

Let our reason then employ all her strength, in the sight of God, first to recognise that the Scriptures are from him, and then to study them. Let her bow more intensely every day, over their divine oracles, to correct herself by them, not to correct them by her; to seek there the meaning of God, not to put upon them her own; to present herself before their holy word as a respectful servant, attentive, tender, docile, and not as a noisy and foolish sybil. Let her daily prayer, during the darkness which surrounds her, be constantly that of that child of the tabernacle: "Speak, speak, Lord; thy servant heareth!"—"The law of the Lord is perfect; the words of the Lord are pure words; it is silver purified in the furnace, and seven times refined."*

And on the other hand, let us seek the Holy Spirit; let us be baptized with the Spirit, "let us be anointed of the Holy One;" it is the Spirit alone who will guide us into all the truth of the Scriptures, who will shed abroad by them the love of God in our hearts, and who will witness with our spirits that we are the sons of God, by applying its promises to us, and giving us from them the pledge of the promised inheritance and the earnest of his adoption. In vain, without this Spirit, should we carry this Scripture in our hands for eighteen hundred years, as do still the Jews; we should not there comprehend the

* Is. xii. 6.

things of the Spirit of God; " they would be to us folly; because the natural man receiveth them not, nor indeed can, for they are spiritually discerned."—But at the same time, in distinguishing always the spirit from the letter, let us take care never to separate them. Let it be always before the word, in the word, and by the word, that we seek this divine Spirit. It is by this word he acts; by it he enlightens and affects the heart; by it he casts down, and by it raises up. His constant work is to make our soul comprehend it, to apply it to our soul, to make our soul love it.

The Bible is then of God in all its parts.

It will doubtless occur, that we shall still meet many passages there, whose use and whose beauty are concealed from us; but the light of the last day will in an instant make their splendors flash out. And as it happens in the long concealed depths of those crystaline caverns into which torches are carried; the rising of the day of Jesus Christ, inundating all things, in its glory, will penetrate all the Scriptures with its light, and there revealing to us on every side, diamonds never before perceived, will make them blaze resplendent with a thousand fires. Then the beauty, the wisdom, the proportion, and the harmony of all their revelations will be manifest; and this view shall fill the chosen of God with enraptured admiration, with tenderness incessantly renewed, and with a joy that cannot mislead.

The history of the past should make us already anticipate that of the future; and we can judge by facts already accomplished, of the splendor of the light which is to be poured for us upon the Scriptures, at the second coming of Christ.

See already what vivid light was shed upon all parts of the Old Testament at the first appearing of the Son of God; and conjecture from this single fact, what must be

29

the splendor of the two Testaments, at his second coming.
Then the plan of God will be completed; then our Lord
and our King, more glorious than the sons of men, shall
be revealed from heaven, riding prosperously because of
truth, justice and meekness; then his light shall fill the
hearts of his redeemed; and the imposing grandeur of the
work of redemption will be manifested in all its glory to
the view of the children of God.

See already how many chapters of the Scriptures, in the
age of Jeremiah, or later, in the long reign of the Maccabees, and during the existence of the second temple, from
Malachi even to John the Baptist; see, we say, how many
chapters of the Scriptures, which now shine to us in heavenly splendor, must then have appeared insignificant, and
dull to the eyes of the rationalists of the ancient synagogue. How puerile, vulgar, unmeaning, useless must
they have found many of those verses and chapters, which
now nourish our faith, which fill us with admiration for
the majestic unity of the Scriptures, which cause our tears
to flow, and which have already led so many weary and
heavy-laden souls to the feet of Jesus Christ! What did
they use to say of the 53d chapter of Isaiah? Without
doubt, with the Ethiopean servant of Queen Candace:
"How shall I understand, unless some one guide me? Of
whom speaks the prophet; of himself or of some other?"
What could be the use of that history of Melchizedeck?
Why those long details about the Tabernacle, the garments
of Aaron, clean and unclean beasts, worship and sacrifices?
What could these words mean: thou shalt not break its
legs? What meaning could there be in the xxii, lxix,
and many other Psalms: "My God, my God, why hast
thou forsaken me? they have pierced my hands and my
feet!" Why (they must have thought,) does David occupy us so long, in his songs, with the ordinary details of
his adventurous life? When too, did they divide his gar-

ments and cast lots upon his vesture? What do these words mean: "All they shake their heads at me, he trusted in the Lord, say they; let him deliver him, since he takes pleasure in him?" What then is that vinegar, and what means that gall: "In my thirst, they gave me vinegar; they gave me gall for my drink?" What mean these exaggerated and inexplicable words: "I have not hid my face from shame and spitting. They smote me upon the cheek; they have ploughed my back?" And what did the prophet mean: "Behold, a virgin shall conceive?" Who again is this "King, lowly and sitting on an ass, and upon a colt the foal of an ass? Zion behold thy God; he himself shall come and deliver you." What then is this burial: "He made his grave with the wicked, and with the rich in his death?"

How strange and unworthy of the Lord must all these words, and so many similar ones, have appeared to the presumptuous scribes of those remote days! What human weakness, they must have said, what individuality, what occasionality! (to lend these ancient men the language of our times.) They doubtless taught then in the academies, learned systems and long deviations upon the situation and circumstances of the prophets while writing such details; and found in their words nothing but the vulgar impression of the merely personal circumstances which had effected them.

But what were you then doing, true disciples of the word of life? What were you doing, Hezekiah, Daniel, Josiah, Nehemiah, Ezra, our brethren in the same hope and in the same faith; and you too, holy women who trusted in God, and who looked for the consolation of Israel? Ah! you bowed reverently over all these depths, as do still the angels of light, and desiring to fathom to the bottom; you waited! Yes, they waited! They knew that, in the passage most insignificant in their eyes, there might be, as a Father of the Church has said: "mountains of doctrine." Wherefore, as ˌSt. Peter says, "searching what or what manner of time the Spirit of Christ, which was in the prophets, did signify when it testified before-hand, the sufferings of Christ, and the glory that should follow," they did not doubt that, thereafter, when time and events should have passed their hand over this sympathetic ink, there would start out from them, astounding pages, all stamped with divinity, and all full of the gospel! The day was to come, after the first appearing of the Messiah, when the least in the kingdom of God should be greater than the greatest of the prophets; and that day has come. But we know too, ourselves, that the day is yet to come, after his second appearing, when the least of the redeemed shall be greater in knowledge than were the Augustines, the Calvins, the Edwards, the Pascals, the Leightons; for then the ears of the children shall hear, and their eyes shall see things, which even the apostles "desired to see, and saw not; to hear, and, heard not."

What then the doctors, the prophets, and the saints did with the passages to them yet obscure, and now luminous to us, we will do to those passages which are obscure to us, but which shall quickly become luminous to the heirs of life, when all the prophecies shall be accomplished, and Jesus Christ shall appear in the clouds, in the last Epiphany of his glorious coming.

With what glory, as soon as they were comprehended, have we seen shine forth, so many passages, so many psalms, so many prophecies, so many types, so many descriptions, whose profound beauty had not before been perceived! What evangelical truth has come forth from them! what appeals to the conscience! what an unfolding of redeeming love! Let us then wait in regard to analogous passages, even more glorious, for that day when our Master shall again come down from Heaven; for, says

St. Ireneus, " there are difficulties in the Scriptures, which, by the grace of God, we can now resolve, but there are others which we abandon to him, not only for this age, butf or the next, in order that God may perpetually be teaching, and that perpetually, man may thus be learning of God, the things which pertain to God."*

If the lights of grace have dimned those of nature, how in their turn will the lights of glory throw paleness on those of grace! How many stars of the first magnitude, still invisible, will be enkindled at the approach of that great day, in the firmament of the Scriptures? And when, finally, it shall be fully revealed to the redeemed world without a veil, what harmonies, what celestial tints, what new glories, what unanticipated splendors, manifested to the heirs of eternal life!

Then, we shall see the meaning of so many prophecies, of so many facts, and of so many instructions, whose divinity as yet, is revealed only by detached features, but whose evangelical beauty will shine on every side. Then we shall know all the meaning of those parables, already so imposing, of the Fig-tree, of the Master returning from a far country, of the Bride and Bridegroom, of the Net drawn on the shore of eternity, of Lazarus, of the Invited, of the Talents, of the Husbandman, of the Virgins, of the Marriage-Feast. Then we shall know all the glory of words like these; " The Lord said to my Lord, sit thou on my right hand, until I make thy foes thy footstool." " Thy people, Lord, shall be a willing people, in the day whent hou shalt gather thine army with holy pomp." " The dew of thy youth shall be from the womb of the morning." " He shall tread upon kings in his wrath. He shall destroy the head over a great country." " He shall drink of the

---

* Ireneus adv. hæreb., lib. ii, c. 47. Ινα ὁ θέος διδασκη, ἀνθρωπος δὲ διὰ παντὸς μανθάνῃ παρὰ θεοῦ.

water-brook by the way; therefore shall he lift up the head on high!"

Then too, shall thou manifest thyself to our view in all thy glory, O, Jesus Christ, Savior, consoler, friend of the miserable, our Lord and our God! thou that hast tasted death, but who art He that liveth forever and ever! Then all the science of Heaven will be thyself! Thou wast always all the science of the Holy Spirit, who descended from Heaven. Thou wast all that of the Scriptures; for "the testimony of Jesus is the spirit of prophecy."* Thou art already all the life of the saints; "their life eternal is, to know thee!" O, thanks to God for his unspeakable gift!

Could the celebrated traveler who first brought to us from Constantinople, the only horse-chesnut which had yet seen our Western world, and who planted it, it is said, in the court-yard of his house; could he have told what he held in the palm of his hand, and what was to spring from it? The infinite in the finite! innumerable forests, in a humble fruit, and under its insignificant shell; trees by thousands, decorating with their majestic foliage and their clustered blossoms our gardens and our fields; covering with their thick shade the squares, the terraces and the avenues of our cities; our people celebrating their national festivals beneath their outspread branches; our western kings, in our capitals reviewing their armies beneath their large bowers; our children playing at their feet, and the sparrow of our houses seeking his food in their branches; whilst each one of these trees will itself produce, from year to year, millions of fruits exactly similar to that from which it sprang, and bearing likewise, each one in its bosom, the dormant germ of thousands of forests, to thousands of generations!

Thus the Christian traveler, arriving from the militant

---

† Rev. xix. 10.

church, at his celestial country, and the city of his God, the house of his father, with one of the thousand passages of the Holy Bible in his hands, knows that he bears thither the infinite in the finite, a germ of God, the developments and the glory of which he can already, without doubt, faintly perceive, but the whole of whose grandeur he cannot yet tell. It is, perhaps, the least of all seeds; but he knows that from it is to spring a great tree, an eternal tree, under the branches of which the heavenly inhabitants will recline. In many of these passages of his Savior, he has perhaps not yet seen even the germ, under their rude shell; but he knows too, that, once admitted into the Jerusalem above, under the beams of the Sun of Righteousness, he shall see radiate, in these words of the eternal wisdom, by that light of which the Lamb is the glorious torch, splendors hitherto latent, and still covered by their first envelope. Then, in an ineffable tenderness of gratitude and bliss, he shall discover agreements, harmonies, glories, of which he had here below, only suspicions, or at least, a respectful expectation. Prepared before the foundation of the world in the eternal counsels of God, and deposited as germs in his Word of Life, they shall burst forth under that new heaven, and for that new earth, wherein righteousness shall dwell.

All the written word is then inspired of God. "Open thou mine eyes, O Lord, that I may see wondrous things out of thy law!"

116

CPSIA information can be obtained at www.ICGtesting.com
Printed in the USA
BVOW07s2246110314

347394BV00006B/83/P